Peter Murphy's book examines the tension between the material, economic pressures motivating poetry as an occupation, and traditional notions of the forces of literary history, or poetry as an art. It focuses on five writers in the Romantic period: James MacPherson, Robert Burns, James Hogg, Walter Scott, and William Wordsworth. The first four are Scottish; the economic and linguistic status of Scotland during the period makes its writers especially interesting as examples of poetic ambition. Murphy's study then crosses the border into England, offering a new perspective on Wordsworth's poetic ambition and career. Murphy's engagement throughout with the ballad revival fields fresh insights into some major concerns of the Romantic period: the interest in the primitive and the simple, experiments with poetic form, the problematics of loss, and the emergence of a new literary culture.

Cambridge Studies in Romanticism 3

POETRY AS AN OCCUPATION AND AN ART IN BRITAIN, 1760–1830

CAMBRIDGE STUDIES IN ROMANTICISM

General Editors:
Professor Marilyn Butler   Professor James Chandler
University of Cambridge   *University of Chicago*

Editorial Board:
John Barrell, *University of Sussex*   Paul Hamilton, *University of Southampton*
Mary Jacobus, *Cornell University*   Kenneth Johnston, *Indiana University*
Alan Liu, *University of California, Santa Barbara*   Jerome McGann,
University of Virginia   David Simpson, *University of Colorado*

This series aims to foster the best new work in one of the most challenging fields within English literary studies. From the early 1780s to the early 1830s a formidable array of talented men and women took to literary composition, not just in poetry, which some of them famously transformed, but in many modes of writing. The expansion of publishing created new opportunities for writers, and the political stakes of what they wrote were raised again and again by what Wordsworth called those "great national events" that were "almost daily taking place": the French Revolution, the Napoleonic and American wars, urbanization, industrialization, religious revival, an expanded empire abroad and the reform movement at home. This was a enormous ambition, even when it pretended otherwise. The relations between science, philosophy, religion and literature were reworked in texts such as *Frankenstein* and *Biographia Literaria*; gender relations in *A Vindication of the Rights of Woman* and *Don Juan*; journalism by Cobbett and Hazlitt; poetic form, content and style by the Lake School and the Cockney School. Outside Shakespeare studies, probably no body of writing has produced such a wealth of response or done so much to shape the responses of modern criticism. This indeed is the period that saw the emergence of those notions of "literature" and of literary history, especially national literary history, on which modern scholarship in English has been founded.

The categories produced by Romanticism have also been challenged by recent historicist arguments. The task of the series is to engage both with a challenging corpus of Romantic writings and with the changing field of criticism they have helped to shape. As with other literary series published by Cambridge, this one will represent the work of both younger and more established scholars, on either side of the Atlantic and elsewhere.

TITLES PUBLISHED
Romantic Correspondence: Women, Politics and the Fiction of Letters
by Mary Favret
British Romantic Writers and the East: Anxieties of Empire by Nigel Leask
Edmund Burke's Aesthetic Ideology: Language, Gender and Political Economy in Revolution by Tom Furniss

IN PREPARATION
In the Theatre of Romanticism: Nationalism, Women, Coleridge by Julie Carlson
Keats, Narrative and Audience by Andrew J. Bennett
Romance and Revolution: Shelley and the Politics of a Genre by David Duff
Allegory in Romantic and Post-Romantic Culture by Theresa M. Kelley

POETRY AS AN OCCUPATION AND AN ART IN BRITAIN 1760–1830

PETER T. MURPHY

Department of English, Williams College, Williamstown, Massachusetts

CAMBRIDGE
UNIVERSITY PRESS

Published by the Press Syndicate of the University of Cambridge
The Pitt Building, Trumpington Street, Cambridge CB2 1RP
40 West 20th Street, New York, NY 10011-4211, USA
10 Stamford Road, Oakleigh, Melbourne 3166, Australia

First published 1993

Printed in Great Britain at the University Press, Cambridge

A catalogue record for this book is available from the British Library

Library of Congress cataloguing in publication data
Murphy, Peter T.
Poetry as an occupation and an art in Britain, 1760–1830 / Peter T. Murphy
p.   cm. (Cambridge studies in romanticism)
Includes bibliographical references and index.
ISBN 0 521 44085 8 (hardback)
1. English poetry–18th century–History and criticism.   2. English poetry–19th
century–History and criticism.   3. Literature and society–Great Britain–History.
4. Poetry–Authorship–History.   5. Romanticism–Great Britain.   I. Title.   II. Series.
PR571.M87   1993
821.609–dc20 92–33949 CIP

ISBN 0 521 44085 8 hardback

*In memory of my mother, Judy Jean McCamant Murphy,
who taught me that strength and weakness
are mortally interwoven in us all*

Contents

Acknowledgments

When I was younger, I found acknowledgments and prefaces a painful part of any academic book, with their stiff generic features and their insistence on the crude machinery of production: why go to the trouble of creating voice and style only to peek behind them in this way? But that was before I understood the extent of my debts, and before I understood both the inevitability and desirability of acquiring them. It was before I was capable of writing this book, which takes looking behind voice and style as its central project. We cannot repay intellectual debts; we can only hand them on, and we can savor the pleasure of acknowledging them. No part of this book was written without help. These people have helped me in ways too important to appear in footnotes, and I want to thank them:

My Father and Mother, for an idiosyncratic intellectual heritage; Nicole Feldman, Daniel Georges and James Banko, for inspiration and sophistication, early and late; Audrey Thier, for salvation; Jay Gillen, John Guillory and Mike Cadden, from whom I learned how to think; Samuel and Paula Thier, for making so many things possible; Jerome Christensen, for returning the pleasures of scholarship; and my colleagues at Williams, for support and interest and rigor.

More specifically, Ron Paulson provided crucial guidance early on, and Jerry Christensen read every page of every version over many years; Michael Fried and the Humanities Center promised and provided perfect freedom; Neil Hertz, Peter Berek, Steve Tifft, Jeff Wallen and Barbara Winn worked on various parts; Michael Bell read all and insisted on honesty and quality; Karen Swann read and commented and insisted with tireless energy, pressing me to make this book more like I wanted it to be.

Alan Liu offered sympathy and encouragement at a most crucial time, and James Chandler likewise, along with the most personable and intelligent editorial advice; these two people have offered support and actual labor far beyond the call of duty. The National Endowment for the Humanities and Williams College provided financial support without which this book simply would not have come to be; and Mark Taylor and the Williams Humanities Center gave me an astonishingly beautiful setting in which to write it. I would also like to thank the editors of *ELH* for allowing me to reprint some material from "Fools Gold: The Highland Treasures of MacPherson's Ossian" *ELH* (Fall 1986), 567–91.

Finally, though this book was written in spite of Aaron and David and Ruth's impatience with such things, and though my wife did not type or edit or read or file, I thought about them all with every word and sentence. Without the abiding presence of my wife, Audrey Thier, whose acuity and strength and moral intensity I admire and aspire to, everything I do would be less interesting.

Introduction

In spite of the Scottish cast to the list of writers on the table of contents, this is not a book about Scottish writers. In its largest sense, this book is about what all books about Romantic poetry are about: the Romantic interest in the primitive and the simple; Romantic experiments with form; Romantic problematics of loss; the emergence of a new literary culture during the Romantic period. These subjects all appear under the rubric of the "ballad revival," a concern with which informs the progress of this book at every point. These issues all border one another, and I find that in traversing the territory of one I inevitably encounter the others. In the same way, the "minor" writers I discuss border on the more major ones; the local becomes the general. Indeed, the practice of the book turns this assertion into a method, and rather than "focusing" on minor or Scottish writers, the claim is that a discussion of one of these writers inevitably, in a sense, becomes a discussion of the others, until the larger discussion inevitably becomes a discussion of the most central concerns of the period.

In the chapters themselves, my materials are linked through metaphors of limitation and boundary, limit and border; in their figurative capacity I mean these metaphors to reproduce the simultaneous action of culture. The most common use of this metaphor is the description of the limitation literary precedent places upon the possibilities of expression; the narrowest is the limitation the poetic line places upon the expressive possibilities of that line. Other members of the family are the cultural limitations suffered by my disadvantaged writers, the border between Scotland and England (which figures in turn the border between local and literary culture, between oral and written, between backward and refined), the invisible but intractable boundaries between classes. The broadest border or limit in this book is the boundary to human life: the

I

condition of mortality, both as it is figured by literary history (the live presence of dead poets; the possibility of undying fame) and as it is present in everyday life, in the form of material needs and other mortal concerns. The action in the larger story and individual stories I tell occurs when a poet steps across a border: when the oral encounters the written, when Burns goes to Edinburgh, when Wordsworth accepts and exploits the continual "crossing" imposed by ballad form. The lesson of the story is that crossing any border is the simultaneous crossing of many others.

Crossing the border always makes a difference, and distinctions that might not be otherwise apparent can be highlighted by such crossings. One of the consequences of critical travel between (say) James MacPherson and Robert Burns or William Wordsworth is that one suddenly feels the absence, in contemporary criticism, of an energetic evaluative vocabulary. The fact that critics want to talk about Wordsworth more than they do MacPherson is a fact, and in what follows I try to deal with that fact. Part of my argument is that assertions of quality, and evaluations of quality, are extremely complex in their motives and cultural sources; one of the consequences of this assertion is that I will not try to summarize or reduce the analysis of poetic quality here. I will say that I try to take up this subject when it arises, and that I conclude with the assertion that there is high critical value for us in encountering the need for distinctions between writers. The distinction I will end with is that between Wordsworth and Walter Scott, but distinction is a fundamental part of every discussion the book offers.

Connected to the problem of literary quality – connected by the thin but strong thread formed by the remnants of the New Criticism – is the strength and interest of discussions of form. In the same way that I found myself in need of qualitative distinctions, I found myself wanting ways of discussing the life and power of poetic form without losing the historical specificity of my materials. The intertwining of poetic structures with other cultural and personal structures is the central subject of each chapter. The material consequence of this interest for the conduct of the book is that most of the arguments move from the local to the general by moving outward from the detail of the poetic line to other details and other structures. This is an example of both the borderland methodology of the book and the borderland argument of the book. One thing, quite literally, leads to another, because borders are marks of distinction and connection at once.

Turning to the specifics of the contents: this book describes, in some detail, the writing of poetry by five writers in the Romantic period. I try to specify the forces that work to produce the poetry that these writers write, and the forces that cause them to choose poetry writing as a job in the first place. Four of the five writers are Scottish, and I would justify this by noting that the economic and linguistic status of Scotland during the period I am concerned with makes Scottish writers exceptionally interesting as examples of poetic ambition. Three of the five (MacPherson, Burns and Hogg) begin life, in differing degrees, at a serious social and economic disadvantage. That they choose poetry as a means of escaping into the world of higher life puts poetry in a most material and homely setting. Most of the poetry in these careers has the plainest of material purposes, and much the same status as any other thing a person might make and sell for hopeful profit. By delineating with particularity the sorts of pressure that result in poetry in these lives, I hope to return poetry to the plain and everyday world of human motive and need, and in this sense this book is deeply historicist.

This historical picture will have value for us to the degree with which it succeeds in showing poetry, in the plainest terms, to be something that people might choose to write. Since poetry is not something that we (speaking generally) choose to write, it is hard for us to see it as just that: a possible choice, an occupation, a kind of work. Whatever value we can give to poetry now, it would seem to me that it would have to rise out of a humane picture of the functioning of poetry within culture. For instance: when Robert Burns attempts to find his way into the literary world of Edinburgh, his most obvious challenge is that of class difference, as manifested in the simplest ways: lack of acquaintance, a rustic accent, lack of money, stained and work-spoiled clothes. The society he wishes to enter is a decorous one, and he is not a decorous person. When this same literary culture begins to read to Burns' writing, exactly the same terms reappear, this time in literary form: politeness, decency, propriety, rustic interest and dress. Society is ruled by form, and poetry is too: these forms share the same culture. The example of Burns, in short, shows clearly that writing poetry in a culture in which poetic form is alive is a way of behaving. Poetic propriety and "social" propriety mix and become indistinguishable. For the ambitious, a poetic "mistake" has exactly the same consequence as a social mistake: the threat of failure, rejection by the world that the ambitious writer wishes to enter.

All Scottish writers, at this period, also begin life at what we might call a linguistic disadvantage, since the literary marketplace, where they hope to sell what they make, is defined largely by the literary English of greater Britain. All four Scottish writers I discuss manage to turn this disadvantage to their advantage, and sell what they have ("Scottishness"; more generally rustic "northernness") at a profit generated by exactly that which they wish to escape from. In sorting through the various strategies by which these writers accomplish this transformation, I hope to describe in detail exactly what sort of literary movement the "ballad revival" was, and what cultural forces allowed for these Scottish writers to find their way into the literary world.

Walter Scott and Wordsworth do not begin with the disadvantages of the other three, and so their ambition has a different cast. Their careers show, however, how generally interesting the small details highlighted by the careers of the other three writers are. Scott shows how spectacularly profitable the marketing of northernness could be; Wordsworth shows how full of literary and expressive interest the northern material was for Romantic culture. Wordsworth is not Scottish, but he comes from the north, and the charge of his "real language" has metaphorically the same charge as the oral and pastoral materials produced by the other four writers. Wordsworth also helps us remember that these socially "low" materials came, during the Romantic period, with the label "real" attached, in some form. The seemingly insatiable Romantic demand for what the northern, ballad-influenced writer had to offer is produced and satisfied by writers whose "rustic" persons authenticate the northern writings they produce. This feature has its own interest (the production of "pastoral" during the period), but also indicates what we might call the moral side to the careers of the writers involved. That is, one of the most compelling historical interests of the use of ballad and oral material is that it is also the use of one culture by another; most generally, the use of the oral by the culture of the written. Such a relationship entails responsibilities, and so the literary movement called the "ballad revival" involves moral choices as well as formal ones. Choosing to write ballads (or songs; or "romances") is more than a choice of medium. In what follows I chronicle the relationships these marketers of oral interest had to their sources, and I try to judge them in that regard. The most exploitive and disrespectful of these writers is James MacPherson, who wanted from oral culture only what he could get, and let the consequences fall where they might; in contrast, Robert Burns and William Wordsworth exhibit extremely careful and sensitive attitudes, and I reward them with an epithet: "integrity." I mean for this term to describe a relationship which not only relishes the oral material but which acknowledges the cultural interests and identity of the source. Both Wordsworth and Burns refuse to simply vend the oral source to the public (though with very different motives), and both of them know that such material has its own interests and beauty, quite apart from its possible place in a culture it has no real notion of. Walter Scott has a unique position in this regard, and I can only say I will try to do justice to it; he is, one might say, a deeply respectful exploiter of the oral.

The foundation of such an innately historical project upon formal analysis is enough of a departure from current practice to warrant comment. In recent years many literary critics, myself included, have turned with relief and even exhilaration to "history," that relief and exhilaration rising out of a sense of rescue from older and now tired formalist ways of talking about literature. A skeptical perspective – or just a short-term memory – shows us how often this happens, how frequently literary critics feel the need to aggressively announce their departure from their precursors and teachers. At the moment, it is bracing to recall how vigorously the criticism that began the forty-year trend towards formalism, the New Criticism, announced its sense of rescue from the historicist criticism that preceded it: New Criticism celebrated its rescue from history, and during the last ten years we have celebrated history's rescue of us (at some remove) from New Criticism. This is Cleanth Brooks, in the Preface to the *Well-Wrought Urn*:

We have had impressed upon us the necessity for reading a poem in its historical context, and that kind of reading has been carried on so successfully that some of us have been tempted to feel it is the only kind of reading possible ... Any attempt to view it *sub specie aeternitatis*, we feel, must result in illusion.

Perhaps it must. Yet, if poetry exists as poetry in any meaningful sense, the attempt must be made. Otherwise the poetry of the past becomes significant merely as cultural anthropology ... [1]

As recent debates on the canon have taught us, the "eternity" referred to here is attained by achieving the heaven of transcendent language, and "poetry" is essentially a judgmental term (a "normative judgment"), a reward for the accomplishment of the "miracle" of decontextualized, transhistorical communication.[2]

We may note the meta-structure of recurring critical rescues, but certainly we needed to be rescued (for many reasons) from New Criticism's forceful imposition of critical acumen, and from the rhetoric of interpretive purity generated in the chapters that follow Brooks' Preface. The world changes, and even if we still share many things with the New Critics, we at least needed a new style, a less pure rhetoric. In this book I practice a historical criticism, and it will be seen quite appropriately as another installment in the continuing rescue from decontextualized reading. As I have noted, I especially try to take the kind of focus on form and poetic detail typical of New Critical readings and describe these features as part of a world where history and material needs are forces. So, for instance, in the chapter on Robert Burns, my descriptions of the form of song, which Burns found so congenial, are attempts not only to illustrate the features of that form but also to describe where their interest for Burns comes from, and even where the force of the form itself, in a broader way, comes from. Song is a literary form, but it functions in the same broad world that people work and sing in: it does things for people, and it did things for Burns. I pursue this sort of argument in all the chapters that follow, and the largest way of describing the purpose of this argument is that I want to contextualize poetic form in a convincing way; I want to rescue "close reading" from formalism by producing a compellingly human picture of the force of form.

Like many critics, though, I also think that we (already) need rescuing from history, from context, and I try to do that by rescuing "normative judgement" from Cleanth Brooks. That is: any discussion of the writing of poetry which does not include some notion of success, of accomplishment, is simply inaccurate, even from the most hard-headed of historical perspectives. Poetry is language in the grips of unusually clear and demanding rules (a simple definition of poetic form); literary history, the example of precedent, presents the writer of poetry with the oxymoronic gift of possibility under the sign of restriction. The presence of rules creates the place for success or failure, for ignorance, capacity and invention. The material world provides context, a context linked to the person and world of the writer, but literary history is a context too, a context which is, quite precisely, by definition, a transhistorical, more than personal context.

In what follows I do not wish to recreate the poetic heaven that Brooks gives us, but I try to acknowledge at all times that some poets are more capable than others, and that this fact must exert an important pressure on our evaluation of the place and identity of poetry.

To revocalize Brooks, in a new key: if it is worth talking about poetry as a distinct form of culture, then we must talk about poetic success and failure. We must grant poetic form life. We must admit that decisions about form matter, and can go awry, and we must not let the interest of reference blind us to the energy of form itself, the energy brought to bear in the literary realm of what we once called the "poem itself." Beginning with MacPherson, I try to define a term for poetic accomplishment, "integrity," through which I can refer to and describe a poetic accomplishment which understands and makes use of the resources created by the constrictions of poetic form. The source of the new key is that I partner my descriptions of the force of form, at all times, with the deeply historicist and material descriptions I have learned from recent critics. Poetic form, literary history as a force of its own, does not transcend the material forms of culture the poet must deal with; it is one force among many. At the same time, material forces do not co-opt or eliminate literary ones. The restrictions of poetry do contain expressive possibility, resources that can be used or abused, contained in the more than personal world of literary history, which visits itself on the poet whether the poet wants it to or not.

If poetry as poetry exists in any meaningful form for us, we must find a way to talk about what makes poetry different from other forms of writing: we must talk about the life and energy of poetic form. In what follows I try to understand poetic form in the context of an historical criticism, and to describe the resources and value of poetry in the plain terms that a historical criticism makes paramount. The most interesting consequence, for me, of this attempt is the way in which formal evaluation dovetails with the broader kind of cultural or humane evaluation the moral side of the ballad revival makes necessary. Writing poetry is a human activity, and partakes of human complexity. Formal choice is always, in some register, moral choice.

My interest in a truly complex description of poetry results in some particular formal features. A generally sympathetic colleague has described certain important terms in my vocabulary as "not in the

critical lexicon since before Lovejoy." This is true, I suppose: these
terms would be ones like accomplishment, art, happiness, beauty,
freedom. We feel a reasonable discomfort with such words, since (as
teachers) we know how often such large terms are used to cover over
vague notions, unpleasant assumptions and unfinished thoughts. I
hope the seriousness of the argument in what follows will justify these
terms for me. That is, I hope the depth of my analysis gives serious
content to these words. I have used them because I have faith that in
their very looseness (and persistence) they do work that cannot
otherwise be done. The reason we need them and continue to use
them is that they respond to the complexity human culture offers. In
the same spirit (as I have noted) I organize each chapter in essentially
figurative ways, with each central metaphor or figure descriptive of
a relationship to border or limit. In the MacPherson chapter, this
metaphor is that of translation (easy transfer over borders); in Burns,
it is smuggling; Hogg is captured and retained on the Border; Scott
blithely steps over borders while never going anywhere; and
Wordsworth tensely stumbles over any border he meets. I organize
the chapters in this way, again, out of a faith that figurative language,
as the poets should teach us, does work that cannot otherwise be
done. In particular, I use these metaphors to organize the several
levels of argument (as I have described them), since their connection
in truth has all the reality of figure.

This book does attempt general argument, and I have tried to give
general descriptions of that argument. At the same time, in some
ways I try to say everything at once, and so the individual chapters
are meant to have a separable identity. They may seem in this regard
to be repetitive; outside of the valorization of repetition that I will
describe in discussing Wordsworth's poetic practice, my hope is that
their repetition is of the ballad kind, incremental and cumulative. I
try to tell each story with respect for its energies, what is unique to it;
because there are real connections between them, these individuals
eventually train into an argumentative progress. I hope that this
method does not seem needlessly thick or dense; my justification must
be that the material itself demands it.

CHAPTER I

James MacPherson

It is conventional to begin modern discussions of the life and work of James MacPherson, creator of the Ossian poems, with a rhetoric of rescue. MacPherson was once famous; he has now lapsed, and when we turn to him we must first raise him up from oblivion. In spite of the ironies of frequently claiming that no one speaks of your subject, there is no question that, from the perspective of literary history, James MacPherson does need rescuing. It is equally true that quite possibly he would not have cared about the lapse of his literary reputation. He died a famous and influential man, and, during much of his life, his primary activities and interests were not literary. He was a Highland squire, member of parliament, historian, and what I think we would now call international businessman or statesman (agent for the Nabob of Arcot).[1] Born in undistinguished circumstances in the most isolated and materially backward part of Britain, MacPherson found fame and fortune, and eventually returned to his birthplace as landlord, a pale version of the vanished clan chief. In many ways, his life, as far as value might be attached to it now, does not stand or fall by literary criteria.

The basic challenge for a discussion of the Ossian poems, the primary literary work of James MacPherson, is that it must in all honesty begin with this sort of disclaimer. For MacPherson, literature – poetry – was in the plainest of ways a vehicle for his ambition, and while he rode it with extraordinary success, its place in the story of his life is relentlessly practical. The final irony is perhaps that in spite of his passing beyond poetry in the practice of his career, and in spite of the general contempt and condemnation heaped upon his productions by generations of criticism, he persists now as a literary figure. As I will try to show, this irony is an illustration of the extraordinary nature of the Ossian poems, which turned all responses to account, negative and positive. The recovery of MacPherson that follows

9

shares this irony, since I will eventually claim that from some points of view there is every reason to condemn his literary accomplishments. What is worth our attention is the extraordinary success of MacPherson's strategies for fame, and the ways in which we can admire how the Ossian poems enabled this success. MacPherson's poetry worked hard for him. How it worked put pressure on contemporary formulations of where poetry comes from and what poetry might do; as we review it now, it puts the same pressure on us.

Hidden in the Highlands in the late 1750s, after a college career at Aberdeen, James MacPherson's contact with the literary world would have been of the most constricted sort. We know he read and published in the *Scots Magazine*, and this seamlessly genteel periodical may safely represent the sort of participation in literary culture that was available to him. Each issue contains a poetry section of unembarrassed artificiality; we might complain that its poetry is undistinguished, but certainly distinction of any clear sort is not what such a magazine pursues. As happens during any period with a popular common style, the poems in the *Scots Magazine* even relish their undistinguished characteristics. In the issue for October 1759 the first poem is an elegy, beginning thus:

> Wake! awake! the plaintive strain,
> Sister of the tuneful train!
> Goddess! thou to whom belong,
> Mournful dirge, and solemn song.
> HALDANE's dead, around his urn
> Weeping virtues silent mourn ... [2]

Four more elegies (three on General Wolfe, recently dead) follow this one, each presenting us with its goddess, personification or classical figure in the first stanza. The small burst of elegies in this issue is set off by General Wolfe, but almost every issue of the *Scots Magazine* contains at least one elegy, usually more than one, and a large number of courtship poems of various types. The balance is filled out by poems of a national cast and some miscellaneous items. The poems are never attributed to their authors by name, though they frequently are marked by initials. In this October issue, there is some reason to believe that the other elegy that is not on General Wolfe is by James MacPherson. In this elegy, "To the memory of an officer killed before Quebec," the subject is christened "Daphnis" by the inspired poet. The poem works the sentiment of his subject's death instead of

its glory, after the style of Young's *Night Thoughts*, though in couplets
instead of blank verse:

> Ah me! What sorrows are we born to bear!
> How many causes claim the falling tear!
> In one sad tenor life's dark current flows,
> And every moment has its load of woes...
>
> *(Scots Mag.*, p. 527)

This poem is signed "J. MacP." There is also some reason to believe
that it is not by James MacPherson, but rather by someone else with
the same initials.[3] The impossibility of confidently attributing this
poem to anybody would seem to be a permanent one, and illustrates
the challenge posed to MacPherson's ambition by his literary world.
The very quality that admits his work, the easy and shared
conventional "taste," assures that the poems he writes will not be
distinguishable from their neighbors in the magazine.

MacPherson may have published this poem; he more certainly
published others that sound very much like it:

> On Mem'ry's tablet mankind soon decay,
> On Time's swift stream their glory slides away;
> But, present in the voice of deathless Fame,
> Keith lives, eternal, in his glorious name.[4]

As far as escaping the Highlands goes, such publications could do
very little for him; what MacPherson needed above all was what the
time called "notice," distinction rather than absorption in the
crowd. From the practical point of view, he would have been better
off if he could have published this instead:

My love is a son of the hill. He pursues the flying deer. His grey dogs are
panting around him: his bow-string sounds in the wind. Whether by the
fount of the rock, or by the stream of the mountain thou liest; when the
rushes are nodding with the wind, and the mist is flying over thee, let me
approach my love unperceived, and see him from the rock. Lovely I saw
thee first by the aged oak; thou wert returning tall from the chace; the fairest
among thy friends.[5]

This is the first "poetry" that would meet the eyes of a reader of
MacPherson's first book, *Fragments of Ancient Poetry*. Whatever we
might say about such writing, it is clearly distinguishable from poetry

like MacPherson's early lyrics. It is even ostentatious in its desire for us to call it different, "original." This sort of writing got MacPherson the notice he wanted, but it may also serve to illustrate what sorts of problems would go along with this notice. He did not publish poetry of this sort in the *Scots Magazine* because he could not: it is not poetry. That is, since its measure is (as I will discuss shortly) only figuratively "poetic," poetry sections would not accept it. When individual Ossianic pieces do appear in poetry sections, they are inevitably versified. The curious syntax of this modulated prose also asks for explanation, and indeed readers demanded such explanations, which MacPherson would provide in the form of a claim that his works were translations of traditional Gaelic verse from the Scottish Highlands. This explanation would delight some readers and appall others. Notice inevitably brings with it scrutiny, and distinction brings exclusion. MacPherson's brilliance is in the way he anticipated, encountered and exploited the energy of these potential double-binds.

In May of 1759, MacPherson, grappling with his desire for originality (and fame), and the seemingly intractable problem of finding it, would have come across a compelling and specific description of originality in his favorite and probably only magazine:

Learning ... is fond and proud of what has cost it much pains; is a great lover of rules, a boaster of famed examples. As beauties less perfect, who owe half their charms to cautious art, she inveighs against natural unstudied graces, and small harmless indecorums; and sets rigid bounds to that liberty, to which genius often owes its supreme glory; but the no-genius [sic] its frequent ruin. For unprescribed beauties, and unexampled excellence, which are characteristics of *Genius*, lie without the pale of learning's authorities and laws, which pale genius must leap to come at them: but by that leap if genius is wanting we break our necks; we lose that little credit, which possibly we might have enjoyed before; for rules, like crutches, are a needful aid to the lame, though an impediment to the strong.

This is from the fascinating, epigrammatic *Conjectures on Original Composition* by Edward Young, author of *Night Thoughts*, as excerpted in the May 1759 issue of the *Scots Magazine* (p. 275). The forceful interest of Young's essay comes from combining the above topos of genius with the following, as presented by the summary in the magazine:

He supposes originals to be now few, not because the writer's harvest is over, the great writers of antiquity having left nothing to be gleaned after them, but because illustrious examples ingross, prejudice and intimidate the mind, preventing a due inspection into ourselves, lessening the sense of our own abilities, and repressing our strength by a false diffidence. (p. 274)

This is close paraphrase; the strong vocabulary is all Young's. Young's immediate purpose, oddly enough, is to point out the genius of Addison's *Cato*, but more generally he wishes to encourage his fellow authors to originality. The poet who is an imitator, a performer by rule, "makes one of a group, and thinks in wretched unanimity with the throng";[6] learning surrounds itself with the fence of literary history, the pale that pale genius must overleap. Outside are liberty, "natural unstudied graces," supreme glory and indecorums. Like so much mid-eighteenth-century encouragement, though, Young's gives and takes, offering the ambitious writer a choice between tiresome pedantry and the risk of total failure and a broken poetic neck. Originality may be possible, but it is also dangerous; MacPherson's challenge is to take advantage of the energy residing in Young's primitivist commonplaces while avoiding the possible indecorum of exposing himself as simply primitive. Young's advice presents a possible opening, but protects that opening with paradoxical defenses.

A broken poetic neck (the failure of a book, say) is not only a psychological problem, and so MacPherson's encounter with literary precedent and possibility has a large practical element. Poetry is his chosen method for escaping from the Highland scenery which literally and figuratively closed him in, and his accomplishment of his purpose demonstrates a real brilliance. In the end, MacPherson's brilliance is a practical, strategic brilliance, and his career grows out of scheme after scheme. The Ossian books are quite remarkably well-made, in their own way, and because they are well-made, the strategies which give birth to them are interlaced and mutually dependent. Separating these strategies is difficult and somewhat artificial. Still, for purposes of clarity, I will make three rough categories: MacPherson's publishing strategy, his literary strategy (the "content" of the poems) and his broader cultural strategies (which give rise to the "Ossianic Controversy"). I will trace the first of these first. In some ways MacPherson does this too; his first book is small and tantalizing, and functions primarily as a sort of teaser, an opening move.

I have already quoted the beginning of the *Fragments*, with all its misty Highland interest. I will try, later, to problematize the originality of this writing, but for the moment there seems no reason to refuse the term to it. It *looks* (in any case) original. It participates in the literature of sentiment, but its tone and style are truly its own.[7] The simple claim of a Gaelic heritage also sets it off, of course, but here at the beginning the interest of the Gaelic heritage is supported, I think, by the formal interest of the "prose" itself. Poetry had been translated into Edinburgh from the Highlands before. In particular, a man named Jerome Stone had published a translation of a Gaelic ballad which he called "Albin and the Daughter of Mey" in the *Scots Magazine* for January of 1756, but this ballad was rendered in rhyming quatrains.[8] MacPherson refuses ballad form, and in exactly the same way that his Highland pieces demonstrate a new combination of heroism and sentiment, MacPherson's peculiar, arresting, passionately modulated prose sets his works off definitively. As I noted above, the singularity of this curious prose poetry confuses anthologists of the time; when Ossian poems are anthologized in poetry collections, they are inevitably versified by other hands, turned into real verse in the place of MacPherson's "poetry."[9] In this first miscellaneous book MacPherson begins small, with "fragments" whose general weight is on a lyric scale, but these fragments quite aggressively present themselves as generic enigmas. They refuse by their diction and expression to be simple short narrative, while the length of the individual fragments makes them lyric in physical presence; they can be fit easily into reviews, poetry sections of magazines (when versified), and so on. They are labelled as poetry in the title of the volume, *Fragments of Ancient Poetry*, but clearly they cannot simply be called poetry, since they are not in verse. Their distinction is heightened, or solidified, by their status as translations: by calling this measured prose a translation of "poetry," Mac-Pherson asks that while reading we march shadowy Gaelic feet through exotic Gaelic meters, but in the vaguest of ways. He is consistently somewhat foreign in his English, and the effort of translation is always before our eyes. His most constant marker of foreignness is inversion, as when, in my example, he begins his sentence with an adjective: "Lovely I saw thee first."[10] I can readily believe that the foreignness of the prose reflects the Gaelic original, but the more important point is surely that the poems have been left partly untranslated, since the translator's job is to rid a work of foreignness. MacPherson chooses the appearance of literality over a completely Englished version. James MacPherson, the translator, has brought treasures down from the Highlands, and he makes sure that his pieces demonstrate how difficult the trip was, how much work he has done. Something that looks like the mist of the Highlands hangs about these "poems." Taken together, these formal and atmospheric elements make up a style of originality, by which I mean a style which presents itself quite aggressively as original, unusual. Whether we feel that this claim is true is less important, at this stage, than recognizing that the poems themselves loudly make the claim. They seem to demand a new generic category, or a new thematic category, or a new linguistic category, of which they would be the only members.

The *Fragments* cleverly and very successfully conjure extra-poetic elements contained in the Highland mist, clinging associations that form a large part of the effect of all of MacPherson's efforts. The *Fragments* mostly conjure; that is, the Highland mist and imagined context of the poems take precedence over more implicit or essential qualities. The mist itself, figured in the obscure and confusing syntax and the broad, gestural diction, stands in the way of specificity. The simple success of MacPherson's designs (his creation of a fascinating and distinctive container) may be seen with interesting clarity in an enraptured response to the *Fragments*, contained in a letter sent to William Shenstone in June 1760, along with the book. The writer begins by quoting Gray's "Elegy," in reference to blushes unseen, and goes on:

Thanks to the taste and love of the ingenious translator, that [sic] we have not to lament the utter loss of these pieces, which reflect so much lustre on the memory of the original bards. Here we see poets framed by the hand of nature; their manners rude and uncultivated, as the wilds they inhabit; unacquainted with *Aristotle* and *Horace*, but pouring the (I had almost said) involuntary effusions of Minds filled with true poetic fire, deeply interested in the themes they sung, devoid of all rules, they attach and warm the heart, by an amazing though secret power, the constant effect of copying nature, but copying her justly; to which the languid efforts of art bear scarce so interesting a proportion as the shadow to the substance ... [11]

There is a lot in this letter, but nothing specific about the poems, no memorable lines quoted, except for Gray's. All the remarks are atmospheric, environmental; for this reader, for almost all readers, the poems are above all part of an inspired, ancient Highland scene, somehow saved and presented by MacPherson. Reference to Gray's verse is perfect here, since this reader is convinced that through some

miraculous overhearing he is hearing the mute Miltons, seeing the
blush unseen, the paradoxical but powerful pleasures of which he
records. MacPherson has calculated the source of this excitement
perfectly: he knew how happy his readers were to literalize Young's
metaphors about the powers of genius, which inhabits a land beyond
rule, and certainly beyond London. Remembering that it is just
1760, it is important to emphasize that MacPherson has needed to
calculate carefully because under this rapture – indeed, giving rise to
this rapture – is a tightly bound sense of propriety. Behind this
reader's dizzy perception of rudeness and absence of rule is a still
functioning and forceful context of art and constraint. His rapture is
pointedly a rapture of relief. It is crucial to the success of the *Fragments*
that they do not try to make this context of constraint disappear.
Because they are presented as "ancient," they do not ask that the
reader would write in this style, or that contemporary poets use it:
they simply provide a brief vacation, "enjoyment." They allow the
reader to forget contemporary constraint briefly by enveloping him
in obscuring clouds of mist. So the Preface to the *Fragments* (a sales
pitch written by Hugh Blair) begins not with discussions of poetic
merit, but with claims of historical authenticity, and notes on the
poems' antiquity. He then moves on to a discussion of the Highlands,
and only finally arrives at the poems themselves, in a paragraph
which begins: "Of the poetical merit of these fragments nothing shall
here be said" (vii).

The smallness of the *Fragments* is purposeful, a posture of humility
appropriate to apprentice work. MacPherson's next strategic move is
an impressive and bold one. Blair's Preface to the *Fragments* mentions
that some of the fragments are apparently part of a larger whole,
fragments indeed, from a "lost" epic that might still be recovered.
This canny advertisement, a message Blair has picked up from
MacPherson himself, shows the depth of MacPherson's plans, and
the extent of his ambition. Rapture, based on relieved forgetting like
that of Shenstone's correspondent, comes and goes. MacPherson
finally wants an impressive solidity, a solidity he can parlay into a
foundation for his fortunes. The *Fragments* inspire rapture, and gain
MacPherson attention; he consolidates his position by publishing his
epic. In producing an epic, MacPherson is asking for the establishment to bring all the definitional mania of mid-century scholarship to bear. This is a gamble, but the gamble is worth it to him. In
1760, it is still more important to win the establishment than the

popular ear; for the career that MacPherson eventually follows out, it is more important to associate with the important than to sell a large number of copies. "Notice," followed by acceptance, can create a spot for him in the select society of the ruling class. Money and influence circulate in this world, and once there MacPherson aggressively and successfully gets his share. In this sense the famous disdain of Samuel Johnson is less important to MacPherson than the parallel opportunity to move about London society with James Boswell (which he did in 1763). In other words, MacPherson calls *Fingal* (what the "lost" epic will be named once found and published at the end of 1761) an epic so that it will at least be tentatively admitted into the close and rigorous circle of criticism and learning. The *Fragments* get brief mention in the periodicals; as a result of its epic pretensions, *Fingal* gets major mention, and frequently takes up the first page. *The Monthly Review*, for instance, extended its review over several issues, and mobilizes an incredible weight of learning.[12] In almost all the reviews and mentions, *Fingal* is tried at the Aristotelian bar. It is sometimes found wanting, as it was in the end by *The Monthly*. Hugh Blair, a relatively forgiving classicist, exonerated *Fingal*, even celebrated it, by his version of the same criteria, as did the *Critical Review*.[13] The important feature, for MacPherson's purposes and mine, is not the verdict, but rather the engagement of critical machinery itself.

The brilliant part of MacPherson's presentation of *Fingal* is that in spite of the claim for neo-classical respectability, *Fingal* is also protected by the tartan plaid, the same historical and geographical material the *Fragments* mobilize so effectively. Since Ossian (a speaker in the *Fragments*, now elevated to author) wrote outside of and before the English tradition, in a dark and barbarous time, he cannot be totally accountable to the hard schemes of the neo-classical epic. Even the basically hostile reviewer in *The Monthly* admits this:

Our readers must not, hence, however, imagine us so hypercritical as to expect, that Ossian should have composed with as much poetical propriety as Homer or Virgil. (p. 43)

He decides, however, to take Ossian to task anyway, making this shrewd observation:

It is with reluctance we should enter into a strict examination of the work before us, as an epic poem; however, we conceive ourselves, in some measure, obliged to consider it, as many of its admirers have allowed it consummate merit *as such*, and have risked its reputation, perhaps a little unadvisedly, on a comparison with the more perfect works of the kind among the ancients. (p. 43)

Even though *The Monthly* goes on to refuse *Fingal* epic honors, that refusal is tempered, and perhaps rendered almost inconsequential, by the obscuring Highland mists. In order to condemn *Fingal* on legal grounds, a critic must invest so absolutely in pedantic insistence on prescribed rule that the argument becomes embarrassingly arid, and so almost all critics take a little edge off their rules before applying them.

The Monthly's writer was surely right, though, in observing that the poem asks for such pedantry by its very title. As the verdict of *The Monthly*'s review shows, MacPherson's gamble was in fact a gamble; thus begins the famous "Ossianic controversy," which I will treat later. That the *Monthly* takes several issues to arrive at its qualified conclusions shows equally clearly that MacPherson wins even when he loses, since respectable and serious attention is what he is after. Many readers in fact accorded *Fingal* qualified success, forgiving faults on the grounds of foreignness. *The Critical*'s reviewer gives this version of the status of Ossian outside of the canon:

It would be as absurd to examine this poem by the rules of Aristotle, as it would be to judge a Lapland jacket by the fashion of an Armenian gaberdine. (p. 410)

Typically, this reviewer does in fact go on to make some Aristotelian observations, as I mentioned above. The important thing is that MacPherson has claimed the importance of this sort of response, and that his book is just obscured enough to make reviewers hesitate.

In sum, whether Highland mist or epic claims, the extra-poetical material that the Ossian poems bring along with them is crucial to their reception and identity.[14] The context this material creates is, however, a compromised one. In the plainest sense, simply calling *Fingal* an epic gets it long reviews, a bulky sort of attention, but also compromises it with the weight of generic classification. At this level, the possible extent of the success of the poem is qualified, pedantic and chancy. *Fingal*'s simultaneous identity as ancient Highland song creates a more useful compromise. To quote the description in *The Annual Register* for 1761: "If we owe [Ossian's] imperfections to the times in which he lived, we are also not a little indebted to them, for

the numberless beauties by which our author is particularly
distinguished" (p. 281). The *Register* goes on to attribute both the
luxuriant, figurative style of the poems and the "pathetic and
terrible" union of sentiment and violence to the same source, "the
times." This is the balance MacPherson benefits most from. Ossian's
Highland antiquity gets him outside of the bright glare of critical rule
(so we may forgive his imperfections), and the same Highland
antiquity lets him come in and enjoy the benefits of acceptance, lets
his virtues be appreciated without trespass of critical propriety.
MacPherson does not want to trespass: he profits from Ossian's
difference, but he also wants the world of propriety to be just as it is,
and he wants to be a part of that world. This description of
MacPherson's gamble helps us understand why establishment
readers were so obsessed with what seems to us to be the dullest part
of the whole business, proofs of Ossian's antiquity. To mid-century
readers, antiquity is the founder of Ossian's fortunes. It underwrites
and legitimizes the unlearned, heroic-sentimental pleasures that are
the real substance of the poems. Without antiquity, the whole
comfortable house of establishment acceptance falls down like a
house of cards. Lest this seem an exaggeration, hear the reviewer
from *The Annual Register*:

But if, notwithstanding these marks of antique genuineness, which add so
much weight to the editor's assertion, this extraordinary piece should prove,
after all, a modern composition; then would its faults admit of little
extenuation, its beauties sink in that peculiar value which they derive from
primitive simplicity; and the poem, however well imagined, and happily
executed, and with all the merit of a fine original, be nevertheless esteemed
but as a grand imposture. (p. 282)

Easygoing as we are, this argument may seem extraordinary now,
since this writer is essentially claiming that he might not be allowed
to enjoy these poems even if he wants to. MacPherson's readers, as
much as they want to, are afraid to make the leap. They need the
reassurance that they will land on conceptually solid ground.

This brief depiction of the careful strategy of MacPherson's
Ossianic publishing will not surprise the modern reader, since he has
been depicted for so long as an ungainly opportunist. He was not,
however, ungainly in the least, and the story of MacPherson's success
is not simply a story of publishing acumen. The Ossian poems may
quite effectively obscure themselves, but it would be wrong to argue

or imply that what they are about is somehow unimportant or secondary. The great popularity of Ossian's works was supported by the way the texts themselves accept and deny the scrutiny that followed upon readerly enthusiasm. There is an inside to the Ossian poems, in spite of the seeming superficiality of MacPherson's ambitions. Evaluation of MacPherson's accomplishment must rise out of a closer look at the poems; this is the second of the categories I proposed earlier. His contemporaries thought so too, and in their case the closer look, when turned aside by these baffling texts, led naturally to the Ossianic controversy.

Their impenetrable density helped to fuel speculation about them and also helped to resist discovery; given free reign, imagination creates an identity for the poems that competes vigorously with the ill-perceived facts. The open and closed nature of Ossian's poems can be illustrated by looking at one of the features that contemporary readers liked best: their strikingly modern quality. By this I mean passages of feeling like this one:

Often did I turn my ship; but the winds of the east prevailed. Nor Clutha ever since have I seen, nor Moina of the dark-brown hair. She fell in Baclutha, for I have seen her ghost. I knew her as she came through the dusky night, along the murmur of Lora: she came like the new moon, seen through the gathered mist; when the sky pours down its flaky snow, and the world is silent and dark.[15]

Ossian's heroes are not only violent and capable, like those of (say) Homer, but they also melt with feminine feeling, valuing not only female beauty but also female swoons of sentiment. They love the dark, the cold, bad weather, and are given to feeling (while out in Nature) belated, old and melancholy. These features please Ossian's readers, but alarm follows upon the pleasure, and provided the impetus for the first investigations of the poems' actual identity. How could they be so modern in spirit? After all, MacPherson claimed that they were from the third century. All explanation of Ossian's modernity is created after the fact, and imagination so outruns the facts that the facts did not catch up for a full century and more. I will take imagination and fact in turn, dealing first with contemporary figurative explanations for the poems' modern appeal, and secondly with some of the facts that we can now discern. With facts in hand, imagination and fact can be re-mixed together: the mixture produces the Ossianic effect.

Hugh Blair, previously mentioned Edinburgh literatus (he would publish *Lectures on Rhetoric and Belles-Lettres* two decades later), was one of the readers whose pleasure led to alarm and a need to explain. What Blair found so attractive in these poems, and what troubled him, can be seen clearly in his "Critical Dissertation on the Poems of Ossian" of 1763. For purposes of comparison, Blair introduces a prose translation of some runic poetry, which he uses to illustrate "barbaric" verse. He then goes on:

[The runic poetry] is such poetry as we might expect from a barbarous nation. It breathes a most ferocious spirit. It is wild, harsh and irregular; but at the same time animated and strong... But when we open the works of Ossian, a very different scene presents itself. There we find the fire and enthusiasm of the most early times, combined with an amazing degree of regularity and art. We find tenderness, and even delicacy of sentiment, greatly predominant over fierceness and barbarity. Our hearts are melted with the softest feelings, and at the same time are elevated with the highest ideas of magnanimity, generosity and true heroism. When we turn from the poetry of Lodbrog to that of Ossian, it is like passing from a savage desert into a fertile and cultivated country. How is this to be accounted for? or by what means to be reconciled with the remote antiquity attributed to these poems? (p. 96)[16]

If the special something of Ossian's poetry is tightly linked to his place outside of the niceties of neo-classical poetic tradition, how are we to explain his very nice, deliciously timely sentiment? Blair explains it by reproducing the literary tradition in Celtic garb. He describes the institution of the bards (of which Ossian was conjecturally a member) as a stable and historically continuous one. Because poetry was institutionalized, it could be cultivated, and the product of cultivation is refinement:

From all this, the Celtic tribes clearly appear to have been addicted in so high a degree to poetry, and to have made it so much their study from the earliest times, as may remove our wonder at meeting with a vein of higher poetical refinement among them, than was at first to have been expected among nations whom we are accustomed to call barbarous. (p. 98)

Blair's sense of literary history is of the most unclouded sort: practice makes perfect. The type of hero that we find in Ossian, for instance, is a result of a healthy, ever-improving tradition, where a sense of the past does not burden or constrict the poet. The example of precedent produces healthy rivalry and above all progress. The bards "rivalled and endeavoured to outstrip those who had gone before them ... is it not natural to think that at length the character of a hero would appear in their songs with the highest lustre?" (p. 99). Lustre results from assiduous polishing. Blair is one of the critics who refuses to condemn Ossian by strict neo-classical rules (though he does his own brand of Aristotelian criticism), and perhaps some of his placid acceptance rests upon the fact that he has snuck classicism into the Ossianic story. In his view, these extra-classical poems are themselves classical, produced by and engaged in a literary history with a strong sense of tradition; he gets to have his primitivism and his neo-classicism too. His learned justification of the sentimental pleasures of Ossian is a common one, in a more general form, and it points out the central accomplishment of the poems, which is to sell refinement under the cover of primitive simplicity.

Factually speaking, Blair is, oddly enough, not entirely wrong in his description of the source of the "refinement" of the Ossian poems. MacPherson's poems were the product of a long tradition, a tradition that had many classical features. MacPherson's Gaelic sources have been outlined again and again, so I will only briefly summarize here. The rise of the actual Ossianic ballads lies 1,000 years later than Blair imagines, in the fourteenth and fifteenth centuries, but their history is a good bit like what Blair describes. Bardic verse, which flourished under the healthy clan system of this era, apparently had many classical characteristics. It was highly aware of itself as a tradition, developed a diction particular to itself, and worked in the forms associated with patronage: eulogy, elegy and the depiction of military exploits. Stories of the Finn, a military clan led by Finn-Macoul (whom MacPherson calls Fingal, and who is Ossian's father), had been part of the Irish bardic repertory for centuries. The Irish material is in fact not what MacPherson knew, but rather the source of his sources. MacPherson's knowledge is mediated by the Highland Bards (often trained in Ireland); the Ossianic ballads are popular descendants of this body of classical material, and seem to have been most vigorous from the fifteenth to the eighteenth centuries.[17] One of the best early recordings of this popular verse is the well-known *Book of the Dean of Lismore*, compiled around 1512. Modern scholarship has shown that MacPherson had this manuscript in his possession, though it is doubtful he could fully understand it.[18] The ballads recorded in this book were in fact primarily oral, and part of a strong and stable oral tradition.[19] This sort of tradition is different from the accumulative and literary (written) tradition that Blair has in mind, but it is a tradition, and the quality of the poetry in it indicates its vigor.

Very little concrete information has survived as to exactly what ballads MacPherson knew. MacPherson had grown up in the Highlands, and he would have had the local and familiar knowledge of the native; but he does not seem to have been literate in Gaelic (i.e., able to read the older manuscripts he came in contact with, or write in Gaelic himself). Much of the narrative in his productions comes directly from traditional sources, and occasionally his "poetry" will run quite close to some recorded oral version of his era. Deciding exactly how close MacPherson's version may run to eighteenth-century oral material is obviously made more difficult by the variability that may have existed in different oral versions, all of them unknown to us. Derick Thomson believes MacPherson knew thirteen or fourteen ballads of various types. So, to be brief, the relationship, on a factual level, between MacPherson's works and traditional ballads is actual but extremely loose. At the same time, it is important to hold onto the fact that MacPherson has drawn his inspiration from this traditional verse. That is to say, the inspiration is not his: he is not, in general, making things up. Whatever we actually call his works, they clearly come under the wing of traditional Ossianic ballads, which really did, which really do, exist.

Blair clearly invents reasons for the sentimental nature of Ossian's poetry. Again, though, in all his ignorance, Blair is right in a way. One of the most striking and interesting parallels between Mac-Pherson's version and traditional ballad versions is indeed the "modern," melancholy, twilight tone. Here is another example from "The Songs of Selma,"[20] which is more thoroughly infused with this spirit than many of the other pieces (thus its lengthy quotation at the climax of *Werther*). It ends with this lament by Ossian:

But memory fails on my mind. I hear the call of the years; they say, as they pass along, Why does Ossian sing? Soon he shall lie in the narrow house, and no bard shall raise his fame! Roll on, ye dark-brown years; ye bring no joy on your course! Let the tomb open to Ossian, for his strength has failed. The sons of song are gone to rest. My voice remains, like a blast, that roars, lonely, on a sea-surrounded rock, after the winds are laid. The dark moss whistles there; the distant mariner sees the waving trees! (p. 292)

This heart-wringing, in MacPherson's extravagant style, is clearly closely related to the themes of many Ossianic ballads. Here are some excerpts, from a ballad in the *Dean's Book* (the numbers refer to stanzas, rendered in prose here):

1. Time passes wearily in Elphin tonight: last night I thought it passed wearily too; and though wearily I find to-day go by, yesterday lacked nothing in its weary length.
2. Wearisome to me is each succeeding day: it was not so we used to be, with no fighting, no raiding, no learning of athletic feats.

*   *   *

8. The last of the Fian [Finn], who won fame, I am great Oisean, son of Fionn, listening to the voices of the bells – Time passes wearily in Elphin tonight.[21]

Ossian calls himself the last of the Finn because, both in tradition and in MacPherson, his father and son have died before him, leaving him as a discontinuous, fragmented presence in history. In both Mac-Pherson and in tradition, this melancholy fate is the source of much reflection. MacPherson heightens these moments, partly by heightening Ossian's self-consciousness, but this self-consciousness is already relatively high in the traditional ballads. Both MacPherson's Ossian and the traditional Ossian take solace from their singing, in which they conjure up the past as compensation for its loss, and their isolation. One could speculate that the melancholy of the traditional Ossian (most often spelled "Osein") drew MacPherson to him originally. In any case, his melancholy is the foundation of the poems as MacPherson presents them, and we see MacPherson's hand as he molds the traditional characters into heroic sentimentalists. This conjunction of the heroic and the sentimental is important, and is glued together by a sensitivity to "tradition," produced by Mac-Pherson as a feeling for the weight of history. That is: the compensation for the losses of history that Ossian derives from his singing forms the essence of his sentimental posture; it is the obsessive subject of MacPherson's stories, and forms the substance of what makes them "heroic" poems.

Conceptually, heroic verse is oxymoronic: such verse sings the immortality of its subjects, an immortality created by surpassing valor, but the poetry is called into being and required by the fact that immortal heroes always die. The mortal and the eternal encounter each other as Ossian sits and sings alone: this encounter is the source of his "spontaneous" verse. In the terms I proposed for this book,

Ossian encounters the limits of mortality; the result of this encounter is poetry which sings of limitless fame. This oxymoronic or paradoxical encounter resembles other paradoxes that MacPherson encountered. Poems like MacPherson's early lyrics are tellingly mortal, confined in time by their interest in a confined conformity, but they also curiously affirm the impersonal survival provided by literary history: the force of precedent, which perpetuates itself by creating them. Convention arranges a meeting between the forceful but dead material of precedent and the conventional sentiment of the live reader. No wonder that this encounter so often produces the refined elegy, which reproduces in turn a mixture of luxurious contemplation and melancholy loss. Secondly, this is the same meeting Young describes and encourages. The dead past has such life that it kills the present; Young's Bloomian advice is that the oppressed, live poet find expressive life by declaring literary history dead. Thus MacPherson's challenge: to squeeze a livelihood out of the forceful yet lifelessly rule-driven world of establishment criticism and literary history.

MacPherson's Ossian poems arrange the encounter of life and death with busy but gentle sentimentality. His heroes demonstrate a constant but pleasingly gentle awareness of both the loss imposed by passing time and also the life conferred by heroic verse. Towards the end of his epic, Fingal says this to one of his vanquished enemies, whom he has forgiven:

Swaran ... to-day our fame is greatest. We shall pass away like a dream. No sound shall remain in our fields of war ... Our names may be heard in song. What avails it, when our strength hath ceased? O Ossian ... you know of heroes that are no more. Give us the song of other years. (p. 353)

Fingal questions the value of living on in song instead of in body, as a way of expressing the evanescence of his prowess, but he also takes comfort in the songs of past heroes. Heroic verse comforts the present (shielding it from the future) by summoning up the past; Fingal's sense of (impending) loss is soothed by the depiction of past loss, now immortalized in heroic verse. We hear of this moment from Ossian, of course, because this moment of song is also recorded in song. In spite of the continuity that the heroic celebration seems to produce, however, in both MacPherson and in tradition Ossian sings the oxymoronic heroic strain naturally, because he is a paradoxical Bard. Ossian has no Bard to sing to, to pass tradition on to. His son and

father have died before him; he is " the last of the Finn. " No chiefs are
gathered to hear him, because there are no more. Recognizing this
paradox, late eighteenth-century readers called the pleasures of
Ossian's sublime and melancholy posture "the joy of grief," a phrase
taken from the songs themselves. The joy of Ossian's grief springs
from the purity of his melancholy, a melancholy unstrained by
anxiety. Ossian is infinitely close to being overwhelmed by his past,
made small by it, but because he is part of the past (he is singing his
own elegy), recalling it is exhilarating instead of sickening.[22]

Like Gray's Bard, Ossian produces history and tradition at the
moment it is about to disappear.[23] In spite of this troubling end to the
story, which I will come back to, MacPherson's Ossian depends on
and expresses a healthy, empowering sense of tradition. History may
not be able to survive him, but it has produced him, and it produces
song; it is the very subject of song. In a precise parallel to Blair's
history of Gaelic poetry, the poems themselves recapitulate the
tradition they sadly claim to be left out of; they exhilarate us with a
sublime description of the liveliness of a past on the verge of death.
The marketing of the poems emphasizes the vigor of earliness, and I
have noted the relieved rapture this earliness allows to MacPherson's
readers. This rapture is produced (before it is retailed) by the stories,
which, early as they are, depict the very lateness they allow an escape
from. Having expired, MacPherson's Ossian may be left out of our
literary history, but he retains his relevance and his interest by
making the burden of history the subject of his song. No doubt this
formed part of these poems' powerful charm. Ossian is the ultimate
product of tradition, its perfection and also its end. His poems can
serve as a focus for both historical vigor and historical anxiety, for
abundance and loss, mixed in a paradoxical package that mirrors the
state of contemporary verse, verse produced by a tradition that is
both dead and vigorously, imposingly alive. Ossian looks like a poet
who finds tradition (memory, history, bardic precedent) empowering, but he is also dead, long ago. Vigor and extinction go hand in
hand.

Paradoxical pleasures are intense but troubling, since in some way
the partakers of such pleasures must blind themselves to the difficulty
presented by the paradox. This the readers of Ossian did, with gusto:
I have shown Hugh Blair vigorously filling in the blanks. Unlike
Blair, many readers understood the tenuous nature of MacPherson's
claims, and sharply attacked him, giving rise to the "Ossianic

controversy." In discussing this controversy, I want to make two claims. The first is that both MacPherson's allies and his opponents willfully blinded themselves to what was really wrong with the Ossian poems. His critics have much to say about his faults, but these accusations are spurious, and I will try to uncover their source. At this point I can indicate their source generally by noting that Ossian's lonely depiction of extinction reminds us strongly of the extinction of traditional Highland culture, the most precipitous phase of which exactly coincides with MacPherson's publications. My second claim comes on the heels of the first: there *is* something wrong with the Ossian poems, and that something can be clearly described. It can only be described, though, by looking through and past the original terms of the Ossianic controversy.

In some ways, the controversy can be compressed into an argument over naming, and I begin by noting the various names which have been applied to the process which produced the Ossian poems. Two possible names oppose each other, "forgery" and "original"; a third, "imitation," sits between these. The poems call themselves by a fourth name, dimly related to all three of these: "translation." My summary of MacPherson's relationship to traditional sources was brief, but I hope it was enough to make clear that "forgery" does not work particularly well as a description of MacPherson's activities. MacPherson attributes the poems to "Ossian," but so does the tradition he worked from; several poems in the *Dean's Book* are entitled "The Author of this is Oisin." Certainly there are dishonesties in his presentation, particularly in his refusal to state clearly what material was his own, so perhaps it would be best to say that he was not simply a forger. The poems are in fact imitations of a sort, but that term does not do justice to MacPherson's inspired transformation of his sources. "Originals" has its applications here, but does not help in describing his obvious and almost total indebtedness. So we are left with MacPherson's own term, "translations." "To translate" has lost some its linguistic interest since 1760. It used to have a whole array of interesting concrete and abstract uses. First among them is the simple act of moving something from one place to another, to transfer: it can describe the transport of a person to heaven without death, or (of Ossianic relevance) it can describe the moving of mortal remains from one place to another. It can also describe a sort of rapture, a figurative use derived, one supposes, from "translation" to another state of being. These various meanings form a linguistic array which pictures the Ossian poems perfectly. Translation is the right term, and in tracing out what MacPherson means by translation we find our way to the heart of the controversy.

I have already foreclosed on the accusation that MacPherson simply made it all up, which is the substance of most of the accusations levelled at him by his contemporaries. Undeniably, though, a lot of things happen to the traditional material as MacPherson translates it from its home to the wide written world. One of the things that happens, which annoys modern readers, and annoyed the more knowledgeable of his contemporaries, is that the two main strands of Gaelic heroic tales, the Cu Chulainn and Finn cycles, are mixed promiscuously together. Derick Thomson is forgiving on this issue, pointing out that tradition had begun to mix them during MacPherson's time anyway: "MacPherson carried to its logical conclusion a tendency which was already becoming apparent" (p. 12). He goes on to say, however, that MacPherson had carried this mixing "far beyond" what folk tradition indicated, and that he "arranged his material in his own way." When conjuring up his prose, MacPherson commonly worked from several versions of his stories, taking what he wished from tradition and adding what he wished from his own imagination. The nature of what results from this process is described by Alfred Nutt, a late nineteenth-century scholar of Celtic tradition:

For the student, whether of Celtic myth or saga, of Celtic Archaeology, or of Gaelic style and literary form, MacPherson's poems are worthless; they disregard the traditional versions of the legends, they depart from the traditional representation of the material life depicted in the old and genuine texts, and they utterly ignore the traditional conventions of Gaelic style.[24]

Hardly translated by Ossian's beauties, Mr. Nutt participates here in the spirit of oral tradition, which abhors novelty of all kinds. Oral traditions are deeply conservative: for instance, the health of Gaelic tradition in the Highlands during this period can be measured by the fact that ballads collected in the *Dean's Book* in 1512 look very much like ballads collected in the eighteenth century. Mr. Nutt has absorbed oral conservatism as a rule, and in the historical structure of Celtic tradition which he envisions he can give MacPherson no place. If we ask why MacPherson can't put Cu Chulainn and Finn together, or contrive a new death for Oscar (Ossian's son), tradition will answer, like any good authority figure, "because he can't." In this sense, oral tradition is like literary history as I have described it, and the reward for agreeing to be bound by its rules is to be included, to find a place. MacPherson can't or won't hear this injunction, and, ignoring the interior energies of Gaelic tradition, "arranges his material in his own way." This independence could in fact be seen as the independence of the translator, who is required to be both within a particular linguistic tradition and also outside of it.

That this independence should be the source of recrimination instead of congratulation is interesting. Taken together with the common modern accusation that the poems are conventionally sentimental, the net result looks like a conspiracy to deny Mac-Pherson credit for his exertions, since he is called both weakly derivative and offensively independent. Factually speaking, we can say that in his search for a way to make his voice distinctive, and so find his way out of Highland poverty, MacPherson finds and mines a rich seam that runs precisely between Gaelic oral tradition and written "western" tradition. Just as his use of inversion and other stylistic quirks gives the Ossian poems the feel of slight foreignness, of being partly untranslated, their material, as I have described it, stops somewhat short of total translation into something else. Mac-Pherson's Ossian is not the traditional Ossian, but neither is he simply an eighteenth-century author. As a result of this balancing act, MacPherson was regarded with suspicion on both sides of the linguistic divide by the end of his life. I don't know if this bothered him. He died a rich man, and an important man. He was buried in Westminster Abbey, though (truth be told) he bought this privilege with his hard-earned money. His money gave him what his time called "independence," and so the judgments of his critics eventually became an abstract problem for him. His independence is his great accomplishment, as translator and career-man. It is also, though, his great flaw, and his independence eats the heart out the Ossian poems.

As I noted, independence is at least potentially an asset to the translator, and MacPherson was very interested in his own in-dependence, in all its senses: others were too. One of those senses is material, but for MacPherson the most immediately important senses are literary in implication; in the end, the material and the literary fatally intertwine. In discussing MacPherson's independence, ob-servers, with fascinating frequency, adopt as an explanatory meta-phor that most integral and inertly independent of elements, gold. MacPherson picks it up in describing his success in a Preface of 1773:

That they have been well received by the Public, appears from an extensive sale; that they shall continue to be well received, he may venture to prophecy without that gift of that inspiration, to which poets lay claim. Through the medium of version upon version, they retain, in foreign languages, their native character of simplicity and energy. Genuine poetry, like gold, loses little, when properly transfused; but when a composition cannot bear the test of a literal version, it is a counterfeit which ought not to pass current. (p. 20)[25]

MacPherson's claim is a complex one, and takes some deciphering. This passage is from the end of the Preface; the Preface as a whole begins with a cynical reflection on the vagaries of taste and the fickleness of reputation and reception. At the end taste (reception as marked by sales) is recuperated as a measure and an assurance of authenticity and pure, independent quality. MacPherson's immediate point, though, is to justify the fact that his translation is prose instead of verse. To justify this fact is to justify the generically undecidable, genetically unknowable nature of the poems. Mac-Pherson reassures himself by saying that the "literal version" (a gentle way of saying "prose") tests the authenticity of the supposed original by removing its form, whisking away its skeleton of rhyme and meter. In MacPherson's picture, the poems' genuineness, their inherent poetic nature, places them beyond form. Ossian's works have the full expressive independence of genius. This golden independence makes them eminently translatable, and so from the Highlands to London (this preface is dated from London), to Germany and Italy and beyond Ossian's poems are Ossian's poems, integral, themselves. Genius, like gold, is a universal currency, accepted everywhere.

MacPherson is actually rewriting a passage from Hugh Blair's "Critical Dissertation," published ten years earlier:

Elegant, however, and masterly as Mr. MacPherson's translation is, we must never forget, whilst we read it, that we are putting the merit of the original to a severe test. For we are examining a poet stripped of his native dress: divested of the harmony of his own numbers. We know how much grace and energy the works of the Greek and Latin authors receive from the charm of versification in their original languages. If, then, destitute of this advantage, exhibited in a literal version, Ossian still has power to please as a poet ... we may very safely infer, that his productions are the offspring of true and uncommon genius. (p. 19)

Blair not only sets form aside: he also makes the violation of traditional oral form into a mark of MacPherson's integrity and Ossian's genius. The word "violation" is authorized by the undressed Highlander who appears in the midst of Blair's metaphors, but I want to set this figure aside for a moment. Here we can see, simply, how masterful MacPherson's calculations are in this context: he has marketed Ossian's genius flawlessly. If the magic of Ossian is a local product, dependent on his location in ancient times and Highland fastness, how wonderful, how strange, that he reaches international fame because he doesn't mind being put into a container that refuses locality, even the broad locality of a specific language.

How wonderful, that is, that MacPherson could balance these two demands. His balance is very much like the balance he strikes, in his own description, between the symbolic and literal identity of gold. He moves easily from the sale of the book, the vulgar world of currency, to what he claims the currency stands for: the independent, unstamped gold of the poems' essence. In this picture gold descends from magnificent metaphor (for genius) to pedestrian symbol (the commercial success of a book) to a weight jingling in MacPherson's pocket, something he can take with him when he moves to London and goes to parties with Boswell. Gold is a good metaphor for integrity, but it is also a good metaphor for a sort of symbolic hollowness, since in its function as a medium of exchange it can literally become anything. In the same way, the elaborate presentation of the Ossian poems' beautiful independence from the constraints of form is itself contaminated by the commercial foundation of MacPherson's description. MacPherson's boldness in associating genius with a sort of avarice and smug self-satisfaction may shock us, but in fact it is explainable. It is part of the rhetoric of translation: these are not his poems.

MacPherson can compliment Ossian's poems so extravagantly because he claims to be merely a translator, independent of his own productions, which represent the gold of someone else's genius. MacPherson represents himself as an admiring sort of midwife, introducing the innocence of ancient Gaelic culture into the broad world, where its native integrity protects it from evil: that is, translation has no effect on its being, just as gold has value everywhere, and crosses borders without diminution. The money, currency, accrues to MacPherson; the golden integrity is added to Ossian's account. Translation is accomplished without deformation.

What a delightful picture of the complex working out of the various cultural forces present here. Gaelic becomes English; poetry becomes prose; MacPherson becomes famous; the Highlander becomes a citizen of the world; literature is circulated to admiration; and golden genius becomes gold sovereigns. This whole stable picture of integrity is underwritten by independence, the independence which MacPherson describes and which he attributes to the poems. Translation is accomplished without deformation because this independence erases borders, transcends difference: in short, because the poems are somehow beyond or above form.

We already know that independence has its dark side for the poems' fate in the canon, and in the same way this magic picture conjured up by Blair and MacPherson has its dark side too. We have seen this darkness, briefly, in the odd, lonely appearance of the stripped Highlander in Blair's description: "we are examining a poet stripped of his native dress"; the other epithets are "divested" and "destitute." This naked character is the next step on the way to understanding the force and interest of the Ossianic controversy. In order to appreciate his shadowy and sudden appearance, though, it is necessary to detour briefly through the Highlands of 1760.

The Jacobite rebellions of 1715 and 1745 mark the entrance of the Highlands into British culture. At the beginning of the eighteenth century, the Gaelic-speaking people of northern Scotland were a mystery to the rest of the population of the island, though they were a feared mystery, descending periodically to prey on the lowlanders. At the end of the eighteenth century they were a different kind of mystery: a culture whose strange ways were a subject of great curiosity (mystery made into a cultural commodity), a culture that was rapidly disappearing into the legends of history. It is common to fix the date of the Highland's decline at 1745, the year of Bonny Prince Charlie and the Great Rebellion, and certainly there is reason to do this. The martial spirit of the clans had made its one, final, all-too-conspicuous appearance, the Hanoverian establishment had noticed it, and decided to eliminate it. The policy of elimination took several paths, but all focused on destroying the functioning of the clan, which they took (correctly) to be the central feature of Highland culture.[26] The policies actually put into practice aimed at reducing the isolation of the Highlands, at mixing this durably foreign culture in with the rest of Britain. The hereditary jurisdiction of the chiefs was abruptly ended, curbing their despotic control over their clans, and the substitution of British law was accomplished by the quartering of troops in the region and the large-scale construction of military roads.[27]

Inaccessibility, which helps produce the Highland mist that shrouds the poems, was also an important force for the Highlanders themselves in the eighteenth century, for good and for bad. It preserved them from conquest by and mixture with the rest of Britain, but it also made them exotic; their invisibility makes seeing them (in poems and stories, in travelogues, or even in person) interesting. The isolation of the Gael was compounded by their very foreign tongue, which has very little connection with what we call "Scottish." As early as 1716, the teaching of English was seen as a way of reducing the Highlands.[28] The problem with Gaelic, what made it so foreign, was not that it was especially difficult to learn, but rather how it had to be learned. It could not be learned from books; in the mid-eighteenth century there were no Gaelic grammars, and a few religious texts made up the whole of printed Gaelic. There was, of course, a very large population of fluent speakers to learn from, but they added a different kind of inaccessibility to the already formidable linguistic barrier. They were the primitive Highlanders themselves, who not only spoke an exotic tongue but who also were ignorant, desperately poor, dirty and mysteriously violent. Gaelic had to be learned from the mouth of an actual speaker, and, because the upper classes so eagerly abandoned their native ways as they mixed with British society, the only reward for learning Gaelic was the ability to talk with lower-class Highlanders.

Both of these methods of including the Gael (building roads and attempting to suppress Gaelic) sought to rend the shroud of secrecy that surrounded them, or which seemed to surround them. So it is not a simply gratuitous pun on my part to include in this category the outlawing of "Highland garb" as one of the most effective methods of eliminating the crucial and dangerous difference of Highland culture. The distinctive way in which the Highlanders shielded themselves from the elements provided a sort of badge of culture, separating them from others and identifying them with each other. Walter Scott explains the purpose of this tactic best:

The system of disarming the Highlands had been repeatedly resorted to upon former occasions, but the object had been only partially attained. It was now resolved, not only to deprive the Highlanders of their arms, but of the ancient garb of their country; a picturesque habit, the custom of wearing which was peculiarly associated with use of warlike weapons. The sword, the dirk, the pistol were all as complete parts of the Highland dress as the plaid and the bonnet, and the habit of using the latter was sure to remind the wearer of the want of the former. It was proposed to destroy this association of ideas, by rendering the use of the Highland garb, in any of its peculiar forms, highly penal.[29]

As Scott describes, the government cannily fixed upon a kind of metonymical linchpin of Highland culture: not crucial in itself, but through its connections, its associations, leading to the very heart of Highland identity. The tartan goes with weapons; weapons go with clanship; clanship goes with the Highlander's dangerous independence from the rest of Britain. In terms of its specific goals, this law was very effective, for though it was repealed only four decades later, the tartan as such did not reappear.[30]

The legal repression of Gaelic culture was terribly successful, but the Highlands were opened to this repression by internal causes, and the success of its repression must be at least partly attributable to this vulnerability. The close-knit, purposefully cohesive and isolated social structure of the clan was under pressure throughout the seventeenth century, and in the early eighteenth century this pressure intensified and expanded.[31] Chiefs felt ever more strongly the attractions of Lowland life (sons were regularly sent out of the Highlands for their education). The old communal economy, where rent was paid in kind (and in blood, in the form of periodic military service), was not designed to satisfy the needs of this new way of life. The chiefs needed a transportable medium of exchange, something to translate their local wealth into a true British wealth. They wanted to live in Edinburgh or London; they wanted the accoutrements of the British manor house; they wanted to travel to the continent.[32] This material translation is effected by money, and the eighteenth-century Highland chief began to feel the need for it. There were a number of ways to get more money out of a given estate, all of which involved "improvement," methods of increasing cash return through increased productivity or a change in the product itself. Improvement usually implied enclosure of previously communal land, and the new product was (in most cases) wool, which implied not only enclosure but depopulation. These methods were entirely destructive of the old communal life, and substituted for it a new focus on the individual and individual holdings.[33] This mixed cultural and economic process is emotionally described by an observer in 1801:

The Lairds have transferred their affections from the people to flocks of sheep and the people have lost their veneration for the Lairds ... It is not a pleasant change.[34]

This is the situation that MacPherson found on his tours in the early 1760s, the tours he took in order to collect his materials. He was able to obtain the manuscripts he did because their value and contents were becoming increasingly unclear. In the Outer Hebrides (in South Uist) he met the present generation of the bardic family associated with the McDonalds of Clanranald (Lachlan Mac-Mhuirich, or MacVuirich), who gave MacPherson manuscripts that were otherwise being used for tailor's measures. Lachlan himself could not read them.[35] A journey to South Uist is still no small project, and so this anecdote illustrates by the way that not only did MacPherson in fact gather "authentic" or local material, but he took considerable pains to do so.

The Highlanders were very well aware that things had changed, and their descriptions make the Highland Society's *Report* on the Ossianic controversy, published in 1805, fascinating reading. The report itself offers this explanation for the fugitive condition of the Ossianic tradition:

[There has been] a change of manners in the Highlands, where the habits of industry have now superseded the amusement of listening to the legendary narrative or heroic ballad, where consequently the faculty of remembering and the exercise of repeating such tales or songs, are altogether in disuse, or only retained by a few persons of extremely advanced age and feeble health, whom, it is not easy to discover ... (p. 12)

This is part of their explanation of why answering questions about MacPherson's methods has been so difficult. There are several interesting things referred to here, things which return in the delineation of the controversy; note especially that the decrepit ballads are found in the mouths of decrepit people who look a lot like Ossian himself. "Habits of industry" is a slogan for the new commercial order, and is described in a more partisan key by a voice from South Uist, also quoted in the *Report*:

We can easily prove, that the noblest virtues have been ruined, or driven into exile, since the love of money has crept in amongst us; and since deceit and hypocrisy have carried mercenary policy and slavish, sordid avarice into our land. Before this modern change, our Chiefs cherished humanity.[36]

The profound sense of loss that this man feels tends to overwhelm writing about the Highlands in the second half of the eighteenth century, and it is the articulation of this sense of loss rather than the actual circumstances of decline that seems to begin around 1745. This is not the "joy of grief" that will become a fashion through MacPherson's efforts, but real grief over the destruction of a culture, arising from the sudden realization that things have passed away. It is also certainly nostalgia, and a highly colored way of describing the violent hierarchy of old clan society. Various ideologies compete over the wreckage in the Highlands, in a spectacle familiar from imperial encounters everywhere.

In the midst stands Blair's undressed Highlander – to bring him back – forbidden to wear his traditional clothes, expelled from his old way of life, poor but no longer to be feared. To whisk away the tartan leaves him naked, prey to the prying eyes of touring foreigners, of whom Dr. Johnson was only one. As we follow the tides of emigration to the new world, and even as we read the misery depicted in various traveler's accounts, we can at least see that the Highlander's translation to the world that is "Britain" is not accomplished without deformation. Around him cluster the things Ossian's poems bring up; his foreign tongue, his air of violence, the sentiment and nostalgia with which he is viewed; the avarice, the lust for gold, that has changed the Highland economy to one which exports various products in order to generate cash, gold, a useful, translatable medium of exchange.

MacPherson was one of the greatest of Highland exporters, and the Ossian poems drew more attention to the Highlands than anything else, the rebellion of 1745 excepted. They were the source of countless tours, for both aesthetic and scholarly purposes. The scholarly visitors went there to try and determine the authenticity of the poems, to try and find them in their natural state, the "originals." Outwardly, this would seem to have been a simple problem. MacPherson had been difficult about showing his manuscripts, and so the solution could be to go where he went, and see what there was to be found. William Shaw, who wrote a tract about the Ossian poems, and who took considerable effort to explore their sources, describes his frustration in a delightful working of the gold metaphor:

If a man says he has a gold watch in his pocket, and I deny it; if he has it, is there anything easier than convincing me, by shewing it? But to persist in affirming that he has it, and publishing dissertations to prove it; to rail, and abuse all who will not believe him, is an insult to the party, and a degree of stubborn audacity ... [37]

Either MacPherson refused to take his Highland gold out of his pocket, or he could not. We know now that he used traditional materials, but this has been verified through sources other than MacPherson himself. He claimed that he had put his manuscripts in a bookseller's shop for inspection in 1762, but no one saw them (or at least no one who could read them). In 1807, the Highland Society published what looked like the gold watch, the Gaelic originals. As late as 1870, an editor fell upon these "originals" with Highland pride; the title of his edition is *The Poems of Ossian, In the Original Gaelic*. The "Dissertation" attached to this edition fiercely defends the integrity of the Gaelic originals against the ignorance of lowlanders with no knowledge of Gaelic. As we begin reading the "literal" translation into English which the editor provides, and compare it to MacPherson's (which is strung out across the bottom of the page), we find that on this evidence MacPherson's translation is tolerably exact, if idiosyncratically hazy.[38] Is this the gold watch? In fact, no. By the end of the nineteenth century, these texts were understood to be a sort of pidgin Gaelic, cooked up for the occasion by translating from MacPherson's English: "The sentences may be English, or Latin, or Greek, may, in fact, be specimens of a new universal language, but they are not Gaelic ... "[39] The fact that this is not made clear until the late nineteenth century is at least as interesting as MacPherson's apparent concoction of the texts, and is perhaps more important for tracing the source of the controversy. Behind this century-long wait is the undressed Highlander again, and the curious, painful insulation of Gaelic from educated, English-speaking observers.

As I have said previously, in various ways, the Ossianic controversy feeds off the confusion surrounding the Ossian poems, and so describing the controversy naturally produces a kind of summary of the various perspectives on the poems which I have explored so far. Exoticism, the difficulty of translation, the poem's generic vagueness, and the isolation of Gaelic Scotland all reappear as forces of confusion. The controversy is intimately bound up with the complex genealogy and exotic subject matter of the poems. Even the simplest facts about them tended to add to their mystery. The argument against MacPherson's claims is most often represented by Samuel Johnson:

I believe that [the Ossian poems] never existed in any other form than that which we have seen. The editor, or author, never could show the original; nor can it be shown by any other... He has doubtless inserted names that circulate in popular stories, and may have translated some wandering ballads, if any can be found ...

He goes on to add, using the currency version of the gold metaphor:

It is said, that men of integrity profess to have heard parts of it, but they all heard them when they were boys... They remember names, and, perhaps, some proverbial sentiments; and, having no distinct ideas, coin a resemblance without an original.[40]

The positive side of the controversy is well represented by Blair, above, or by Shenstone's enthusiastic correspondent.

It is hard, even from a modern and better-informed perspective, to find our way between these opinions. For MacPherson's contemporaries, and even for MacPherson himself, the insulation of Gaelic tended to frustrate attempts to see it. Take as an example the experience of one highly motivated reader of Ossian, Thomas Jefferson. Reading his books in the wilds of America, Jefferson decided that in order to fully appreciate the beauties of the Celtic bard he would need to ponder the original, and learn a little Gaelic. He wrote to an acquaintance of his in Edinburgh (also named MacPherson) requesting the necessary materials, and received this discouraging reply:

Excepting the specimen of *Temora*, Ossian's poems in the original, never were in print. Sorry I am that a copy of the Gaelic manuscript, of these poems, cannot be procured... I do not at all wonder that *you* should be "desirous of learning the language in which Ossian thought, in which he sung." But, alas, I am afraid that this will be attended with insuperable difficultys. A few religious books aside, we have no publication in the Gaelic language, no dictionary, no grammar.[41]

MacPherson (James, that is) had replied to Jefferson's friend's request for a manuscript with a lament that the orthography of the manuscript was so idiosyncratic that only he could comprehend it, and that he simply did not have time to create a written, translatable "original." This defense is ingenious, partly true, and very difficult to argue with. At this time Gaelic was singularly unavailable to those out of earshot. Spoken by thousands, it had lapsed out of texts. Even the Highland ministers, who delivered sermons in Gaelic, were largely illiterate in Gaelic itself; they were taught to read and write in English.[42] Among those who could read and write Gaelic, the standards of orthography were not fixed, and would not be for another century. The *Dean's Book*, Derick Thomson says, "is written in a peculiar phonetic script, which is not easy to decipher."[43] What MacPherson himself could read of his manuscripts is entirely unclear. In any case, he was quite right that his manuscripts were of a peculiarly unenlightening sort, not absorbable by the rules of a grammar book. Ossian may have written an epic, but Jefferson could not study it as he studied his Homer. On the other side, these same factors strengthened Johnson's assertion that if manuscripts of the Ossian poems existed they had to be fakes because Gaelic was a language without texts, unwritten; it merely "floated in the breath of the people."[44] Johnson's point is double. He insists, quite incorrectly, that "Gaelic MS" is a simple contradiction in terms, since Gaelic is accused of being entirely oral.[45] He makes this mistake because he disbelieves in the possibility of an oral tradition. For Johnson, literary tradition means literary history, which means writing. This is actually the more important of Johnson's accusations, and I will return to it shortly. Without the refinement generated by the presence of writing, Johnson says, all development is short-circuited: "diction, merely vocal, is always in its childhood" (p. 116). One can sense in these small extracts the disorientation imposed on Johnson by oral materials. Without writing, and hence without literary history, precedent, and rule, Johnson can literally see no literature at all. Oral verse looks to him like the disenfranchised Highlander, wandering childishly through his Highland home. If all one gets for Highland pains is the capture of this illiterate, then surely it is not worth the trouble; and surely he could have nothing to do with the sophistication, the modern appeal, of the Ossian poems.

When Highlanders said that they heard the Ossian poems in their youth, they were telling the truth, as far as they knew, for MacPherson's poems were at least partly made up of the poems they had heard. The problem of identity, I have shown, is a *real* problem, and should not be dismissed as simple-mindedness or stubborn national pride. The Highland Committee, attempting to discover exactly what poems MacPherson had in his possession, was faced with answers like this from their Highland correspondents:

I shall make no difficulty of thinking that the editor of Ossian's works has translated those parts of the original which were repeated in my hearing, I will not say with servile exactness, but on the whole inimitably well.[46]

This qualification repeatedly interrupts attempts to pin down exactly what MacPherson did. People who speak in this way squiggle around the problem of form in much the same way that Blair and MacPherson do. MacPherson is defended as having tapped the (golden) essence of the poems, even while transforming what this essence looks like. Such indeed could be a translator's business. If one believes translation without deformation to be possible, then this is what strong translation would look like. Form is accidental, a local feature, which may be left behind when introducing Ossian to higher and foreign spheres. Worrying over local detail looks small, "servile." This is another form of what I have labelled MacPherson's independence. Factually speaking, the presence of this conception of translation of course renders research quite difficult. Lord Webb Seymour, who took a tour in the Highlands and dabbled in Ossianic research, had poems recited to him in Gaelic and then translated. He also spoke to people who claimed to have compared the English and Gaelic versions; but all he was able to say was that "in slight outline" the versions corresponded, or that he "found them to vary but little."[47] The investigator, instead of confidently dividing sheep from goats as he would like, the false and derivative from the true, finds himself confronted with a curious mixed breed, neither one nor the other. If the task is not one of matching words, what is left of the problem?

This vexing and seemingly unavoidable confusion fueled the controversy. Argument about the creation of MacPherson's poems always threatened to degenerate into an argument about the theory of translation, removing the focus of the critical eye from the existence of MacPherson's originals to his relationship to his originals, from forgery to skill. This detoured version of the Ossianic puzzle, though not solvable in any clear way, would have disappeared quietly enough if satisfying originals had been available; people could have made their own decisions, and at least they would have been arguing a question of poetics. MacPherson's refusal to produce his originals was taken as proof of their forgery, as well as a proof of the general perversity of the man. But what could he have shown? manuscripts that no one could read, for one. As for the records of poems taken down from oral recitation, all that he could show would be papers in some contemporary handwriting, perhaps his own. "Original," as a place of reference, begins to shift and slide. Would the original be the poem one would obtain if one asked the same oral source, now? Would it be the words spoken to MacPherson, originally? Because they constitute the problematic element in the argument about translation, these difficulties of verification are the center of the voiced controversy.[48] I do not wish to exonerate MacPherson from fabrication, and am happy to admit that he was difficult over these issues because he had much to hide. The best summary of MacPherson's presentation of his texts is from Joseph Ritson, an exceptionally hard-headed ballad scholar most active in the 1790s. On the flyleaf of his copy of the works of Ossian, he wrote:

> To maintain that Fingal inhabited, in whatever age, any part of the present Scotland, and that his son Ossian composed poems, of many thousand lines, preserved to this day by Highland tradition, and actually here given to the publick, in an English dress, is of the essence of falsehood and imposture.[49]

Stated in this simple factual way, there can be no argument. The claims of factuality advanced by MacPherson, of an actual Highland history and an actual third-century author named Ossian, are false.

The original issues of the controversy end here, unproductively, with impossibilities all around. Progress can be made, though, by changing the view, and shifting issues. When we do this we can see that the voiced, public controversy is merely a symptom of the real problem, the source of which is the tension created by the encounter of oral and written cultures. We have already seen this tension in Johnson's blind and angry accusations. William Shaw (whom I mentioned previously), a native Gaelic speaker and author of the first Gaelic grammar and dictionary, illustrates quite precisely where the problem lies. In his "Enquiry into the Authenticity of the Poems Ascribed to Ossian" (1781), he describes asking some Highlanders to produce some poems of Ossian. He expects his witnesses to produce manuscripts,

> but instead of going to their cabinet for manuscripts, or copies of them, as I expected, application was made to some old man, or superannuated fiddler, who repeated over again the tales of the 15th century ...[50]

There is deep irony in Shaw's disappointment in this veritable Ossian, an old man who is the repository of tradition, and his disgust is the disgust of the outsider, to whom this tradition is meaningless, as

well as the disgust of the literate for the illiterate, and the young for
the old. Shaw cannot see that the "superannuated fiddler" is Ossian
himself, venerable container of a long tradition, the concrete
manifestation of "bard." He sees only an old man. His tour in search
of Ossian is hilariously (if painfully) full of this sort of self-rationalizing
contempt for his very mission. For instance, he insists that the blind
are the best informants remaining, but insults everything they give
him, blind himself to the picture of the blind old Ossian that these
people represent. That is, the beautiful literary blindness of Homer
and of the "real" Ossian cannot be the contemptible or simply
pathetic blindness of dirty Highland inhabitants.[51] When blind old
Homer made up poetry, it was literature; when blind old Highlanders
sing, they sing debased and derivative songs. If Ossian represents a
refuge from time, then clearly the painfully time-bound Highlanders,
so expressive of mortality, cannot give him to us. If they cannot, then
(readers such as Johnson and Shaw conclude) we cannot have Ossian
and the "original" such readers searched for could only have been a
record of MacPherson's originality, now valueless. The conclusion of
such researches is that the relief Ossian brings is unauthorized,
palpable but fictional and hence unusable.

Looking at Ossian from the dead-and-alive perspective of written
literary history, Johnson and Shaw can find stability and refuge from
mortality only in the written record itself, in history. Hard-headed,
they do not want Highland Mist: they want remains, real remnants
independent of 1,000 years of time. With every reason, Johnson
figures faith in Ossian as a resemblance coined without an original, a
sentimental transaction carried out with paper currency. This kind of
skeptical reader refuses Ossian his golden integrity, perhaps correctly,
but for pleasantly figurative reasons. On the lookout for a noble
tradition, William Shaw looks over and past the reality of that
tradition, subliming oral poetry into "breath" and making old and
sad Highlanders singing the tales of loss into "superannuated
fiddlers." The paradoxes return: in pursuit of earliness, "genius,"
Shaw limits his researches by looking for "Ossian" himself, a poet
defined as being both dead and perfectly immortal (like "Homer").
Not finding anything, he concludes, with an angry vigor, that there
is nothing to find.

Ossian's defenders had to counter these charges, and many readers
struggle to solidify conceptual models for the integrity of oral
tradition. They do so, however, as Shaw would, and the mystery of

oral tradition is explained without leaving the primacy of writing behind. The lack of writing is turned from "ignorance" to "purity," and this new metaphor is applied to a retouched picture of "the breath of the people." This is MacPherson:

At a distance from the seat of government, and secured, by the inaccessibleness of their country, [Highlanders] were free and independent. As they had little communication with strangers, the customs of their ancestors remained among them, and their language retained its original purity.[52]

"Independence" returns here, the corollary and source of purity. We should not be surprised, then, when rather later the Highland Society's *Report* draws the same picture by making use of the coin/gold metaphor:

Language is changed from its use in society, as coins are smoothed by their currency in circulation. If the one be locked up among a rude, remote, and unconnected people, like the other when it is buried in the earth, its great features and general form will be but little altered. (*Report*, p. 147)

Tainted, perhaps, by an acquaintance with Johnsonian skepticism, the *Report*'s gold is both debased and pure. That is, as coins, Highland culture has no golden independence from form, but then the coins are buried and so preserved from loss. Such is the power of figure: in this model the activity of Highland culture disappears without writing, and the *Report* insists that the Highlanders cannot wear out their language just by speaking it: strangely, miraculously, they do not use it.[53] In the same way, MacPherson insists that remoteness produces purity. As in a sterile culture dish, any stains or strains upon language must come from outside. These conceptions are part of a broader context, of course: they are familiar *topoi* of the eighteenth century. These *topoi* extend as far as poetics, and primitive people are said to "display themselves to one another without disguise: and converse and act in the uncovered simplicity of nature," making them naturally poetic.[54] This state is usually described as coming before commerce, and before Art, and in MacPherson's picture of remoteness it also comes before the need for translations of any kind, since no one is disguised or wrapped in cultural or linguistic difference. The simplicity of such primitive poets is always tied to boldness, boldness of imagination, and in the anthropomorphic historical model (where ancient history is the childhood of humanity), this boldness is attributed to youthful culture just as it is naturally the domain of actual youth:

The powers of imagination are most vigorous and predominant in youth; those of the understanding ripen more slowly, and often attain not to their maturity, till the imagination begin to flag. Hence, poetry, which is the child of the imagination, is frequently most glowing and animated in the first ages of society. As the ideas of our youth are remembered with a peculiar pleasure on account of their liveliness and vivacity; so the most ancient poems have often proved the greatest favorites among nations. (Blair, p. 90)

In the language I applied to the poems, the losses of age are compensated by the memories of youth, and the natural result is that the memories of youth are contained in the oldest of poems, as old Ossian contains his past. To his defenders, Ossian's compensation offers delicious compensation to them too, since Ossian's posture reflects or mimics their own belated cultural weariness. To his critics, this compensation is a figment of weaker brains, since Ossian's posture is faked and dependent upon a tissue of fabrications.

I can begin to conclude by noting what is perhaps an obvious irony of these pictures of Ossian's credibility. Highland boldness, vigor and resolute independence are quite precisely the qualities that Hanoverian Britain resolved to crush out after their surprising and frightening appearance in the rebellion of 1745. In a process familiar from public discourse about conflict everywhere and always, refined admirers of Ossian blindly and placidly sublime figures out of the Highlands and toss the Highlands themselves away. The lesson of the controversy is that both sides come to the same thing, views from within the definitions of written culture. The "reality" of the "original" Ossian became the subject of dispute, and this translation saves both sides from having to confront oral poetry and its singers. This translation is effected by insisting on golden independence, which underwrites the lapse of form.

Though MacPherson was willing to exploit the appeal of the poems' antiquity, his insistence on an infinitely translatable, formless essence necessarily leaves history out (it is another kind of protection): in the end, Ossian is as independent of time as immortal Homer himself. His antiquity and his Highland remoteness are purely decorative. They have no content, and they engage nothing whatsoever. Ossian and MacPherson both pay for the freedom thus bestowed. Ossian himself expires, lonely, and his mortality is paralleled by that of MacPherson, whose originality perishes along with his works. This is because form is not just a local decoration: it cannot be left behind without consequence. Poetic form may be the same as poetic appearance, but appearance, as an anthropologist would say, is a deep matter. It is only by forgetting the depth of form that appearance can be made superficial. Specifically, in the same way that money slips in underneath the pure disinterestedness of gold, Highlanders themselves crowd in under the metaphors of purity and integrity. As currency undermines the independence of gold, Highlanders undermine the pleasures of the primitive Highlands by assigning more graphic, concrete meaning to the word "primitive." Abstraction is darkened by physical presence or reality, and the controversy is the tug of war between these two levels. Controversy is inevitable because the isolation of the Gael is only partial, not ideal; or, to shift registers, because the Ossian poems are in fact not independent of form, by which I mean their physical presence and their identity as Gaelic ballads or English prose.

Those who criticize MacPherson say one of two things: either that he refused to be guided by the rules of inheritance, deforming and re-forging what he received by "translating" it into something else, or that the whole ethos of earliness is nonsense, that "primitive poetry" is an oxymoron, and that MacPherson is only trying to escape the consequences of the lateness of the age by palming his own originality off as primal simplicity. In both cases he violates what we might call laws of currency, laws of a system in which something stands in for an original. In the first, he undermines the value of the translation by not properly fixing the relationships of representative to original, and in the second he is guilty of pretending that he has a gold original when in fact all he has is the translation. What MacPherson actually did is interestingly lodged between these two versions. He both violates originals and also works without originals; he is also perfectly faithful, in some ways, as both a translator and a folklorist.

Those who value the Ossian poems enjoy and accept and even relish the contradictory nature of Ossian's identity. Poetry enjoyed as a relic of a bygone age is thought of as independent of time; poetry praised as vigorous, youthful and refreshingly unartful is savored for its up-to-date sentiment and gentleness. These contradictions stand on top of a contradictory, or oxymoronic, arrangement of youth and age. Because of their extreme age, the Ossian poems are productions of humanity's youth, and remind us of that youth; because of his extreme age, Ossian is reduced to singing about his youth. Because the Highlands remained retarded, youthful, these productions of old age were preserved from the deformations of younger times. This oxymoron appears on the most basic of levels, in the fact that the person behind the hoary persona is the 25-year-old MacPherson. The Highland Committee encountered a social or practical version: the purest vision of the youth of the tradition that underwrites Mac-Pherson's effort is found in the memories of the superannuated, those who have lived beyond the destruction of their culture, or, worse yet, *was* in their memories, for they may have died. Real old people repeat the brinkmanship of Ossian himself (or they are its original).

The darkest Ossianic paradox is that of Highland purity. This paradox will continue to be an important one throughout this book, since it lies in wait for all complex users of pastoral or primitive simplicity. I have described it previously as the meeting place of the mortal and the eternal. If the preservation of the Ossian poems depends upon the purity of the isolated Highlands, and if their charms come from the beautiful independence of the Highlander from commerce, then – obviously – reading the Ossian poems in an English book in London is to see, in your hands, the palpable evidence of the destruction of the source of your pleasures. If the poems have been collected, then isolation has been breached and cultural purity sullied, and if Ossian's lonely inspirations have been overheard then they have been removed, somehow, from the heard and spoken world that has protected them from the ills of written culture they so deliciously counteract. The very existence of the book pushes Ossian over the edge of his sublime melancholy; purity is no more, commerce has appeared, and the coin of Highland peculiarity and genius is circulating in Britain.[55]

So it is not rhetoric but simple truth to say that pure Ossianic simplicity cannot, by its very nature, be seen or read. If spontaneous song appears in a book, some trick has succeeded. The reader who savors Ossian in a book enjoys the tension produced by this underlying paradox and at the same time regards the tension as somehow resolvable or forgettable. Here we can finally describe what is wrong with MacPherson's poems. Their flaw is not his violation of the canon, of Aristotle's rules, or of the etiquette of translation; it is not in violating Gaelic tradition, or in making things up; it is not, even, in his smug profiteering. MacPherson's flaw is in his ease, his claim that he can hand Highland mystique to the jaded sophisticate with one easy gesture. He claims that the tartan can be whisked away without leaving someone naked. Again, this is not a purely metaphoric way of describing his crime; the Highlander is forcibly mixed into British culture by literally disrobing him, forbidding his tongue and dress. MacPherson covers this up by throwing his poems into a hazy past, long dead, where the drama of cultural destruction (the content of the poems) can be enacted beautifully instead of sinfully. There, the old singer is sublime instead of disgusting (remember William Shaw) and Gaelic heroism wonderful instead of empire-threatening and unpredictable.[56] All the while the High-landers themselves, alive, speaking Gaelic, are left out of both the commerce of publishing and that of praise.

Necessarily – crucially – this fraud, which covers the death of a culture, is paralleled by another, perpetrated by whisking away form. With form killed off, the translator can pretend that the text can be handed into English with no formal pain. He can reassure the reader that Gaelic need not be read to access the originality of Ossian, and that the "original" can be found without personal or social trauma, without consulting blind Highlanders. The simplest practical benefit of the death of form is that the English prose can be matched to the Gaelic verse in an essential way. Translation is complete and also completely transparent, painless. This claim of formal independence is the crucial structural element in MacPherson's project as a whole. It is a claim, made in bad faith, that the tartan is simply removable, a surface layer instead of an essential metonymy. The Ossian books, with their stories and their atmosphere, are the enormously successful packaging of the two kinds of fraud I have described, the physical and literary sides of MacPherson's coin. The result, as I have said, is a powerful elixir for curing the ills a highly wrought culture develops. The crime is in the claim that preparation of the tonic does not, in some way, destroy its source.

What sort of poetry is this, and what sort of poetic status can we give to James MacPherson? We must grant the brilliance of his accomplishment. Not only do his books rescue him from Highland obscurity, but they themselves use the energy of what we think of as their faults to their advantage. The controversy and the curiously opaque fraud of the poems work in MacPherson's favor, since he wants notice above all. He can't lose: I have tried to show who does lose, but MacPherson cannot. His ambition is fulfilled with ruthless freedom, and as long as he is free he will simply ride the wind of the storm he raises. I would insist that his canonical death is justified, though, because he has committed a literary crime. He is a brilliant but utterly unpoetic poet. His contempt for form is a contempt for real literary beauty, and the divine emptiness of Ossian's poems is the result. He is a calculator, a poet for whom poetry is quite simply a possible road to success, and so he happily leaves literature behind as he rises to country squire and imperial functionary. Especially after the reworked inspiration that the high romantic poets give to us, MacPherson's motives, and what they produce, look appalling. I think we should insist on the ugliness of MacPherson's poetry, but not on the ugliness of his motives. Such motives have produced more poetry than we often admit. Ambition is a human passion and partakes of human complexity. In tracing this complexity, I want to push my exploration of literary ambition further by following another highly ambitious (Scottish) poet, who pursues his schemes some twenty years later: Robert Burns. Burns' ambition matches that of MacPherson, and he creates a career for himself in a very similar way, by retailing simplicity to the jaded sophisticate. But Burns was a poet, and he could not blind himself to the consequences of form. This sensitivity derails his career, and he dies romantically young and destitute; but he wrote some beautiful things.

CHAPTER 2

Robert Burns

In January of 1783 a very young sounding 24-year-old Robert Burns wrote to his former schoolmaster, John Murdoch, with the intention of telling him what had become of a prize pupil. As the measure of biography and the world goes, what had happened to Burns was pretty much nothing; but though he has no aims, he wants to have them; and though he has no accomplishments, he feels he should have. That is, he has no compelling story to narrate, since he has been living the life of a young Scottish man with small income and moderate station, and the events of his life simply do not dramatize well. He has been reading, though, and he tells Murdoch what:

In the matter of books, indeed, I am very profuse. – My favorite authors are of the sentimental kind, such as Shenstone, particularly his Elegies, Thomson, Man of Feeling, a book I prize next to the Bible, Man of the World, Sterne, especially his Sentimental journey, McPherson's Ossian, &c ...[1]

To the modern reader, who most likely thinks of Burns as a poet of the folk tradition, this list of the ultra-refined might be surprising; but Burns was a well-educated man, and most of his earlier poetry is anything but folk poetry. When Burns says he has been reading Shenstone's Elegies, it means he has been savoring such tidbits as this one, from the first Elegy:

> Ye loveless Bards! intent with artful pains
> To form a sigh, or contrive a tear!
> Forego your Pindus, and on — plains
> Survey Camilla's charms, and grow sincere.[2]

Time has done its merciless work on verse such as this, and Shenstone's recommendation to descend from Grecian heights (Pindus) to — plains (and so replace Art with Simplicity) looks ridiculous. His plan substitutes one sort of artificiality for another,

49

and his pastoral viewpoint, which looks down at rusticity from the heights of refinement and wealth, sees a blurry figure which he idealizes and christens "Camilla." So deliciously general a figure is she that Shenstone cannot put her anywhere, leaving her to float on the abstract plain of "—." Whatever our flaws, at least Camilla no longer charms us; the second half of the eighteenth century adored such figures, and the artful artlessness that this stanza expresses had a powerful appeal. Strange as it seems, Robert Burns felt this appeal as strongly as anyone, even though his position in life would have rendered him as blurry to Shenstone as Camilla is. Stranger still, Burns actually wrote his own artfully artless verse, verse which makes much the same claim that Shenstone's does about the especially real and beautiful life of the rural folk, in a style equally sweet and vaporous. Fully one-third to a half of the verse in his first edition of poems (1786) could be described as being of this general type.

What appeal could such hopeless idealization hold for an actual farmer? Why would Burns write such verse? In the first half of this chapter I will try to answer these questions as thoroughly as I can; there are many compelling answers available. Burns eventually asked such questions himself, and (largely) stopped writing such verse. In the second part, I will explore his reasons for stopping, and try to describe what he wrote instead. Artificiality is easily exposed as false, but artificiality has its place and especially its purposes. Burns' career, successful in some ways and quite unhappy in others, is made from a series of engagements with the artificiality that the literary world thrust upon him. In this chapter I will step through a number of these engagements, ending with a poor poet writing song lyrics with every appearance of satisfaction.

The best place to begin understanding Burns' early, literary and artificial verse is "The Cottar's Saturday Night," which Burns' contemporaries loved above all his other poems. The most common effusion that readers gushed over this poem was that it was, in some way, "true." More than twenty years after it was written, even the often stern Francis Jeffrey made the claim:

Its whole beauty cannot, indeed, be discerned but by those whom experience has enabled to judge of the admirable fidelity and completeness of the picture.[3]

The poem presents the Saturday night rituals of a Scottish farmer and his family as they go through their meal and prayers. Only if it is seen through the lenses of the pastoral can such a poem be called "complete" or true. The readers who praise the poem's fidelity do not mean of course that there is indeed *one* family whose home life is as lovely as this one; they mean that there is a blurry class of people, "Scottish farmers," whose family life is sentimentally pure and pious. The poem asks perfect generality for its subjects, members of this imaginary class: Camilla could sit down to dinner and feel right at home. The poem's description of daily routine is diversified by brief excursions into other areas. Typical of the poem's sentimental roots is a rumination on the hypothetical "rake" who would or could invade the cottage and steal away the virtue and happiness of the eldest daughter, Jenny; thankfully, her "strappan youth" is a fine young farmer himself, highly respectful. The major contemplative excursion of the poem concerns the piety of the family, and finishes with this delicate stanza:

> Compar'd with this, how poor Religion's pride,
> In all the pomp of *method*, and of *art*,
> When men display to congregations wide,
> Devotion's ev'ry grace, except the *heart*!
> The POWER, incens'd, the pageant will desert,
> The pompous strain, the sacerdotal stole;
> But haply, in some *Cottage* far apart,
> May hear, well-pleased, the language of the *Soul*;
> And in His *Book of Life* the Inmates poor enroll.

This interestingly sacred version of the pastoral – a sort of easy-going protestant sectarianism – blends with more classic versions:

> O SCOTIA! my dear, my native soil!
> For whom my warmest wish to heaven is sent!
> Long may thy hardy sons of *rustic toil*
> Be blest with health and peace and sweet content!
> And O may heaven their simple lives prevent
> From *Luxury's* contagion, weak and vile!
> Then howe'er *crowns* and *coronets* are rent,
> A *virtuous populace* may rise the while,
> And stand a wall of fire, around their much-lov'd ISLE.[4]

The emphasis provided by the italics was added, as far as I can tell, by the Kilmarnock printer (Burns' correspondent Mrs. Dunlop makes fun of it at one point). These stanzas are in high artificial mode. Like Shenstone's "— plains," Burns' delicate place-name,

"Scot ia," names its thing with considerable embarrassment. The use of such a word belies a worry that the plainness of the thing referred to might make it unpoetic or distasteful. Using quasi-Latin pushes the word itself in front of its object, and cushions the blow the low thing might inflict. The effect is especially noticeable in this poem because of the rhetoric of fidelity: "To you I sing, in simple Scottish lays/ The *lowly train* in life's sequestered scenes" (lines 5–6). Through a not-so-subtle process of abstraction or sublimation, what the artificial eye of the refined pastoral enthusiast sees is evaporated out of "Scotland" and then returned to the world in the form of the imaginary place "Scotia." Farmers in late eighteenth-century Scotland were a mixed bag: some of them were no doubt pious and quiet, and some others were inattentive and adventurous like Robert Burns, who fathered his first illegitimate child with a servant on the family farm in 1785, a few months before writing "The Cottar's Saturday Night."

There is a moderate amount of sturdy Scots diction in "The Cottar's Saturday Night"; not too much, but enough to be noticeable. At one point, for instance, the wife's prized cheese is given the highly substantial epithet "well-hain'd kebbuck." Substantial, I should say, to the speaker of standard educated English, having as it does not only the substance that foreign words have naturally, but also the good, solid, harsh sound of old-style English words. A poem that uses a Latin tag to refer to Scotland cannot also be a Scots effusion, so this sort of diction cannot be present "naturally." It does not retire behind some dramatic scenario, like dialogue; it stands in the midst of rarified poetic English, calling attention to itself. "Kebbuck" is anthropological, telling us what they call cheese in Scotland. The effect of such a word is less visible now, I think, since this poem is read (especially in the United States) mostly by scholars, who are used to difficult reference and foreign words.[5] Many of Burns' readers found the Scottish words very intimidating, which made them one of the most noticeable features of Burns' poems. The full title of the first edition is *Poems, Chiefly in the Scottish Dialect*, information provided because it was seen as important, even in the provincial Scottish town where it was published. Sometimes readers found the words too Scottish, and failed to understand. William Cowper wrote entertainingly to a friend about this problem:

Poor Burns loses much of his deserved praise in this country through our ignorance of his language. I despair of meeting with any Englishman who will take the pains that I have taken to understand him. His candle is bright, but shut up in a dark lantern. I lent him to a very sensible neighbor of mine; but his uncouth dialect spoiled all; and before he had half read him through he was quite *ram-feezled*.[6]

The highly local has on the one hand anthropological interest and on the other pure, off-putting foreignness. Interestingly – crucially, I would say – Scots diction had an equally strong effect on Scots readers, though they could understand the words. Educated Scots of the later eighteenth century had painfully conflicted feelings about their native dialect. "Scottish" was at once their own tongue, a mark of essential identity, and also a mark of backwardness, a sign of provinciality that kept them, in an Ossianic way, from blending in with the powerful, who now lived not in Edinburgh but in London. In other words, English (accent and diction) had become the language of ambition, Scots the language of home. This is an inherently pastoral arrangement. To the refined (or ambitious) Scot, who looks down on his or her own Scottish-speaking youth, Scots is the language of the simple and the young, English the language of writing and the broader world.[7]

Francis Jeffrey describes this figurative arrangement plainly, in the review I quoted earlier:

[Scots] is by no means peculiar to the vulgar, but it is the common speech of the whole nation in early life, – and with many of its most exalted and accomplished individuals throughout their whole existence; and, if it be true that, in later times, it has been, in some measure, laid aside by the more ambitious and aspiring of the present generation, it is still recollected, even by them, as the familiar language of their childhood, and of those who were the earliest objects of their love and veneration. It is connected, in their imagination, not only with that olden time which is uniformly conceived as more pure, lofty and simple than the present, but also with all the soft and bright colors of remembered childhood and domestic affection.[8]

Jeffrey refers to his generation, the next after Burns', but the previous generation was if anything more thoroughly embarrassed about Scots (Jeffrey had Walter Scott and Burns himself as allies and precedent). Burns' generation, and indeed the generation before his (the generation of Adam Smith and David Hume), as is well known, had gone so far as to hire "elocution masters" to aid them in ridding

themselves of "Scotticisms."[9] For both the English and the educated
Scottish, Scots is highly local, attached to places: for the former, it is
a picturesque language, smelling of the virtuous (foreign) poor; for
the latter, it is the language of a lost home, a place of Scottish identity.

The pastoral force of Scots explains the mixture of Scots and
elaborate English in "The Cottar's Saturday Night." The Scots is
there because it is what the pastoral vision sees, the local object
peered at from on high; the English and quasi-Latin are there to
control the specificity of the local things by presenting them in a
refined and imaginary setting. The local objects displayed, often in
italics, thus take on an interesting abstract substance: they are
especially real, being country things, but they are set in an extremely
artificial frame that makes them highly figurative and expressive.
Scotland itself, as "Scotia," is transformed into a place where Real
poor people Really live, but which cannot be found except in the
minds of the educated. The poem is an elaborate scheme, the target
of which is to speak words like "kebbuck" without being tied to a
possibly unpleasant reality by such a word's sturdy reference. As in
all pastoral writing, the net effect is a paradoxical style of truth.
"Kebbuck" looks substantial, like the truth, but it also evades the
consequences of reference that speaking the truth might bring. This
artificial truth is what readers reacted to: it is what gives poems as
artificial as this one their sense of referential triumph, so clear in the
snippets I have quoted.

Our versions of pastoral have changed, and though the artificialities of the poem may sound flat to us they can aid us in appreciating
Burns' accomplishment, for the poem really does show off a rustic
genius. Like many a "rustic genius" before him, he has not written
rustic poetry, but has carefully, painfully, jacked himself up and out
of the country so that he can then look down upon it and refine it into
(acceptable) poetic material. In his sweet, careful performance of
pastoral convention, Burns shows himself to be a poet, an enthusiastic
newcomer in the reading and writing world, where poetry is not only
a technical accomplishment (the ability to write in Spenserian
stanzas, for instance, taken from Shenstone), but also a demonstration
of conventions learned, of culture absorbed and appreciated. Great
effort has been expended in writing "The Cottar's Saturday Night,"
and Burns tries to cover over the exertion with the rustic fiction of
"spontaneous singing" that he was careful to personify, especially in
the Preface to the Kilmarnock edition:

Unacquainted with the necessary requisites for commencing poet by Rule, he sings the sentiments and manners, he felt and saw in himself, and his rustic compeers around him, in his and their native language.[10]

This fiction domesticates Burns' class origins by making them obvious. If he says he is a spontaneous singer, then he is not a social climber; under the cover of the fiction of the spontaneous singer, poems such as "The Cottar's Saturday Night" can be seen as poetry instead of an elaborate attempt to imitate the forms of the poet's betters. Seen from on high, such an imitation might look like an unpleasantly knowing ambition. Preceded by the delicate fiction of spontaneity, this poem instead offers itself as a indirect kind of courtship poem, a poem which politely asks that the poet be included inside the circle of refinement. Burns produces a persona which is rustic, the "them" of the pastoral world, but writes poetry in the mode of the refined, the connoisseurs of pastoral delights. Compare this posture, for instance, to the purer pastoralism available to the Oxford-educated Shenstone. To use a metaphor from the Excise (Burns' eventual career), Burns is attempting a kind of conventional smuggling: himself under the cover of the rustic singer, his materials on board a refined vessel.

In Burns' Scotland, the circle of refinement was very nearly a physically perceptible item; it corresponded to the confines of Edinburgh. Published in the provinces, in Kilmarnock, Burns' book asks to come to Edinburgh. The Edinburgh elite, reading Burns, were astonished at what they saw – rightfully so, I think – and duly invited him there. This invitation was extended in a diffuse but unmistakable manner. The grand and already old man of Edinburgh letters, Henry MacKenzie, wrote an essay in (what happened to be) the final issue of his genteel periodical *The Lounger*, which ended like this:

I do my country no more than justice, when I suppose her ready to stretch out her hand to cherish and retain this native poet, whose "wood-notes wild" possess so much excellence. To repair the wrongs of suffering or neglected merit; to call forth genius from the obscurity in which it had pined indignant, and place it where it may profit or delight the world; these are exertions which give to wealth an enviable superiority, to greatness and to patronage a laudable pride.[11]

This extract illustrates both the unabashed nakedness of the courtship that Burns is engaging in, and the cheerful recognition that the courted extended to him. MacKenzie recognizes that refined readers would recognize that "The Cottar's Saturday Night" is directed at them, under the cover of spontaneity, and gratefully makes use of Burns' self-presentation as a rustic singer to arrange a pastoral connection between Burns and his betters. MacKenzie calls the superior place in this relationship "enviable" because it seems so justified and so stable: everyone may play his or her part with confidence. Here, then, is one of the purposes of artificiality. Burns asks, and because he asks well (performs convention with grace and good faith) his betters recognize and answer him. The transaction is "false," but that does not inhibit the business being conducted. Burns eventually found his part appalling, as his betters eventually found him to be, and the whole thing fell apart, but that is a matter for later.

The courtship of "The Cottar's Saturday Night" may properly be called smuggling because it must be read out of the poem. One need not try very hard to see it, but then smuggling is often just as easy to interpret, like the big cars of drug kingpins. Most courtship poems written before 1800 see no need for ruses; that is, courtship is often the acknowledged subject, pursued with plain clarity and gross flattery. Burns wrote some poetry of this type: it does not fit well with our picture of the poet of "A Man's a Man" and "Love and Liberty," but he was indeed a writer of the eighteenth century and he did indeed write patronage poetry. The plainest example is a longish (for Burns) poem called in its published state "To Robert Graham of Fintry Esquire, with a request for an Excise Division" (no. 230). Burns sent it to Graham in a letter which details the business end of his request. Indeed, as far as this sort of thing goes, Burns comes off with a fair amount of dignity; the letter reflects mostly his clear sense that Graham could help him where he could not help himself. At the same time, he does observe the proprieties in his own way. Here are a couple of paragraphs from the letter:

I again, Sir, ask your forgiveness for this letter. – I have done violence to my feelings in writing it. –

> – "If in aught I have done amiss,
> "Impute it not!"

My thoughts on this business, as usual with me when my mind is burdened, vented themselves, in the inclosed verses, which I have taken the liberty to inscribe to you. –

You, Sir, have the power to bless: but the only claim I have to your friendly Offices, is my having been already the Object of your goodness, which indeed looks like producing my debt instead of my discharge. (vol. I, p. 315, no. 269)

The quotation is a misquotation from that oft-quoted (now forgotten) classic, Addison's *Cato*. The capital letters, in "Offices" and "Object,' appear because the writing is formal; they are the equivalents of the capitals and italics in "The Cottar's Saturday Night." Burns does not elevate nouns in this way when writing to familiars. Burns presents the fiction of spontaneity especially aggressively here, and the distance between "spontaneity" and the formal poem referred to is as clear as it is in the case of "The Cottar's Saturday Night." The conventionality of the claim to spontaneity is delightfully clear in this case, since Burns had sent a draft of the poem to Mrs. Dunlop at the beginning of August 1788, a full month before he wrote to Graham.

The plot of the poem ingeniously allows Burns to be less self-effacing than is usual in such a poem; he spends most of his time discussing his need instead of his patron's abundance. Still, the form demands praise, in payment for patronage, and Burns has to include obsequious moments:

> But come, ye who godlike pleasure know,
> Heaven's attribute distinguished, – to bestow,
> Whose arms of love would grasp all human-race;
> Come, thou who givest with all a courtier's grace,
> Friend of my life (true Patron of my rhymes)
> Prop of my dearest hopes for future times. –   (lines 65–70)

Burns does his best, but this is still a poem of naked ambition. The ambition here is not even figured as literary ambition; behind this verse is the most prosaic sort of request for a job. Though it feels paradoxical, the plain source of this poetry also explains why it is so formal, so strained: the poem is a special kind of asking, and the "poetry" marks Burns' sense that he is not simply a man speaking to an equal: "ye"; "thou"; "givest." Equally plainly, a poetic request is appropriate to Burns since his skill as a poet constitutes his claim for special attention from his betters. His poetry is the something he has instead of social and economic status. His ritualized flattery accepts the hierarchy of patronage as completely as Mac-Kenzie's notice of Burns does; some of the poem is given over to a defensive contemplation of this acceptance, but the acceptance is here nevertheless, as it should be. The convention that produces this poem is a strong sort, convention shading into the wider social functions of ritual, and Burns is playing his part.

It was important that he do so. Burns was a lyric poet of the eighteenth century. He could not amass a fortune by publishing, in the way that Pope had, or Byron and Scott were soon to do; his troubles are more like those that Wordsworth was to experience before the family money came through. His first book is a thin line of smoke from the woods, notice of talent and need. What he wants is what MacPherson achieved: for his writing to make him a figure, to gain him an entry that he could then make use of. The poem to Graham is the clearest example of the kind of poetry that this motive led to. Burns needed for his poetry to set him up in life: it could not be a source of money in itself. In some moods this use of poetry bothered Burns immensely (he calls it "sodomy of soul" or "prostitution"), but it was a fact he recognized. His friend Mrs. Dunlop spent a fair amount of time going over career possibilities for him. Her letters on the subject are eminently practical:

You have already told us that "Cash your pouches wad na bide in." This makes it doubly needful for you to form a wish, and communicate it to some one that could assist its completion, as there is no time they would find it so easie as when the world are in eager expectation. Just before the longed-for publication, or at the moment it is first seen and in every mouth, would be the time some active friend might drop some useful hint to forward any favourite scheme which you thought could make you happy.[12]

The event the world expects is the publication of the Edinburgh edition, which appeared in April 1787 (this letter is dated February 26, 1787). Burns did not take her up; her favorite idea would eventually be to make Burns a "Salt Officer," whatever that might have been. That is, he did not follow her advice about timing, since his first letter to Graham is not written for another year.

Remembering that Burns wrote patronage poetry teaches us essential things about his motives and the shape of his career. Of course Burns wrote many other sorts of poems, poems which should not be called patronage poetry, though much of it is courtship poetry in the romantic sense. But the world that the patronage poetry delineates is the world that Burns had to live in, as a writer. It is a very small world, closely interconnected and hyperaware of novelty and intrusions. It is populated not by more or less anonymous readers, but filled instead with people who know each other and who keep a sharp eye on social business. When Burns appears in this world, he does so self-consciously and as a formal object of interest, imported with the approval of the elite. He found the obsequious posture oppressive, as any person would, but I think that the structure itself was perfectly congenial to him. Burns is a poet of occasions, and his poetry is almost always social in some way; speaking to nameable people, in commemoration of some real event. The poem to Graham came along in a letter for ritualistic reasons, but Burns' letters are always full of poetry anyway, and frequently poetry that he did not publish elsewhere. For Burns, the carefully worked language of poetry goes with the special attention due to friends and others in the course of daily activity: poetry is a social form, an interactive form, a special way of talking. His poetry is often intimate and personal in tone, and it is also frequently actually intimate and personal, taking an active part in personal interchange. Above all, in the small world Burns was writing for and in, writing circulates; it does not, as in our time, live primarily in books and other publications, read by oneself. Poetry shades into the social. Poems are part of gatherings, evenings; songs are sung at parties; the events and people that inspire verse are known to people other than the poet. In short, all poetry, in this world, is in some way "occasional."

That being said, occasions can be very different, and they will make for very different poems; as different, say, as the poem to Graham of Fintry is from the song "The Blue-Eyed Lassie" (no. 232), each of which formed parts of letters sent to different correspondents in the fall of 1788. Burns' ambition – to put it another way – has various goals, as different as a successful career is from a seduction. These two kinds of ambition, social and erotic, meet, of course, in Burns' need to portray himself in an attractive light, and in the ways in which writing can serve that purpose. Burns' social ambition, his desire to know the great (especially the great of Edinburgh), peaks out in early 1788, after which period he lives almost uninterruptedly in Dumfriesshire. This peak naturally coincides with the peak of his "English" verse, since this verse is the vehicle for his social ambition. I have explained Burns' English, artificial mode as purposeful, and hence comprehensible, but I do not wish to demystify such poetry too thoroughly. It is poetry of "feeling," what we see as falseness, but it is also true, and even contains a kind of fervor. This fervor is hard but important for us to see. Burns inherited and put to use a remarkably artificial literary culture, and his use of that culture is in part plainly practical. At the same time, his erotic and social ambitions were real, keenly felt, and inscribed within the world that this artificiality defines and rises out of: so these artificial modes inevitably carry a high emotional charge. Indeed, the peak of his ambition corresponds with a bizarre and ecstatic faith in the power of literary expression. Right at this peak, explaining and comprising it, is the material I wish to use to illustrate Burns' ecstatic faith, his fervor: the correspondence between himself and a luscious Edinburgh matron named Agnes M'Lehose, in the winter of 1787–8. This correspondence, carried out (quite seriously) under the pastoral *soubriquets* of "Sylvander" and "Clarinda," brings together in one burst Burns' social and erotic ambitions, and also makes painfully clear the strained high point of his faith in the high artificialities of English literature, and educated literary history, as a medium for his ambitions.

One of the interpretive keys to this episode is that Burns was confined to his room for the larger part of it. In early December he bruised his knee falling from a coach, and did not stir until the middle of January; the Clarinda business peters out in early February. Through most of the letters his infirmity is referred to daintily as a bruised "limb" (not an unconnected fact). The almost unbelievable style of the correspondence can be demonstrated by quoting Burns writing while he is still confined, and burning with a sort of neo-Augustan heat:

You have a heart form'd, gloriously form'd, for all the most refined luxuries of love; why was that heart ever rung? O Clarinda! shall we not meet in a state, some yet unknown state of Being, where the lavish hand of Plenty shall minister to the highest wish of Benevolence; and where the chill north-wind of Prudence shall never blow over the flowery fields of Enjoyment? if we do not, Man was made in vain!... what unprovoked Demon, malignant as Hell, stole upon the confidence of mistrusting busy Fate, and dashed your cup of life with undeserving sorrow? (vol. 1, p. 190, no. 166)[13]

The sorrow Burns laments is Clarinda's life: abandoned by an uncaring rake of a husband, who squandered her fortune and then evacuated to Jamaica, she was living in Edinburgh with her two small children, depending for means upon her powerful uncle, Lord Craig, a member of the MacKenzie/*Lounger* set. Forced to maintain a sad sort of respectability – since she was still actually married – her life can only have been of the most confined sort.

The capital letters in this extract denote courtship, here both erotic and social; they also fit into the chokingly "passionate" style, so difficult for the modern reader to swallow. The foundation of this style is personification, which overwhelms most of these letters; passions, moral features and ideas run about with manic energy. Indeed, personification sets up the framework for the whole of the correspondence. The style of both Sylvander's and Clarinda's letters is a dramatically sincere one: intimate thoughts come on stage and act out their identity for the breathless audience. The things personified in this artificial way gain stature in their transformation, but they also lose content.[14] What exactly is "Prudence" here? or "Enjoyment"? Certainly not sexual restraint and sexual abandon, respectively, though with equal certainty whatever content these large things have derives from these plainer things. Personification translates its objects to the plane of abstraction, where they can relate to other exalted abstractions, but where they lose touch with the world that gave them birth. Sylvander and Clarinda could Enjoy themselves without Prudence while living in Scotia; but what can Robert Burns and Agnes M'Lehose do in Scotland?

Not much, physically speaking, and hence the letters. Burns begins with physical distance exaggerated by his injury, and gradually he sublimes everything away into his crazy epistolary world. After a while, the artificiality of the relationship becomes positively painful, for them and for the reader. In the first week of January Sylvander and Clarinda arrange for Clarinda to walk about in front of Burns' lodgings, so that he may glimpse her; she comes, but does not look at the right window, sending Sylvander into despair. After Burns is able to visit her (about the middle of January), their letters begin to record the difficulties of encounters where the physical closeness that Burns desired (and was used to) must be pushed away, with fear and trembling. In these circumstances, the high artificiality of the correspondence becomes more understandable, perhaps even moving and pathetic. The purpose of "The Cottar's Saturday Night" was to say "kebbuck" and give no offense: Sylvander and Clarinda's letters go further, trying to get beyond the need for such words, even for such things. Thus the replacement of "knee" with "limb"; thus the loss of even their own names.

The force behind the lovers' behavior is a desperate faith in the sentimental encounters depicted so passionately in eighteenth-century English literary culture. Constrained almost entirely by their bodies and their social dependency, Burns and Mrs. M'Lehose try to escape under aliases into a world where distinction dissolves. The mechanism here is precisely that of the pastoral verse I was describing earlier. Abstracted away from bordered locality, the pastoral enthusiast can meet and sport with Camilla and Clarinda. The pressure exerted by the physical world is much greater here, though, and the needs of the participants more pressing and personal. It is difficult to attribute sincerity to "The Cottar's Saturday Night," though it may be there, but these letters are sincere. Sincerity made into a style, personified into a principle, but sincerity nonetheless. There is a state of Being in which Enjoyment may be had, and it is in writing. The personifications mark writing that has, like the personifications, both an intrusive hard durability and a vaporous, sentimental abstraction. This writing is a medium of interchange, a common ground, and interchange has been made more effective by getting rid of the local limitations of the subjects.[15] Like a traditional trading language, such a style makes for a place where difference can be formally overcome. Sylvander's letters are packed with quotations from English literature; quotations fit perfectly with the high style, since "Great" authors, agreed upon by convention, constitute a basic currency. As Addison (through *Cato*) did for Burns in his letter to Robert Graham, Great Authors can be introduced to speak for the otherwise unbecomingly personal and local letter-writer. Quotations are also the inevitable product of Burns' ambition, his pursuit of the world of Letters. If the persona who speaks in "The Cottar's Saturday Night" could write letters, he would write letters like those of Sylvander. Here is the end of one of his late-night effusions:

You are by this time fast asleep, Clarinda; may good angels attend and guard you as constantly and faithfully as my good wishes do!

> "Beauty, whether waking or asleep,
> Shot forth peculiar graces – "

John Milton, I wish thy soul better rest than I expect on my pillow to-night! O for a little of the cart-horse part of human nature! Good night, my dearest Clarinda! (vol. i, p. 202, no. 174)

The quotation is from *Paradise Lost*. Milton, so heavily and clumsily introduced, is a sort of guardian angel here himself, standing watch over an act of forced self-inclusion in the abstract, shared world of writing. Sylvander and Clarinda desperately insist that they are sensible members of a beautiful abstract world populated by feelings, quotations and the ghosts of Great Good Authors. This world is a meeting place for the educated elite, and especially for the educated elite of Edinburgh, who always worry that their Scottishness might make them into cart-horses no matter how hard they try.

A biographer of great authority has this to say about the Sylvander and Clarinda correspondence:

The Clarinda episode has more prominence in most accounts of Burns than it deserves. In its beginning and growth it was in fact quite untypical of the man – his one intensive effort to act a part not natural to him.[16]

This is quite true, except that we should add that its prominence has derived from precisely this fact: the intense artificiality of the effort. Burns was acting a part, but he acted it with desperate energy. He was not false to himself – he was a chameleonic person anyway – but rather his correspondence with Clarinda was his last great experiment with high falseness as an expressive mode. For Burns, as for MacPherson, the world of forms, the world we call literary history and convention, was infinitely more than simple literary precedent. As I said in the previous chapter, form is a deep matter. Burns enters into poetry as into a world of possibility. The artificial style of high sentiment seems to offer him a way of living, if not a pure escape from his homely life. It is an Ossianic lesson that this style and this world are created out of paradox, and so (as Burns discovers) this world cannot be realized. MacPherson did not want to realize this world: he wanted it to be as elusive as possible. Burns tries to live in it, but cannot. Sylvander is a beautiful person, made flexible by his mistiness, but Robert Burns is considerably heavier. He had more than a little of the cart-horse part of human nature in him, and the gross physical world was inevitably to rear up and end his strange sentimental vacation in the world of sensibility. Burns had to leave Edinburgh in the middle of February 1788; had the correspondence been successful in subliming away the bodies of Agnes and Robert, this would have made little difference. Once back in the world of farms and the necessity of making a living, though, Burns quickly fails in his promise to write every day, and soon silence replaces the fevered chatter of only a few weeks before.

All kinds of things were happening underneath the level of beautiful abstraction. Burns had been venting his sexual frustrations with at least one lower-class woman of Edinburgh (named Jenny

Clow); it was far from a liaison in the abstract world, and Jenny would eventually produce yet another illegitimate child. During these months Burns had also been pursuing Robert Graham and his commission to the Excise, a project essentially concluded by the time he left town.[17] By the end of March he had publicly acknowledged Jean Armour as his wife; earlier in March she had given birth to her second set of twins fathered by Burns, both of which had died within a few weeks.[18] Clarinda eventually got wind of all this (their world was very small) and did not communicate with Burns again for a full year. When eventually they do exchange letters again, it is as Robert Burns and Agnes M'Lehose. Agnes had troubles of her own; people in Edinburgh were talking, and her uncle had heard of her dalliance with the now-tarnished poet. For Agnes, this was a serious business, since Lord Craig paid for her maintenance. Biographers frequently make implicit fun of Mrs. M'Lehose's Calvinist principles, and her prudery; but purity was not simply a moral issue for her. If she had produced one of the many Burns children, her life would have fallen apart; as the single mother of two children, she had a lot to lose. Sylvander and Clarinda pushed their experiment to a kind of sublime extreme, and created a world which had to collapse.

Mrs. M'Lehose's indiscretions, and their possible consequences, point to the fact that Burns' ambitions, and his attempts to fulfill his ambitions, were not without their dangers. These dangers were real, or at least real enough to be called dangers. By the middle of 1788 Burns had accumulated considerable responsibility, both moral and financial. In spite of his frequent claims to the contrary, the "heav'n taught plowman" was not a good farmer; his health was always indifferent, and his skill was not the greatest either. His brother Gilbert was the farmer; Robert was, truly enough, a sociable man with what we would call more professional capacities. The Excise eventually offered a serviceable outlet for his bookish skills, and, as far as we can tell, he was a responsible and hard-working Exciseman. Withdrawal to a Cottar-like seclusion and independence was not available to him. He needed a job that would pay his bills, and getting such a job depends upon things like status and character and prosaic capacity. Character may be abstractable, but it has its plain social side. For Burns too indiscretion offered real dangers.

The lesson I wish to draw from Sylvander and Clarinda is double. On the one side is the hopelessly passionate use of high literary expression, and its inevitable failure. This mode fails because Burns tries to live it, and his body refuses to be idealized. Literary mode and everyday life cross, destroying both. This is clear enough, and an Ossianic lesson anyway: the energy of oxymoron ("the poetic plowman" in its smallest form) is literally painful if realized. The other side of the lesson keeps us from separating the literary and the bodily too completely. In spite of their refusal to mix, these two worlds are also utterly interdependent. Burns' poems, abstracted as they are, are the vehicle for his ambition, while the object of this ambition is physical, a way of providing for bodily needs. Mistakes in one lead to the failure of the other.

I will pursue this lesson through the rest of the chapter, eventually finding my way to what Burns learns from it. In reference to the conduct of Burns' career, what this lesson teaches is that it will be very difficult. If too much of the body destroys the artificial, and if the purpose of the artificiality is the accomplishment of plainly practical ambitions, trouble is seemingly inevitable. Burns' marketable talent is his ability to sublime away the physical grossness of the world, in high pastoral mode; the crucial feature of that talent is that he is especially bodily, a rustic genius, the "poetic plowman." In other words, all of Burns' strategies had to negotiate the tricky border between local and general, between coarse Robert Burns and the airy Poetic Plowman. The inevitable flaw in all of his schemes for material advancement is his simultaneous dependence upon and inability to control the appearance of his coarse side. For instance, the mixture of modes, of voices, in Burns' first editions of his poetry reflects rather than conceals his mixed nature. He never published his coarsest work, of course, but what he did publish offered a broad range of styles, ranging from the earthy joking of his verse-epistles and poems like "Tam O'Shanter" and "Holy Fair" to the purities of "The Cottar's Saturday Night." The rougher poetry contained plenty of what leading Edinburgh lights considered indecency.

Eventually Burns' person came to be regarded as presenting the same sort of mixture of high and low, and hence the distaste Lord Craig had for his niece's affair of the heart. In my terms, the coarser voice of some of his poetry and – by readerly extension – the coarser parts of his person interfered with the smuggling that Burns tries to accomplish through poems like "The Cottar's Saturday Night." He reveals himself as a smuggler, and so gets caught, and sent home. Twenty years later, Francis Jeffrey was still highly sensitive to Burns' ambitious tactics, sensitive enough to read them out of his poetry:

However refined or eloquent he may be, [he] always approaches his mistress on a footing of equality; but has never caught the tone of chivalrous gallantry which uniformly abases itself in the presence of the object of its devotion. Accordingly, instead of suing for a smile, or melting in a tear, his muse deals in nothing but locked embraces and midnight rencontres; and even in his complimentary effusions to ladies of the highest rank, is for straining them to the bosom of her impetuous votary.[19]

Jeffrey seems to be ignoring the Sylvander episode here, but one could equally, and truthfully, say that it is because Burns' muse does deal in locked embraces that the M'Lehose affair fails. Jeffrey, who like many good Whigs was highly sensitive to rank, is actually talking in an undertone about a specific poem, "Song, on Miss W. A." (no. 89). This poem illustrates very plainly both the extent and the inevitable failure of Burns' impossible compression of worldly and abstract ambition.

Written in 1786, "Song, on Miss W. A." is generally an attractive example of Burns' English style, and is set to the well-known tune "Ettrick Banks." It begins with a stanza of nature-appreciation, and moves on to an encounter with "Miss W. A." I quote the second stanza and the last two (skipping the first and the third):

> With careless step I onward stray'd
> My heart rejoiced in Nature's joy
> When, musing in a lonely glade,
> A Maiden fair I chanc'd to spy:
> Her look was like the morning's eye,
> Her air like Nature's vernal smile,
> The lilies hue and roses' die
> Bespoke the Lass o' Ballochmyle
> ...
>
> O if she were a country Maid,
> And I the happy country swain!
> Though sheltered in the lowest shed
> That ever rose on Scotia's plain:
> Through weary winter's wind and rain,
> With joy, with rapture I would toil,
> And nightly to my bosom strain
> The bony Lass o' Ballochmyle.
>
> Then Pride might climb the slipp'ry steep
> Where fame and honors lofty shine:
> And Thirst of gold might tempt the deep
> Or downward seek the Indian mine:

Give me the Cot below the pine,
To tend the flocks or till the soil,
And evr'y day has joys divine
With th' bony Lass o' Ballochmyle.

Pastoral is a congenial mode to Burns because it so happily conflates social and erotic ambition: it very often, in fact, makes them the same thing. This song also combines Burns' two favorite ways of describing his methods of song-writing, the one erotic and the other pleasantly pastoral: putting himself "on a regimen of admiring a fine woman" and wandering through pastoral scenes with the tune in his head.[20] The ambition may be read out of the style here, as I have done previously; some context, which I will turn to shortly, makes this reading easier. The song itself of course smuggles ambition under the cover of its denial; enjoying the charms of the Lass o' Ballochmyle substitutes for social ambition (personified as "Pride"). To accomplish this substitution, Miss W. A. must be reduced to a country maiden; and so, as in the Shenstone stanza I began with, there is a sort of appropriation involved in the pastoral rapture. The Lass, encountered in a walk, is ecstatically absorbed into the poet's pastoral vision, and loses herself thereby; he hasn't given her a pastoral name, but he has given her a suitably impersonal epithet. Idealization of this sort is always part of the pastoral vision, but here Burns exacerbates the effect by noting that the song is about an actual person.

The line Jeffrey is remembering is in the fourth stanza: "And nightly to my bosom strain/The bony Lass o' Ballochmyle." Various strains are visible in the strangely concrete emphasis on straining. In general, the pastoral vision adopts Sylvander's methods: it replaces the crudities of physical love and attraction with pretty abstractions. The Lass o' Ballochmyle has "charms" (from the third stanza, unquoted), but she has very little else of a physical kind; she has airs, hues, and participates in the abstract world of Nature and Morning, which are more lovely but less approachable than morning and nature. "Bosom" abstracts the chest and the body of the singer, but still the singer is straining the Lass to him, and this effort cracks the clean surface of innocent abstraction. The addition of "nightly," with its air of both regular and nocturnal activity, only deepens the problem. In fact, I think Jeffrey is right to read this as the eruption of plain ambition in the midst of a pleasant pastoral fiction of the rejection of ambition. Clearly Burns sees no reason why he could not strain Miss W. A. to his bosom, and in particular he sees no reason why he shouldn't imagine himself doing so. To him it is a poetic right, justified by Passion. To Jeffrey, it is the intrusion of low things in the midst of high, and an unpleasant reminder of the crass physical world that lies beneath the abstractions of poetic love. The collapse the "strain" produces is the poetic equivalent to the eventual collapse of the Clarinda episode. The possibility of dealing only with the vapors of the physical world is inevitably voided by the intrusion of that world. No one can, in general, prevent that intrusion, but Burns cannot keep it out of even this short song, just as he could not keep himself away from Jenny Clow while corresponding with Agnes M'Lehose. His imperfectly abstracted self was the reason his career as an Edinburgh literary man did not, and could not, ever materialize.

Burns knew that he was taking a risk in this song. He sent it, asking for forgiveness and approval, in a letter to the subject, Miss Wilhelmina Alexander (of Ballochmyle), in November of 1786. The letter itself is a profuse and uncontrolled example of Burns' most extravagant sentimental style, and essentially retells the story of the song in prose. Here is how he ends:

What an hour of inspiration for a Poet! It would have raised plain, dull historic Prose to Metaphor and Measure!
The inclosed Song was the work of my return home: and perhaps but poorly answers what might have been expected from such a scene. – I am going to print a second Edition of my Poems, but cannot insert these verses without your permission. – (vol. i, p. 64, no. 56)

The letter begins by worrying over the impropriety of the song in a facetious tone:

Poets are such outre beings, so much the children of wayward Fancy and Capricious Whim, that I believe the world generally allows them a larger latitude in the rules of Propriety, than the sober sons of Judgement and Prudence. – I mention this as an apology all at once for the liberties which a nameless Stranger has taken with you in the enclosed ...

"Liberties" is of course a common euphemism for various degrees of rape, and that is indeed the unpleasant suggestion that the poem creates. Burns clearly hoped that the flattery inherent in such a song, and the effort taken with it, would overrule Miss A.'s hypothetical sense of appropriation or violation. In this, it seems, he was quite wrong, and the song was not published in his lifetime.

Burns had already begun to circulate the song by the time he wrote to Miss Alexander. He sent it in September of 1786 to Mrs. Stewart of Stair, along with several other poems. In the cover letter he says that Mrs. Stewart "will easily see the impropriety of exposing [it], even in manuscript ... I have no common friend to procure me that permission, without which I would not dare to spread the copy" (vol. I, p. 52, no. 47).[21] Apparently still without that "common friend," Burns wrote to ask permission himself, but did not receive it. We know this because the MS of the letter, as we have it, has a note, by Burns, attached:

Well Mr. Burns, & *did* the Lady give you the desired "Permission?" – No! She was too fine a Lady *to notice* so plain a compliment. – As to her great brothers, whom I have since met in life, on more "equal" terms of respectability, why should I quarrel with their want of attention to me? ... Ye canna mak a silk-purse o' a sow's lug.

Burns kept pushing his song; in March 1787, as the Edinburgh edition was going to press, he evidently consulted his Edinburgh circle about the possibility of publishing it and another questionable production (he refers mysteriously to "a jury of literati"): keeping up the figure of a song on trial, Burns says that his songs were found "defamatory libels against the fastidious Powers of Poesy and Taste; and the Author forbid to print them under pain of forfeiture of character" (vol. I, p. 98, no. 88). Burns speaks lightly, but the poem was not published. The lesson, to run Burns' proverb backwards, is that you can't make a sow's ear out of a silk-purse.

This small controversy illustrates two crucial facts about Burns' poetry. The first reemphasizes the size of the world that Burns was working in. If Miss Alexander did not want "her" song published, then it would not be, because, in spite of his joke, Burns' character would have been forfeit, and serious trouble could have ensued. His poems are convivial, and there is great pleasure for Burns in their social life; the suppression of this song is simply the down side of that conviviality. To be included within a circle is to be constrained by its limits. The whole episode stuck in Burns' mind, and the note he appended to his letter is not easy-going or socially comfortable. We have the note because Burns included a transcript of the letter to Miss Alexander, as well as the earlier letter to Mrs. Stewart, in a manuscript of his work which he gave to his friends the Riddels in 1791. The Riddels were also his betters; the preface that Burns attached to the manuscript he gave them is all about their social standing, and their consequently generous reception of "Poverty."[22] This is the physical side of the controversy: Burns' poems are things in a world, subject to constraint, active and plainly consequential. They circulate through different circles and are expected to be well-behaved. Because this poem expresses its ambition unpleasantly clearly, that ambition must be frustrated.

A second fact is the literary consequence of the first. Pastoral has its limits, and this poem runs against them. "Ballochmyle" is not a name with pastoral possibilities; it refers not to some part of Nature owned by everyone, but to an estate, and so the "Lass o' Ballochmyle," as an epithet, cannot reach the level of beautiful pastoral abstraction. It can only name Miss W. Alexander, resident of Ballochmyle on the river Ayr. Since Burns so incompletely subsumes his subject, his song remains tethered to the world it must escape in order to succeed as pastoral. In Burns' fulminating letter to Miss Alexander, which crazily encrusts his country walk with sentimental ecstasy, and in the poem itself, the machinery of pastoral is so exposed as to ruin the possibility of pastoral. The pleasures of abstraction founder on what looks like the process of abstraction. The failure is rendered more complete because of the conventional pastoral denial of ambition that the poem enacts. Exactly the same sentiments produced delight in "The Cottar's Saturday Night"; here, they look artificial, forced. This is not simply an illustration of a bad social conscience on the part of Burns' educated readers. Jeffrey's criticism, an accusation of a lack of humility, is a literary one first. In the same way, the humility of pastoral is not primarily a social or personal humility; it is not a "true" humility at all. It does claim truth, but it does so from within the safe confines of literary convention. Within these confines, Burns can with apparent sincerity refer (in the note to the Alexander letter) to his highly conventional and artificial poem as a "plain" compliment. But even though pastoral is one of the most artificial of all poetic modes, it cannot recognize its own artificiality. Since "On Miss W. A." forces this recognition, the song collapses, ironically, under the weight of its artificiality.

In order to succeed Robert Burns must tread a thin path between rapture and disgust. The "Song on Miss W. A." provides an extremely clear example of the width of this path, but in this case Burns wanders off the path because of what looks like a mistake, and this is not always the case. Any author who is marketing him- or herself as a rustic genius must encounter various obstacles that can be extremely difficult or even impossible to surmount. The balance between rapture and disgust presents itself in various forms. One of them I have already mentioned: the pawky punch of Scottish diction, which so easily turns into incomprehension and annoyance at the foreign word. For Burns, the most palpable difficulty he encountered was the difficulty he had in not appearing to be obscene or blasphemous. These two can be lumped together under the general, and common, accusation of "indecency." Hugh Blair, one of the more confined of the many confined souls included in the Edinburgh elite, left a list of notes for the improvement of Burns' poems. All of the suggestions involve the deletion or altering of indecent passages. One of his suggestions refers to some stanzas in the "Epistle to J. R***" (no. 47), a poem conducted in Burns' best plain style. The stanzas Blair is worried about quite humorously, if disconcertingly, parallel a midnight ramble with a woman to a poaching expedition. The poet is arrested for his misdeeds, and "pay't the *fee*." The biographical underlayer is Burns' description for John Rankine of the trouble caused by his first illegitimate child. Blair describes these stanzas hilariously:

The Description of shooting the hen is understood, I find, to convey an indecent meaning: tho' in reading the poem, I confess, I took it literally, and the indecency did not strike me. But if the Author meant to allude to an affair with a Woman, as is supposed, the whole poem ought undoubtably to be left out of the new edition.[23]

Here is the initial stanza of the little allegory:

> 'Twas ae night lately, in my fun,
> I gaed rovin wi' the gun,
> An' brought a *Paitrick* to the *grun'*,
> A bonie *hen*,
> And, as the twilight was begun,
> Thought nane wad ken.   (lines 37–42)

Blair's naive acceptance of the episode as rustic sport quite wonderfully demonstrates the double edge of the pungent rustic thing, here purposefully double-edged.

In reading (if only timidly) both levels of meaning, Blair comes tantalizingly close to perceiving the truth about pastoral sports, which we might say are generally far less abstract than the pastoral suggests. Truth pops its head up suddenly, and with curious artificiality, Blair proposes that the abstract pastoral be restored by simply suppressing this overly physical truth. Even though Blair cannot himself see underneath the surface of the allegory – his censorship is purely conjectural – he still recommends suppression. The Edinburgh world supposes itself large, but the underworld of expression that lives happily under the cover of this allegory is available only to those within the circle of its meanings, a world of indecent verse and poaching jokes. Blair's uncertainty in reading creakily illustrates the simple features of his sort of omnipotent vigilance. It is all a matter of agreement; indecency can only be defined by referring to a more or less vague set of commonly held prohibitions. The Edinburgh circle, or the circle of the refined, includes or interacts with other circles, scribed around words, behavior, ideas. Danger and uncertainty appear when borders are crossed: outside its proper limits, Burns' allegory fails utterly, bringing either pure incomprehension or pure censure. Blair humorously illustrates both of these possibilities. How did Hugh Blair "find" the indecency in the figure? Somehow even he has poached upon some other circle, where the figure is read another way. Translation does not concern him, though: his care is for the common world of publishing, domain of the high style, which must be kept clean.

Such prohibitions, though always laughably vague and hopeless, are never to be trifled with. Literary conventions define a world, or at least they coincide with the rules that define social circles. Transgression may not have the moral effects that the critics always threaten, but it almost always has practical effects, as Burns found. His correspondent and friend Mrs. Dunlop was especially clear and angry on this point. She too made many suggestions for the improvement of Burns' poems (though they do not survive); her general complaint seems to have been that the indecencies of his poems kept them out of the society of decent women. Burns ignored her suggestions as he had ignored those of Blair. When she found she had been ignored, Mrs. Dunlop wrote to Burns in high "peevish" (her word) style:

Think what an exquisite pleasure you might have afforded me at the small expense of half a dozen blots, or rather half that number, cast over what your own good sense must acknowledge to be improprieties, only excusable in a Kilmarnock edition of the dawnings of authors debarred the converse of the world and content with wit in her very worst attire, before her face was washed, because the author had never seen her drest.[24]

How delightfully clear Mrs. Dunlop is about Burns' ambition, his desire to move from one circle to another; she sees with equal clarity the nature of the pastoral vision, which distinguishes between country things and the representation of country things. I include her complaint not only for its clarity but also because it has a simple practical edge. Burns' refusal to clean up his poetry has cost him money; it has "annihilated a scheme" of Mrs. Dunlop's to engage a group of her respectable friends in subscribing to his book. She is not worried about herself, or, it seems, her friends. She knows that indecency will hurt Burns more than anyone else.

A sense of indecency is created when two nearly separate worlds come together and mingle, if only ever so slightly, as when Blair is allowed to glimpse the poaching joke. The sexually and socially ambitious Mr. Burns created such encounters wherever he went: encounters between rustics and the refined, between men and women, between upper and lower classes. The accusation of indecency dogged him everywhere. Whether we call them rustic or no, Burns brought with him certain qualities that the Edinburgh elite could not tolerate. It is hard to pin a character on such a changeable man, but he could not adapt endlessly, and he could not perform the tricks that – for example – Hugh Blair wanted him to. Well-meaning superiors also counseled him about more purely literary matters. People especially encouraged him to write something longer, more substantial, and so allow himself to make a real literary figure. Here is one such suggestion:

these little doric pieces of yours in our provincial dialect are very beautiful, but you will soon be able to diversify your language, your rhyme and your subject, and then you will have it in your power to show the extent of your genius and to attempt works of greater magnitude, variety and importance.[25]

Burns sometimes speaks of such ambitions, but always under compromised conditions. One of the oddest parts of the patronage letter to Robert Graham (quoted earlier) is a promise that a position in the Excise would allow him to write, and that he wanted to pursue something of "the Drama-kind." This idea is created solely by the need to portray himself in a more substantial light than his truer identity as a convivial writer of songs would allow. There is no evidence that he ever seriously intended to write anything longer than what he had already written. It was not in him to do so.

After Edinburgh, Burns, as a poet, was confronted, first, by a stylistic or generic problem. He had shown himself capable of performing well in the most popular and conventional modes of eighteenth-century verse. This success could have been extended, as his well-meaning advisors suggested, by publishing longer and hence more profitable works. He understood literary history and what it had created, and could write the sort of thing it demanded. Unfortunately, as the rise brought about by performance of the pastoral plays itself out, the pastoral becomes impossible. In writing highly conventional poetry a rustic genius inevitably renders him- or herself oxymoronic, since the rise implied by such performances (the rise from obscurity to refinement) always ends up looking like unpleasant social climbing. Pastoral figures ambition as non-ambition, but this fiction must lapse in the face of the physical world, just as its picture of "passion" must also turn into actual passion. The fiction can only be maintained by staying outside of the circle of refinement; socially, such a person will always be like a sort of learned pig, as Burns liked to say, a perpetual miracle never accorded the simple rights of the social elite. As the "Song on Miss W. A." illustrates, for a rustic to write pastoral poetry paradoxically looks like a paradox, and that paradox always stands ready to swallow the rustic up. At the same time – to come to the problem specific to Burns – Burns liked and thrived on conventions, the bread-and-butter of a convivial poet. So literary history, the world of letters, seems to squeeze him out by offering both an enjoyable, socially consequential poetic world and an oppressively ruled and self-defeating set of precedents. What sort of poetry could he happily write in such circumstances?

Burns also faced career decisions. By this I do not mean simply the necessity of finding a way to make a living: Burns was an energetic man and would be able to do that. What bothered him, I think, was trying to decide in what way his poetic talents might interact with his material concerns. He had already failed in making his poetry simply underwrite the rest of his life. His pastoral verse, again, illustrates his problem best. Unlike those of refined poets (Gray or Shenstone, say) the pastorals of Burns have an uncertain dose of reality, and the sentiments expressed in such poetry take on more potential reality than they would in poems from a refined pen. Again, Burns liked the mixing of personal and poetic; it is the soul of his poetry, and he continued to want to write and circulate what he wrote, and to get convivial credit for it. But his presence in his poetry seemed to be exactly his problem. What sort of verse could he write in these circumstances?

The answer to these questions, it turns out, is that he could write songs. It would not be precisely accurate to say that Burns retreated from Edinburgh in 1788 under a cloud; he went away when there was nothing left in Edinburgh for him. His status as an acceptable person of interest to the high and mighty had disappeared, by and large, and there was no prospect of any income appearing, other than what he had already received from his book. His ambitions had come to an end: his social ambitions in the evaporation of his status and his erotic ambitions in his cataclysmic affair with Mrs. M'Lehose. Burns turned his mind to the future, and what he could make of it; he turned his mind to Jean Armour, the Excise, and to two collections of Scottish songs then in the gathering stage, one edited by James Johnson (*The Scots Musical Museum*) and the other by George Thomson (*A Select Collection of Scottish Airs*). All biographers of Burns, with their various moral shades, agree that the two winters in Edinburgh mark a kind of watershed for him, if a life of thirty-odd years can have watersheds, and I agree. Edinburgh was the destination marked out for him by his ambition, and the English verse he wrote during these years was all earmarked for Edinburgh. After 1788, the amount of high sentimental verse dwindles markedly, and the proportion of "Scotch" songs rises dramatically. Actually, longer poetry of all types nearly disappears, replaced by songs and a few other short modes, like epitaphs. I have been rather hard on Burns so far, but I would insist that he really was a writer of great genius, and a poet of integrity and subtlety. After his debacle of failed ambition, he was able to write in a way true to his talents. We remember Burns not for his pastoral effusions; nor, I think, do we really remember him for highly capable and fun poems like "Tam o' Shanter" and the verse epistles: we remember him for smaller things, for his songs.[26]

Before I turn to the songs, the true and effective answer, there is one other spurious answer to my questions that I want to consider. Before finding practical solutions to oppression, any person of an aggressive nature, like Burns, is bound simply to become angry first. Rebellion, in this small sense, is not a solution, but it frequently feels like one. We have already seen an example of Burns' anger, in his addendum to his letter to Miss W. A. There his thwarted ambition expresses itself in the anger of the spurned: cranky and psychologically exposed, his note does nothing but underline his spleen. His life is full of rebellious activity, and he was frequently enough in trouble for his rebellions. I would again call up the metaphor of smuggling: if the front door is closed, go in through the back, and kick something when you get in. For instance, marriage seems to have been, for Burns, one of the institutions he felt oppressed by, implicated as it is in decorums. So he continually went around this institution, in the company of whatever woman he could convince to go with him. Burns uses the metaphor in an early and hopeful letter:

And then to have a woman to lye with when one pleases, without running any risk of the cursed expence of bastards and all the other concomitants of that species of Smuggling – These are solid views of matrimony – (vol. 1, p. 24, no. 18)

Smuggling is of course the great Scottish specialty, as well as Burns' source of livelihood once in the Excise. The strongest poetic parallel to participation in a smuggler's underworld is Burns' lifelong interest in reading and writing "bawdy" verse. Such poetry is designed to be passed around under the nose of such censors as Hugh Blair; in fact, the stanzas Blair objected to in "Epistle to J. R***" come very close to a certain type of bawdy poetry. During Burns' time indecent verse was frequently passed around in manuscript, and enjoyed at the meetings of clubs and other all-male events. Burns had certain correspondents to whom he regularly sent indecent verses, and he maintained a well-known manuscript collection of such poetry, a collection which eventually appeared in the published world as *The Merry Muses of Caledonia*.[27] Indecent poetry offers various sorts of pleasure, only some of which are simply titilating or sexual in nature; it offers, for instance, the excitement of doing the forbidden, the pleasure of secret naughtiness. Indecent verse also powerfully exploits and emphasizes the existence of social circles, each with its set of decorums. It is the very essence of convivial verse, made for private, exclusive, "clubby" enjoyment. Such secret pleasures were attractive to Burns, for the usual reasons. They helped him feel he was not completely captive to his oppressive social world: they allowed him to sneak some simple freedoms into his life.

One of the poems in *The Merry Muses of Caledonia* is called "Ode to Spring," a poem which Burns sent along with a letter to one of his song collaborators, George Thomson, in January of 1795. It is set to a tune ("The Tither Morn"), and is of handy song-length:

> When maukin bucks, at early f—s,
> In dewy glens are seen, Sir;
> And birds, on boughs, take off their m—s,
> Amang the leaves sae green, Sir;
> Latona's sun looks liquorish on
> Dame Nature's grand impetus
> Till his p-go rise, then westward flies
> To r-ger Madame Thetis.
>
> on wandering rill that marks the hill,
> And glances o'er the brae, Sir,
> Slides by a bower where many a flower
> Sheds fragrance on the day, Sir;
> There Damon lay, with Sylvia gay,
> To love they thought no crime, Sir;
> The wild-birds sang, the echoes rang,
> While Damon's a-se beat time, Sir.
>
> First, wi' the thrush, his thrust and push
> Had compass large and long, Sir;
> The blackbird next, his tuneful text,
> Was bolder, clear and strong, Sir:
> The linnet's lay came then in play,
> And the lark that soar'd aboon, Sir;
> Till Damon, fierce, mistime'd his a—,
> And f—d quite out of tune, Sir.   (no. 481)

This little squib has its good points. Its meter is delightfully solid, and the bouncing rhythm not only aids the humor of the song but also participates in the subject, the rhythms of sex portrayed and burlesqued. The typical rapture of the pastoral is repeated and burlesqued too, in Damon's "participation" in nature. Still, the energy of the poem is undoubtably in the dirty words. These words derive their effect by substituting for the conventional diction of songs in the pastoral mode; a word like "ardor," for instance, could be used instead of "pego" (in the first stanza), and would turn the dirty line into a perfectly acceptable line, and a perfectly conventional

line besides. It is funny to see these low-class words masquerading as
something higher, words that might be in poetry. The small thrill of
putting dirty words into an otherwise quite conventional and capable
poem comes from pretending, for the moment, that these hopelessly
common words are the same as other words. The fun of such a
displacement can be exaggerated by rhyme, as in one of Burns'
versions of the song "Green Grow the Rashes, O":

> 'Twas yestereen I met wi' ane,
> An' wow, but she was gentle, O!
> Ae han' she pat roun' my cravat,
> The tither to my p— O.   (no. 124)[28]

Through the rhyme Burns forces "gentle" and "pentle" (a word for
penis) together for a moment, and the pleasure in their contact is the
same coarse pleasure one might get in bringing an ill-bred guest to a
formal party, or in acting ill-bred oneself. Simply put, it is the
pleasure of conventional transgression. As a principle of composition,
indecent diction is just an extreme version of Burns' use of Scottish
diction, where a word like "kebbuck" energizes poetry by its extra
dose of corporeality. Read by the wrong person, the charge the poet
hopes to generate can easily go too far and turn into disgust; such
verse cannot move in all circles. That this song presents only a
relative freedom is illustrated by the only partial actual presence of
the dirty words, covered as they are by that most amusing of
typographical conventions, the "—." The blanks that are in this
poem as it is printed are there in the original letter, a "spontaneous"
composition. This song does not spring free of convention; it is simply
within conventions of a different provenance than those that rule the
usual ode.

Burns' prose setting for this song (the letter to Thomson) is an
interesting one:

I fear that my songs, however a few, one or two, or three, or even four, may
please; yet, originality is a coy feature, in Composition, & in a multiplicity
of efforts in the same style, disappears altogether. – For these three thousand
years, we, poetic folks, have been describing the Spring, for instance; & as
the Spring continues the same, there must soon be a sameness in the
imagery, &c. of these said rhyming folks. – To wander a little from my first
design, which was to give you a new song, just hot from the mint, give me
leave to squeeze in a clever anecdote of my *Spring originality*.– (vol. ii, pp.
335–6, no. 651)

He goes on to describe how the "Ode" was written on a bet, the wager being that Burns could not write an original poem on the spring. The "Ode"'s originality is in its dirty words, since otherwise it is (quite consciously) a completely conventional poem. The problem of precedent that Burns describes so lightly is of course a serious problem for him, a kind of oppression; the indecent poem is written as an escape from this oppression. Since the "Ode" is at heart quite conventional, the whole thing is a joke, a little present to Thomson. As a joke, though, it has several levels that are worth describing. Writing songs is difficult because the subject matter is so unvarying; birds sing, maidens blush, bosoms heave. Burns' model, described in the letter, would explain the repetition of these items by noting that love is always the same, which is at least partly a metaphor for the fact that sex is always the same. Poems on the spring are always about history's repetition of sex; love blooms afresh in the spring, as it did the year before and as it will the next year. The plainest joke that Burns' "Ode" serves up is to demystify the elaborate diction of the many songs about spring, and to call their love and passion sex instead. Damon and Thetis do not woo or swoon: they have sex. This part of the joke is an exposé, a cynic's insistence on corporeality instead of idealized abstraction.

But of course what Burns substitutes for the repetitions of literary history is in itself the very essence of repetition. This is, in fact, what makes it a good joke, since it prevents the song from taking itself seriously. It may look subversive because it replaces indirection with (perhaps offensive) direction, but it says the same thing as its hypothetical decent twin: love blooms afresh in the spring, as it always has. The last lines, where Damon loses time, underline the irony of the song's rebellion by laughing out loud; they knock it off its tracks in a light and uncaring way. The source of the laugh, though, is that Damon loses time because his passion overcomes him, and so the jolly springtime activity of keeping time with the birds is overrun by the frenzy of the actual activity. This laugh also prevents me from taking these lines too seriously; so I will only say that Damon's loss of rhythm is a nice metaphor for Burns' real concerns, which lurk around the edges of this simply successful joke.

After all, the joke that Burns plays on literary history is also a joke on himself, for he quite seriously wrote plenty of manufactured verse, indulged in plenty of indirection and artificial diction. Because it ironically belittles its own voice, this joke leaves him neither the opportunity to assert the dignity of song-writing, nor the opportunity to take the tradition seriously and try harder. Burns could write acceptable conventional English verse, but he knew that his "fierceness," in some form, would always interfere with the harmonies of such performances. He and his works circulate, and he circulates his works with enthusiasm. From time to time an occasional production will wander from its proper recipient. Burns knew this about himself, and knew it was also true of his poetry. He knows that the "Ode to Spring" is not any sort of anything at all, and so it is offered not only as a joke but as a self-effacing joke, a joke that recognizes its limitations. Burns enjoys the thrills his song provides, but he also knows them to be cheap. It may escape from the oppressive circle around high literary convention and the proper matrons, but it is inside an equally tight circle, drawn around the conventionally male rebellions of the "club." His rebellion goes nowhere, and provides no remedy for the coyness of originality. I wanted to discuss this non-solution because it indicates how songs relieved Burns' from the oppression of authorship, though here that relief is ironic. There is poetic integrity in the laugh at the end of the song, and a kind of freedom. The freedom comes from an oxymoronic arrangement of talent; Burns both demonstrates his capacity and easily disappears behind the casual nature of his production. Burns' freedom here is the freedom of a man who knows and understands his limitations. I do not mean by this that Burns had become a happy social dependent, or that the strangely resilient nature of social conventions had ceased to bother him. I mean that his literary ambition has turned in on itself, away from genres not suited to his genius. The joke of the "Ode" works so easily because Burns has no more ambition to write a real "Ode," no sense that the confinement that the joke depends on is a painful confinement. The whole of the letter to Thomson exudes a pleasant poetic confidence, a solid sense of capacity. If Burns has a sincere prose voice, it is in letters such as this.

The limitations that the "Ode" so easily reasserts and jokes about are exactly those of songs in general. The song is an especially diffuse genre. Most importantly, in songs authorial presence is diffused, since songs are performed : the author must share credit with the performer. The texts of songs are set to tunes, which most often come from tradition, and sometimes from composers. Burns did not write any tunes. Imported from elsewhere, the tune sets strict limitations on the possibilities of the verse, dictating rhythm, line and stanza length, as well as, to some degree, tone and subject. A light love lyric cannot be set to a dirge. Songs also circulate far more freely than more ambitious kinds of poetry, since they are easier to remember, and friendly by nature. In this way, traditional songs often outrun their authors, who disappear in the very popularity of their productions. Working as he was within and on the edges of the folk tradition, many songs came to Burns in what he thought of as a nearly finished state; he would change a few things, set them to a new tune, keep a chorus here and rewrite one there. Occasionally he wrote entirely new verses for a tune. Song is also one of the most heavily conventional of genres, and so acceptable subject matter is almost without exception limited to the old stand-bys of love and wine. Out of the fifty-one songs Kinsley includes in the section entitled "Last Songs," for instance, forty-four may be fairly described as about love.

Song is one among many minor genres, but it amplifies minority to an extreme. Writing in 1809, Walter Scott deplored that Burns would have spent his energy working on such small things:

We cannot but deeply regret that so much of his time and talents was frittered away in compiling and composing for musical collections ... even the genius of Burns could not support him in the monotonous task of writing love verses on heaving bosoms and sparkling eyes, and twisting them into such rhythmical forms as might suit the capricious evolutions of Scotch reels, ports and strathspeys. Besides, this constant waste of his fancy and power of verse in small and insignificant compositions must have had no little effect in deterring him from undertaking any grave or important task.[29]

Scott seems to have been taken in by Burns' occasional mention of fake larger ambitions; that is, he pictures Burns distracted from larger tasks. Appropriately, if disapprovingly, his description of the erotic genre of the song is sexually determined. He sees Burns' song writing as creative onanism, absorbing energy that might otherwise go into the respectable parenting of substantial offspring. Scott met Burns when he (Scott) was fifteen years old, and so he had no interaction with Burns: Scott is part of the next generation, but even though he has read Burns and Wordsworth, he is still holding up the solid ambitions his predecessors had for Burns. These ambitions figure the oppression and exclusion which drive Burns from Edinburgh. Paradoxically, the value Burns finds in song comes from their very contemptible smallness, and Scott's reaction points to what

Burns wants. He gives up conventional business for the pleasures of smuggling, and songs are the vehicle. They give him all the convivial flexibility he needs, because they are so small that the critical great cannot see them. Scott may not approve of Burns writing songs, but neither is he pestering Burns with decorous rules of decency. Because Scott cannot look closely at songs, Burns can use them to smuggle poetically and personally satisfying accomplishment into the world.

In other words, underneath Scott's observations is the perception that the Muse of song is an easy-going mistress. There is prudery in his dismissal of songs as a serious outlet for poetic energy, but certainly, as a genre, songs are licentious. Their economy is a sexual one, and their repetitions can only be justified by sexual argument. The subjects of song return as sex does in the spring, as sexual desire returns after its satisfaction; songs may be made from sheer repetition, but this repetition is a sign of vitality instead of exhaustion. The obverse of the limitations of song is that songs do not demand very much at all from their authors; they do not even demand that they (the songs) have a clearly discernible author. What they do demand is all of the things that were most congenial to Burns: they demand an easy familiarity with their tradition, poetic flexibility, and a freely profuse feeling for conventional sentiment; they ask for an easy and adaptable style, and a willingness to work quickly and sweetly, in a confined space. They are convivial in a very broad way.[30] Songs do not insist that their authors be original; that is, songs are perfectly happy with their repetitive nature, and value variation more than novelty. Songs allow Burns to exert his very real powers and also to efface himself, so that he may escape from the pitfalls of self-assertion that he felt so keenly from his ambitious period. This – to close the argument – is the same self-effacement that happens in the "Ode to Spring," but here it is a productive effacement: productive especially of a poetic contentment, a happiness that is expressed in the quality of so many of Burns' songs. Burns' self-effacement is productive because it clears a place for him to work; it is like the effacement of "Ode to Spring" because it clears that space by comfortably recognizing limits, by understanding that the possibilities of song arise from its very confinement.

More frequently than anything else, later readers of Burns have praised him for a sturdy sense of humanity, an earthiness and frankness that make him a strong poet in the folk tradition. I have argued that he was much more than that, and it is simply true that his poetry is much more various than this compliment would indicate. But I would agree that Burns' talents can best be seen in songs and poems of an especially earthy type, songs that take frankness as their style and also as their subject matter. One of Burns' best songs is the early "The Rantin' Dog the Daddie o't" (no. 80):

> O Wha my babie-clouts will buy,
> O Wha will tent me when I cry;
> Wha will kiss me where I lie,
> The rantin' dog the daddie o't.
>
> ...
>
> When I mount the Creepie-chair,
> Wha will sit beside me there,
> Gie me Rob, I'll seek nae mair,
> The rantin' dog the daddie o't.
>
> Wha will crack to me my lane;
> Wha will mak me fidgin fain;
> Wha will kiss me o'er again,
> The rantin' dog the daddie o't.

The "Creepie-chair" is the stool of repentance, on which convicted fornicators were forced to sit in front of the congregation. Burns had his encounter with this institution in 1786. The biographical Burns was allowed to stand in his own pew; indeed, he was actively forbidden to stand next to Jean Armour, his partner in crime and eventual wife.[31] "The Rantin' Dog the Daddie o't" finely and beautifully turns the humiliation of such exposure into love and closeness. Many of Burns' poems depend upon the clear pronunciation of the pungent word or fact; but how different here the role of pungent unembarrassed speaking from the calculations of "The Cottar's Saturday Night" or the "f—ks" of the "Ode."

Sex is a private act, and can be pursued and savored out of the public eye. It is also reproductive, of course, and so the body will often have to publicly own up to what the speaking person would prefer remained concealed. Sex has many abstract features, many imaginative pleasures, but children are a tangible result, and insist by their simple presence on the corporeal foundations of sex. Sadly, woman only is marked by this tangibility, and for the man owning up to the consequences of private passion is a psychological and social matter. In "The Rantin' Dog the Daddie o't" these two kinds of acknowledgement mix and blend with touching, firm fondness, characteristic of Burns' best manner. As in many of Burns' songs, the speaker here is female, and from her plight derives the simple pathos of the song; but the stanzas zero in on the father, ending with him and depending upon him, repeating him as a kind of protection. Dramatically, shame and the loneliness of the woman's situation work out towards tenderness and recovery, and since the song so frankly accepts the father the tenderness is real and solid instead of painful. By the last stanza the song has left the baby and focused wholly on the mother; its sentiments are those of an energetic love song, with only the last line left to underline the urgency of the mother's needs.

The dramatic compression of the song – another Burns signature – comes from its harmonizing different kinds of unembarrassed acceptance. The speaker has been called up to confess and to suffer; for her, confession and acceptance of what is physically unavoidable are not choices but necessity. We, the listeners, are relieved from her pain by the unembarrassed presence of the father, who "will own he did the faut" (from the stanza I didn't quote). Their mutual acceptance turns necessity to sturdiness, and scandal to love. The mother may be left in her fault, but the father will "crack" (talk) to her when she is alone. Under the umbrella of acceptance, life, figured by sexual pleasure, returns again: "fidgin fain" means to be eager and excited, to fidget with excitement. The song as a whole is also a frank one, the kind of song Hugh Blair and Mrs. Dunlop would have found indecent. Not only does this song refuse to be quiet about carnal sin; it also insists on happiness instead of decorous or indirect sorrow. Its drama is the drama of forgetting troubles. The direct speaking of the song supports the acceptance which is also its theme; it turns the exposure of the Creepie-chair to account by emphasizing its irony. If the punishment for fornication is exposure, what better parallel than a loud song? The censors would insist that exposure be accompanied by a shameful silence, covering the sin as "—" does a dirty word. The characters of the song take this pastoral paradox into hand as directness and acceptance; censorship is present (in the song) only through its opposite.

In the terms of Burns' career, the censors would also insist that such a sin must be left concealed in the provinces that gave it birth, that it not be brought into the refined circle of Edinburgh. It was not, at least not directly. This song does not appear in Burns' editions of his poetry, though it was published in his lifetime, in Johnson's *Scots Musical Museum* of 1790. It was signed "Z': the volume explains that "these marked Z are old verses, with corrections or additions." When Burns signed his songs, and why, are questions not fully answered; many songs in Johnson were marked as his, but just as many, if not more, were unmarked. Johnson marked the songs of authors who wished to remain anonymous with letters (such markings are an old song-book convention). After Burns' death, Johnson acknowledged that the letters "B" and "R" marked songs by Burns. "The Rantin' Dog the Daddie o't" is distantly related to a song of Allan Ramsay's called "The Cordial," and so could conceivably deserve the double anonymity of "Z," but Burns' song is an entirely new version, and could with equal propriety be signed by him.[32] I would say that Burns' interest in anonymity in this case arises from smuggler's motives. Clothed as an old Scots song, "The Rantin' Dog" can circulate in the world free of the censure that would be heaped upon it as a published poem of Robert Burns. The author is lost, dead or unimportant; the song lives on by itself, sanctioned by the popularity that we imagine has allowed it to survive its author. The irregularity of its theme is accepted under the banner of old Scots honesty.

"The Rantin' Dog" is not an old song, nor is it an imitation of one. It is a genuine song in the old Scots style, disguised as an old song. Burns was openly credited with some songs, and we assume that in these cases he did not mind. Song credit is always of a mediated sort, anyway; the tune itself always claims a signature (perhaps unknown) other than that of Burns. The subject of "The Rantin' Dog" is irregular enough to threaten Burns with more of the troubles he had already grown tired of, so anonymity makes sense in this case. I will admit that such an explanation cannot be generalized cleanly, since perfectly inoffensive songs were often unsigned too, like "My Heart's in the Highlands" (no. 301), signed Z. The disguise of a mixed anonymity can, however, be understood from a broad perspective. It was a publishing strategy on Burns' part: he was not actually secretive about his authorship of his songs. We know that he wrote "The Rantin' Dog the Daddie o't" because he wrote a note about it in his copy of the *Musical Museum*; there he says that he sent it to the young woman concerned, and there is no reason to doubt that he did.[33] When published, it circulates beyond this small circle of occasion, but only incognito, and so it cannot rebound upon him. By making the majority of his output invisible, Burns not only helped his songs lead less troubled lives, but also reduced his profile, the dangerously clear ambition Scott wishes upon him. In Johnson's *Museum*, for instance, his acknowledged presence is strong but not overwhelming; he looks like a dabbler in song, not like the dedicated and prolific song-writer that he was.

Anonymity was a basic feature of traditional song collections (since songs don't care about their authors), and so in cutting his songs free of his person Burns did not at all leave them rudderless; they were then free to enter the world and be read in the light of the very well-defined (sub)genre of the Scots song. The genre of Scots song, in particular, absorbs with ease the indecency that characterizes many reactions to Burns' signed and higher works. Everything about Scots song is covered and explained by an especially intense version of pastoral simplicity. The *Musical Museum* says this in its Preface to the second volume, in 1788 (the first that Burns contributed to):

> Ignorance and Prejudice may perhaps affect to sneer at the simplicity of the poetry or music of some of these pieces; but their having been for ages the favorites of Nature's Judges – the Common People, was to the Editor, a sufficient test of their merit.

The very tunes of Scots song were thought of in the same figurative terms. Joseph Ritson, an English collector of Scots songs with no great love for the Scottish, refers to the "irregular style and pathetic simplicity" of Scots airs. He also approvingly quotes a Scottish writer on Scots song:

> It were endless to run through the many fine airs expressive of sentiment and passion in the number of our Scottish songs, which when sung in the genuine natural manner, must affect the heart of every person of feeling, whose taste is not vitiated and seduced by fashion and novelty.[34]

Directness, simplicity, and naturalness all sit ready to receive "The Rantin' Dog the Daddie o't" in their sturdy arms; irregularity stands ready to excuse the occasional impropriety. These figures are ostensibly the same that received "The Cottar's Saturday Night," but as attendants of songs they have been naturalized and made more honest. I will not say that these aesthetic categories have lost all of the paradoxical energy of the high pastoral mode, but they have lost a lot of it. The minority of songs does not simply exempt them from the demands of contemporary taste; it does bleed off pressure, and makes those demands more diffuse. Part of this protection derives from sheer numbers, the numbers that Scott lamented. Who has the critical energy to keep track of every little song in a substantial collection? Songs ask to be considered (I have heeded their request) *en masse*. There is also the simple effect of their humility. In repayment for their not asking to be thought important, songs are accorded more space to move around in. These qualities protect Burns' songs even when he did sign them, and the protection is only increased by relieving them of the burden of Robert Burns, the Poetic Plowman.

The irregularity of "The Rantin' Dog the Daddie o't" makes it a borderline case, though, and George Thomson's collection would very probably not have printed it. Thomson was a proper Edinburgh person, and his introductory letter to Burns states his views and rules:

The editors of [older collections] seem in general to have depended on the music proving an excuse for the verses; and hence, some charming melodies are united to mere nonsense and doggerel, while others are accommodated with rhymes so loose and indelicate as cannot be sung in decent company. To remove this reproach would be an easy task to the author of "The Cottar's Saturday Night."[35]

Thomson lived far into the nineteenth century, and his attitude is a forward-looking one. He is an "improver" of song. Thomson's list of the freedoms of old Scots songs which I have been arguing Burns was interested in is negative: freedom in need of suppression, looseness in need of tightening. One of the ironies of Burns' interest in anonymity is that he himself lives on the very edge of the old order, which was slowly but surely turning to the system of accountability that we now know. Thomson is a sign of things to come, an era when looseness of many sorts would no longer be tolerated. For instance, James Hogg, the subject of the next chapter, will have a much more difficult time understanding in what ways his published songs related to his person. Burns did not approve of Thomson's stiffness, but in song mode he was very flexible, and he adjusted to Thomson's delicacy with all signs of good cheer.

Thomson was right that Burns was the perfect person to improve old songs. Thomson's compliment to Burns' abilities is two-fold: he compliments both his talents and his specific talent for pastoral idealization. Burns' mobility caused him frequent grief, but it also made him a supple and faithful translator; one of the delightful effects of embarrassment like Thomson's was Burns' decent versions of older, well-known indecent songs. The best of these, in my opinion,

is his version of "John Anderson, My Jo" (no. 302; actually published
by both Johnson and Thomson):

> John Anderson, my Jo, John,
> When we were first acquent;
> Your locks were like the raven,
> Your bony brow was brent;
> But now your brow is beld, John,
> Your locks are like the snaw;
> But blessings on your frosty pow,
> John Anderson, my Jo.
>
> John Anderson my jo, John,
> We clamb the hill the gither;
> And mony a canty day, John,
> We've had wi' ane anither:
> Now we maun totter down, John,
> And hand in hand we'll go;
> And sleep the gither at the foot,
> John Anderson my Jo.

The indecent version of this song, which is four stanzas longer, was
widely distributed before Burns' time, and also appeared in the *Merry
Muses*. In that song John Anderson is impotent or at least uninterested, so that the woman's lament is at once very similar and
very different. In the obscene song old age looks like this:

> John Anderson my Jo, John,
> When first that ye began,
> Ye had as good a tail-tree
> As ony ither man;
> But now its waxen wan, John,
> And wrinkles to and fro;
> I've twa gae-ups for ae gae-down,
> John Anderson, my Jo.[36]

Burns' decent version is in his best style; it would pass by any censor,
yet it is not an idealization. Like "The Rantin' Dog," it takes its
energy, instead, from a counter-idealization that emphasizes sur-
viving the death of idealization. I have shown Burns struggling with
the fact that the eruption of the physical destroys idealization; here,
the inevitability of physical imposition is made into a source of an
especially concrete fondness. The subject of a conventional love-song
is quoted and superseded: raven locks and a bonny brow turn to snow

and baldness, and the love-song is sung in a different key. What makes "John Anderson" such a happy opportunity for Burns is the nature of the obscene original, a song quite congenial to his genius. Convivial and naughty, the traditional obscene version treats the body with more sophistication than a simple swearing indecent song. The traditional speaker warns her husband that he will be cuckolded if he continues to be uninterested; the song is interested in her psychology and her predicament. Its frankness is attractive, since it treats the woman's needs with enthusiasm and sympathy (Burns was very interested in songs on male subjects spoken by women). In Burns' version the sex is turned to sentiment, but the sympathy and the simple direction about physical infirmity remain. Burns liberates "John Anderson, my Jo" by composing decent lyrics, and yet under the cover of decency he smuggles the plain acceptance of physical facts that energizes the indecent version. In particular, his song simply and sincerely expresses the solidity of fact that the pastoral vision, in its embarrassed and encumbered way, is always looking for and claiming to express. The solidity of the physical world does not destroy what it touches, here, as it does in Burns' career and in his aggressive pastorals; here physicality is embraced, rationalized and turned to account. By clipping the song of four stanzas, Burns creates a compression that works greatly to his advantage. It gives the song an up and a down to correspond to its picture of life's up and down, and limits the scope of reflection to a small, sharply defined place. It is, in other words, a beautifully limited song, a song that takes advantage of the simple confinement that song as a genre offers. The expression of the song is also about limitation and its acceptance: it passes by the amorous ambitions typical of the conventional song, and so arrives at its quiet burial with delightful integrity. This is the poetic space that song offered to Burns, a place where ambition can be acknowledged, and acted out in accomplishment, but also passed by and forgotten in acceptance of the limiting realities of the world and the body.

At the beginning of July 1793, George Thomson wrote to Burns to thank him for his contributions, which were at this time building up to a steady rush. Thomson seems surprised, even a little disoriented, by Burns' enthusiasm, and offers him compensation:

I cannot express how much I am obliged to you for the exquisite new songs you are sending me; but thanks, my friend, are a poor return for what you have done. As I shall be benefited by the publication, you must suffer me to enclose a small mark of my gratitude, and to repeat it afterwards when I find it convenient.[37]

Burns replied with ironic but sincere indignation:

I assure you, my dear Sir, that you truly hurt me with your pecuniary parcel. – It degrades me in my own eyes. – However, to return it would savour of bombast affectation; but, as to any more traffic of that debtor and creditor kind, I swear by that HONOUR which crowns the upright statue of ROBT BURNS INTEGRITY! – On the least notion of it, I will indignantly spurn the bypast transaction, & from that moment commence entire Stranger to you! BURNS's character for Generosity of Sentiment, & Independence of Mind, will, I trust, long outlive any of his wants which the cold, unfeeling Ore can supply: at least, I shall take care that such a character he should deserve. (vol. II, p. 220, no. 569)

During 1793 Burns was doing relatively well, financially speaking, so there was no great pressure, for the moment, to accept the five pounds Thomson had sent him. Burns keeps refusing, though, in leaner years; the only other money Thomson was to give him was a loan requested by Burns during the throes of his last illness in 1796. In any case his position was never one to make spurning money an easy thing. Nothing more dramatically marks Burns' resolution to keep his poetry out of the world of "ore" than this refusal of compensation for what amounts to his life-work. To Thomson, no doubt, Burns' resolve must have been incomprehensible, since Thomson was in the business of song-publishing, and hence the defensively humorous way Burns explains his refusal. For Burns, songs were outside commerce, but not everyone felt that way: his strategy, again, was a personal one, pursued for personal ends. Offered a straightforward, above-board method of publishing, with clear and legitimate profits, Burns chooses smuggler's methods instead.

The smuggling of his talents into the world brought Burns a profit only he could see, a personal profit much more stable and attractive to him than those available through proper channels. Thomson's money would have legitimated his underworld pleasures, and so must be refused. Edinburgh taught him that legitimate poetic pleasures are subject to taxation.

This, then, is Burns' solution, his way of turning the pressures of rule to his side. As it did for MacPherson, high literary history offers Burns models and direction that he cannot use. The circle of possibility it defines marks and coincides with the circle of high social possibility, and these two circles effectively rule out forms of expression natural to him. Acceptance into these circles depends upon a performance of regularity and decorum that Burns was capable of only briefly. MacPherson took this as a challenge, and simply tried harder to break into this higher circle.[38] Burns' solution to his dilemma (a simultaneous desire and contempt for "rising" and fame) is a solution of great poetic integrity, and this sets him apart from MacPherson. By associating himself with the tradition of song, Burns turns the limitations of the world into an expressive mode. MacPherson fraudulently proclaimed the disappearance of temporal, spatial and cultural boundary, and formlessness is the Ossianic sign for all these things. Burns' honesty acknowledges the inevitability of limitation. This honesty is the subject of his best songs, and it is also their form. Withdrawing from expansive example and high inheritance, Burns' ambition scribes itself within song's cheerful constraints. This is an act of discipline, a moral act, and the deep integrity that underwrites it is the source of the songs' beauty.

This is a beautiful, if painful (for Burns) story, and a true one. It is important, though, to acknowledge the purely personal nature of Burns' solution. It did not change the ruled world; it only changed his relationship to it. Smuggling is by nature only an end-run around oppression, and the uncompromising world surrounded him still, even though he rendered himself and his works invisible to it. In particular, Burns may have escaped the weight of "ore" in a personal way, but his output was output, and went out into the world of profit and loss, success and failure. Smuggling can be very profitable, but, as our own times have proved, the profits are rarely distributed equally. Burns took only his idiosyncratic personal profits, and so the monetary profits fell to others. Burns' methods generated, in fact, a thriving Burns industry, whose final product did not appear until Kinsley's edition of 1968, the first actually "complete" edition. Smuggled into the marketplace, altered by Thomson, unsigned, independent, many of Burns' songs (as well as some of his poems) have taken substantial tracking, a tracking which has always brought profit to the tracker. Burns' strategy took advantage of the qualities of song, but the very success of his project undermines the protective coat around his works. The quality of his songs quietly and paradoxically asserts itself and eventually brings the attention of the censorious world. Burns' strategies make for evasion, a temporary solution that looks more substantial in the shade of his untimely death. It worked, but his fame was growing apace: like so many

Romantic deaths, Burns' death looks like an especially drastic but effective part of his solution to his problems. More than most poets, Burns' works were closely linked to his person, and though he could evade this fact through his songster's anonymity, they remained so linked. After his death, Burns scholarship came instantly into being, sewing the things to him that he so carefully cut free. Johnson, for instance, unveils the "B" and "R" conventions at the first opportunity after Burns' death. As much as it desired the beauty of his poems, the world in general had no use for the personal side to Burns' poetic solutions.

With Burns' offensive body out of the way, the literary world happily acknowledged and welcomed the author Robert Burns, now created in its own image. Once he was gone, he could be reinvented, and made into the rustic genius that would behave. The first official posthumous edition appears in 1800, along with letters and a biography, edited and written by James Currie, a moralist whose tendencies to censorship would have satisfied even Hugh Blair. The refined went to work with a vengeance. Jean Burns entrusted Currie with all of Burns' papers, a move that scholarship is still trying to recover from. Currie's sensibilities were so delicate that he could only describe his censorship in delicate terms:

It will easily be believed, that, in a series of letters, written without the least view to publication, various passages were found unfit for the press, for different considerations ... it has been found necessary to mutilate many of the individual letters, and sometimes to exscind parts of great delicacy – the unbridled effusion of panegyric and regard.[39]

Currie's excisions in the letters were legion, often descending to very small alterations of phrases whose offense is now entirely invisible; Currie's biography, the famous part of his production, was equally fastidious, and he also left out many poems that he considered indecent (including the song-drama then called "The Jolly Beggars," now known as "Love and Liberty"). Cromek (in 1809) noted of Currie's edition that "nothing is there inserted which can render [Burns'] works unworthy of the approbation of manly taste, or inconsistent with the delicacy of female taste."[40] At last, the world had its wish: an inoffensive Burns. In particular, it had a Burns who would not indecently step outside of the circle of refinement. Mrs. Dunlop's friends could, and no doubt did, subscribe to this refined edition. I take it that the business of this early Burns industry proves the reality of the pressure I have described Burns escaping from, and the reality of his (temporary) escape. The world insists, commonsensically, on retrieving Burns and his distinctive voice for its use. The bastards of his muse must be identified and named for him, legitimized but also captured. The profits from the Currie edition (on the order of 1,500 pounds) were given to the now-indigent Burns family, and so even the material side of the economy of song is reimposed. I do not suggest that this was a bad thing to do – far from it. But the real need of the Burns family emphasizes how radical a solution Burns had imposed.

The process of reinclusion goes on: certainly what status Burns has in the modern critical world depends more on his songs than the poetry included in his authorized editions. In the end, smuggling is as much a part of the world as any other way of making a living. It looks like a way of avoiding or escaping from the way society rules itself into closed circles with strict boundaries, but in the end smuggling (like obscene verse) creates its own circles, and participates in others. I must admit that this is a commercial lesson, and Burns did not care about the irony it offered to his muse. After all, he made his living as an Exciseman, a man whose job is the eradication of smuggling. The material lesson does, however, help to show the purely literary nature of the space Burns created for himself, and the purely literary nature of his profits. During his life and after, he is hedged around by the contest over his name and body. This contest is created by the life he chose for himself, and no doubt many of its convivial aspects appealed to him. In the midst of it he drew a magic circle about himself, a circle which made him invisible. The irony of this *askesis* is that the literary world recognized, eventually, that Burns' withdrawal produced poetry of high quality and accomplishment. Burns turned his songs into literary contraband, but eventually his songs are legalized, and consumed like any other poetic production.

CHAPTER 3

James Hogg

I have depicted James MacPherson and Robert Burns as in some ways opposite poles, successful poets whose success is achieved by going in opposite directions. I have also tried to bring them as close together as I can. Poetry is something that they both do; the muse visits neither man. All poets have "poetic careers," but the careers of these men are highlighted by their initial obscurity. They not only have poetic careers; they need them, and their subsequent rise is palpable and highly visible. The next poet I want to pull on stage will help illuminate accomplishment and ambition by the counterpoint of failure. James Hogg outdoes both Burns and MacPherson in initial obscurity, and in the end outdoes them, by far, in volume of literary output. In spite of his productivity, he attains neither MacPherson's material and social distinction nor the more simply poetic accomplishment of Burns. His constant difficulties not only indicate the superior coordination of his predecessors, but also demonstrate with agonizing clarity the traps set for the rustic poet ambitious of fame and fortune.

In 1807 James Hogg published a book about sheep called *The Shepherd's Guide*. Though its title makes it sound like various sorts of pastoral literature – Hogg himself later collected pieces under the title *The Shepherd's Calendar* – it is actually pastoral literature, pure and simple: it is a sheep-disease handbook. After nearly twenty years of shepherding, with many of those years spent as head or chief shepherd, Hogg was very well qualified to appear as a published pastoral expert. Hogg grew up on the Scottish borders, and on many border farms of the time sheep represented the major capital investment of the landowner; the chief shepherd was one of the most important people on the farm. Being a shepherd was not a pastoral career, complete with sunny leisure and carefree singing, but rather a position of responsibility and financial consequence. Hogg's book did quite well. It brought him eighty-six pounds, no small sum, and also won two awards from the Highland Society; it was popular enough to get a popular title, and was generally known as *Hogg on Sheep*. Though I know nothing about the diseases of sheep, and less than nothing about the state of sheep-knowledge in 1807, I can say that Hogg's book is well-written; it is not the production of an illiterate shepherd.

Hogg had been publishing small pieces (mostly short poems, and some travel accounts) in *The Scots Magazine* since 1794, and had in fact developed a small reputation. He was already known as "The Ettrick Shepherd"; he occasionally signed himself that way. It was this nascent literary expertise that Hogg felt uniquely qualified him to publish *The Shepherd's Guide*:

It is evident, from the rapid improvement made of late years in our breeding stocks, that the farmers of our country need only to be convinced what scheme tends most to their interest, to put that scheme immediately into practice. But it is also plain, that the greatest part of those who have brought these improvements to the highest pitch, and who, by a steady perseverance, have proved most eminently successful, are men nowise singular for their literary acquirements; and who, though they can communicate their sentiments with perspicuity in conversation, never once think of doing it in writing ... From a continual course of conversation with such men, assisted by daily actual observation, have I collected the following hints ... For [my] purpose, I must be allowed to retain a homely and plain style, with the common phrases and denominations of sheep, herbs and diseases; otherwise, I would be unintelligible to the very class of men to whom these hints can be of any use.[1]

By virtue of his "literary acquirements" Hogg's world extends further than that of the strong speakers he has learned from; he can bring into circulation ideas otherwise locked into a circle of speech. Hogg's tone here is one of superiority; not of a moral superiority, but a cultural superiority, a higher perspective. He can see further. He stands above the obscurities of his native level, and so can see not only his native, local things, but also the world they live in: he knows his native pastoral world has its limits. Because he knows its limits, he can cross them as an ambassador and exporter of local knowledge.

He is an ambassador because he knows two languages. One is his native, homely tongue, which contains phrases like "Rot, or Poke" and "Leg-ill" (two sheep diseases the book discusses). The other is the language of his easy and expressive preface, the general language of the larger, written world. This world is marked not only by English (instead of Border Scottish) diction, but also by the grammatical and referential fluency that Hogg demonstrates in his prose. Like Burns, Hogg seems to have been born with precocious diplomatic talents, and quite by himself raises his head up high enough so that the wider landscape of the world becomes visible and available. Indeed, the effort involved for Hogg was far greater than that required of Burns; born into a much lower social stratum, Hogg had only six months of official schooling before he was put out (at the age of six) to the lowest of all rural Scottish tasks, the herding of cows. Hogg was the kind of person Burns would have hired to work on his farms. At age twenty-four Hogg could not, like Burns, quote Shenstone or Addison; by his own account, he had been literate for only six or so years. He could, interestingly enough, quote Burns, and his first published poem, called "The Mistakes of a Night" (1794), tells a rustic story in the stanza of Burns' "Halloween." [2]

By 1807 Hogg had achieved a kind of standing, and that standing allowed him to write his book. His standing was not all good for him, though. His (superior) position as an observer of his native country was a useful asset (which he could sell in the wider world), but it also destroyed certain local assets. Hogg had already lost his life-savings in an unfortunate and seemingly quite unfair legal disaster in the isle of Harris, where he tried to let a farm. With the money he got from *Hogg on Sheep*, together with the proceeds from a book of ballad imitations (called *The Mountain Bard*), Hogg embarked on another farming project, this time in his native Ettrick, which failed too. By 1809 he was destitute. He had also lost his capacity to make money as a shepherd:

Having appeared as a poet, and a speculative farmer besides, no one would now employ me as a shepherd. I even applied to some of my old masters, but they refused me, and for a whole winter I found myself without employment, and without money, in my native country. [3]

By raising himself up, Hogg has ended nowhere. He has neither the capacity to go down again, nor the capacity to stay where he is. There is a plangent note in his complaint of being without money in his "native country"; to be unemployed among friends is quite different from being unemployed amongst strangers. The place from which he can see the borders of his native Border country turns out to be a kind of no-man's-land itself, not part of the broader world, and not local

Ettrick either. His ability to speak with local authority to the wider world has made him a local misfit. This unpleasantly neutral position can be seen in the targeting of the Introduction to *The Shepherd's Guide*. Who is this introduction addressed to? Not to the people Hogg sees the book as a whole addressing; it is about addressing these people. It is aimed at some vaguely higher spot, at hypothetical readers who are not low, but who are also not the audience for the book. He need not justify the style to those for whom it is appropriate, and equally he need not justify it to those who will not read the book. He is speaking into the thin air he has raised himself into.

Contemporary accounts make Hogg's story less sad, since his losses seemed to involve some inattention on his part.[4] In any case, he loses his rustic concentration, and the man who had not long before been a trusted shepherd was now something else: the "Ettrick Shepherd," a destitute writer from the provinces. At this extremity, Hogg decides to "push his fortune as a literary man," and marches off to Edinburgh. Writing would be his only real source of income for the rest of his days. And so Hogg's literary ambition has a very simple, hard edge of practicality to it, since there is no evidence that he ever thought of his writing as a career before he was reduced to poverty. A man who tries to let a farm in Harris is not thinking of making a splash in the literary circles of Edinburgh. Once he began, at the age of forty, he was remarkably productive, if only partially successful. Here are some of the things he did: he wrote a *Spectator*-like periodical; he collected songs; he wrote long, Scott-like poems; he wrote several historical dramas intended for the stage; he wrote historical novels and short stories, as well as stories of contemporary city and country life; he wrote squibs for magazines and extended, seriously executed poetic parodies; he wrote original songs and ballad imitations; he wrote sermons; he wrote criticism. Walter Scott, Hogg's great friend and avowed mentor, is the only contemporary writer who offers comparable variety, and his variety is less. This seeming inability to find a satisfying voice, to settle on a simple form, is the chief characteristic of Hogg's career. In what follows, I will argue that Hogg's variety derives from the sort of neutrality that informs and deforms the preface to *The Shepherd's Guide*. Ambitious of going somewhere, Hogg always seems to end nowhere. For the ambitious rustic poet, self-presentation is everything, and Hogg can never decide just who he wants to be. I will begin where I began with Burns: with what contemporaries thought of as his best work.

Hogg is known now, if he is known at all, as the author of the dark, insanely detailed story *The Private Memoirs and Confessions of a Justified Sinner*. I think that story is in fact his best work, and deserves whatever reputation it has and more. I am not going to deal with his prose narratives, though, but rather with his career as a poet; in his own time, he was known as "the author of *The Queen's Wake*," a long poem published in 1813. It brought him a certain degree of fame, and was reviewed by Jeffrey in *The Edinburgh Review*. One of the smaller poems it contains, "Kilmeny," attained a canonical status large enough so that E. C. Batho, writing in Britain in 1927, could say that it was "too familiar for quotation to be necessary." [5] I call the *Queen's Wake* a poem because it appeared in a single volume with that name on the cover, but it is not a single poem in the way that Scott's long poems are. It is a narrativized anthology; it is a collection of various ballad-oriented verses set into a narrative framework. Later Hogg said that "having some ballads or metrical tales by me, which I did not like to lose, I planned the 'Queen's Wake,' in order that I might take these all in" (p. 24). The narrative framework is not negligible, by any means, but clearly it is a consequence of the need to make a book rather than the book's inspiration.

The plot of *The Queen's Wake*, as provided by the narrative framework, is a poetry competition sponsored by Queen Mary upon her return to Scotland from France. Mary summons the best bards of Scotland before her, to try their skill and compete for the distinction of her favor. It takes place over three nights, and the poem is divided into three "nights," the equivalent of cantos. There are twelve bards' songs presented in all. As Jeffrey said of the poem, "this, it is obvious, is a plan that admits, and even invites, to every possible degree of variety."[6] Formally, there are actually just two types of poems: ballad imitations, in a ballad stanza, and Walter Scott-like poems, largely dependent on octosyllabic couplets, though sometimes these transmute into couplets in pentameter. The subject matter has a superficial variety, since all of the poems tell a different story, but all but one of the poems may be lumped under the category of "Border poetry." In this bin I put not only stories of the Scottish Borders (four of the twelve), but also stories of border states or border-crossing, especially tales that involve visitation from other worlds, such as "Kilmeny." This expanded category takes care of all the poems except the twelfth bard's song, the story of a romance-like joust.

I do not think that metaphorizing "border" in this way is specious.

The poems collected in *The Queen's Wake* are all quite consciously about border states. The Scottish Border resembles the supernatural border, the line between this world and the supernatural world, in the perilous freedom of existence there. The characteristic violence of Border life and Border stories – the exchange of raid for raid, murder for murder – is generated by the traditional lawlessness of the Borders. Hogg's Border stories, and those of Scott, and those of the tradition they both spring from, always keep this lawlessness before the reader's eye. In the face of lawlessness, Border clans make their own laws by strength and violent encounter. Higher authority can never be appealed to, or hoped for. The border between Scotland and England thus does not designate a change in kings, but rather a loss of kingly authority: the Borders, in Border story, really are a no-man's-land, a place where authority falters. Jealously guarded, crossing the border is perilous; yet because (one could say) there is no law against it, the border is crossed all the time. Thus, in "Dumlanrig," in the third night, the "southern host" raids Scottish land, and the Scots reply with a raid of their own. In exactly the same way, Hogg's supernatural stories depict a border that is relatively easy to cross, yet also dangerous; crossing is one thing, but coming back is another. Kilmeny, a young woman kidnapped by fairies, and taken to the fairy world, does return (sad and wise) to our world, but she cannot stay. She eventually disappears again in the same way she had at first, too good and pure for our world. While in the fairy world she sees visions of the earth; specifically, she sees the Napoleonic wars prefigured in allegory. Mostly, though, she simply sees beyond our world to something better, and finds it impossible to truly return home after her experience of a wider world. "Young Kennedy," the first poem recited and the eventual winner of the prize, involves a father who returns as a ghost to avenge his murder; four other poems involve visitation or kidnapping in some form.

The essence of all of Hogg's stories – and particularly these stories – is perilous freedom; to live on the borders is to be free but also nowhere, subject to dangerous forces. This kind of description has a quite specific application to *The Queen's Wake*, because the connecting narrative of the poem is just such a border tale. This story turns an anthology into a poem; *The Queen's Wake* is not an anthology because the space between poems has been filled with story. Calling the drama of the poem a connecting, border tale describes not only how Hogg made the poem, but also the drama of the poem. The reciting

bards come from every part of Scotland (plus two from the south);
one even recites in Gaelic. They share nothing but the stage, and
their presence on the stage is the subject of the story. One by one they
come before the Queen and expose themselves in the strange,
unrestricted, judgmental space that she has created. Those bards
with natural grace (self-possession) fare well; those with false airs do
not.

I call this narrativized space a border state because it is a place of
contest and freedom; the freedom to sing and the freedom to fail.
Literally speaking, the story of the poem is judgment. The judgment
applied is non-local, and quite specifically so: the bards have been
removed from their native, naturally approving arenas and put into
an abstract space where something like intrinsic merit is exposed.
One bard (from Galloway) finds this exposure leaves him naked:

> With hollow voice, and harp ill-strung,
> Some bungling parody he sung,
> Well known to maid and matron gray,
> Through all the glens of Galloway;
> For oft has he conned it there,
> With simpering and affected air...
> Woe for the *man* so indiscreet!
> For bard would be a name unmeet
> For self-sufficient sordid elf,
> Whom none admires but he himself.
> Unheard by him the scorner's tongue,
> For still he capered and he sung... [7]

Another provincial bard, from the forest of Ettrick, finds another sort
of exposure:

> The next was named – the very sound
> Excited merriment around.
> But when the bard himself appeared,
> The ladies smiled, the courtiers sneered:
> For such a simple air and mien
> Before a court had never been.
> A clown he was, bred in the wild,
> And late from native moors exiled,
> In hopes his mellow mountain strain
> High favour from the great would gain.   (p. 20)

The joke about the name (Hogg, we assume) cements an already
highly personal reference by Hogg. This bard's self-possession, which

wins favor from the women, eventually gains him second prize: a harp from Queen Mary, the very same harp that the speaking persona of the poem says he has inherited, and which he strums as he sings *The Queen's Wake*.

These two bards' fates depict the tension that creates the story of the poem as a whole, and which creates the story I told of Hogg's turn to literary work. On the one hand is purely local talent, which when removed from local context pales and looks provincial and ungainly; on the other is real merit, which because of its intrinsic character survives the transition to the nowhere of judgmental space, and wins the prize. The erasure of local borders and affiliations gives the singers a strange freedom, and especially the freedom to fail. The bards gain a courtly audience of broad cultural experience, an audience capable of detecting superior, "pure" quality, but they lose the homely security of local prejudice. The bard who sings in Gaelic cannot win a prize, since the very language of his song is actually local and not transferrable. In crossing the border you may lose yourself and your place. This sort of peril is very specifically the subject of the song the Bard of Ettrick goes on to sing, in which the fairest Border women are kidnapped by fairies; they are kept in a cave until rescued by stalwart Border men, who are able to assert themselves in the midst of lawlessness. Like the description of the Ettrick singer, this episode in the Bard of Ettrick's song is a fantasy of trans-local inner worth, which is not disoriented (disoriented like the bard from Galloway) by the perilous dislocation that comes from crossing the border. The self-possession of the Bard of Ettrick himself derives from traditional pastoral sources. He retains his pungent local flavor, but the natural dignity granted by pastoral simplicity (the simplicity of Burns' Cottar) gives him trans-local value too. Simplicity keeps him unaffected; the Bard of Ettrick has neither excessive locality nor its opposite, "refinement," that disease of those who have lived too much in the wider cultural world and so lost local affiliation.

Obviously Hogg tells this story because it is a fantasy close to his heart: especially close in 1811, when the poem was written. But he also tells it for plain practical reasons. By giving him the formal freedom Jeffrey noted, it allows him to anthologize. This freedom also allows Hogg to tell his supernatural stories without appearing naive or looking like someone who is pretending to be naive. The various bards absorb the naiveté, and he (the modern voice of the narrative context) is free to manipulate them. Since the practicality of his scheme is so noticeable, the formal freedom Hogg gains has its dangers too. Jeffrey, immediately after noting that Hogg derives freedom from his arrangement, notes that it also prevents him from developing any sustained theme other than the anthologizing story itself. The poem looks like what it is, a book created out of smaller, discrete parts. *The Queen's Wake* lives on the borders of connected story, and as such it is an intently personal statement from Hogg. The several poems Hogg has "by him" compete for attention, and this creates a kind of cacophony, instead of a publishable book: so Hogg makes cacophony itself the subject of the story, and in this way tames, or at least confines, his unruly talent. Like so many other Romantic poems, this one makes itself by making the making of poetry into the subject of the poem. The poem thus created is forced, however, to live in its own border region. The identity of *The Queen's Wake* hovers somewhere between a broadly unified poem (one thing, spoken in one voice) and a pile of discrete poetic localities.

The product of Hogg's singularly practical book-making skill, *The Queen's Wake* illustrates exactly Hogg's capacity and also his peculiar failure. He is a ballad singer, and extension always taxes him. The fortuitous exposure to greatness, and the resulting reward and attention, which he imagines for the ballad singer in *The Queen's Wake* rarely, if ever, actually happens, and so Hogg himself must do something more practical to gain literary attention. Faced with this problem, Hogg thinks up a method of presentation that will take up the ballads he has by him. The result is typical of his career: a "poem" that works well enough, but which is not quite all one thing. In his later life, Hogg divided his time between Ettrick and Edinburgh; just so his poems. Their lack of unity keeps them from succeeding as they might. Hogg (the natural diplomat) has a talent for languages: but as he learns the language of high culture (the culture that asks for a Poem instead of loose ballads), he loses the force of his local dialect. This is in fact the same oppressive double-bind that Burns experienced, and which he escaped by actual instead of pastoral withdrawal. Hogg never escapes, and lives in a literary borderland for the whole of his career.

The Queen's Wake is an interesting poem, or group of poems, and it can stand confidently among the best poetry of the ballad-inspired type. Hogg's most brilliant achievement in verse, however, is not *The Queen's Wake* but *The Poetic Mirror*. It too presents, and takes advantage of, a sort of cacophony, the competition of voice; it is also a striking example of both the profit and the loss that Hogg derives from his talent for languages. This honestly astonishing book, published anonymously in 1817, is made up of imitations that slide into and out of parody. It would be silly to call it a well-known book, but it has had some notoriety for the parodies of Wordsworth that it contains, which are of high and humorous quality. Hogg's conception of this project is full of interest. The "advertisement" describes it in entertainingly false terms:

The Editor claims no merit in the following work, save that of having procured from the authors the various Poems of which the volume is composed ... A number of years have now elapsed since he first conceived the idea of procuring something original from each of the principal living Bards of Britain, and publishing those together, judging that such a work, however small, could not fail of forming a curiosity in literature. On applying to them all personally, or by letter, he found that the greater part of them entered into his views with more cordiality that he had a right to expect; and, after many delays and disappointments, he is at last enabled to give this volume to the public.[8]

This was in fact the original conception, and Hogg had for a couple of years previous been angling for contributions to a miscellany.[9] He hoped that it would turn into a periodical, and hoped especially for something from Byron, which would "turn as it were every letter of our repository into gold."[10] Byron did promise something, but never delivered (Hogg says it was "Lara"); Scott promised for the second number; Wordsworth actually sent something ("Yarrow Visited"). The original idea had several versions. As explained in a letter to Robert Southey, it had a twist:

No names whatever will be put to the various pieces so that every reader will have the pleasure of finding out the authors himself which I am persuaded will very seldom be done aright.[11]

When combined with a disappointing return on his requests, this twist twists further into *The Poetic Mirror*, as Hogg describes it in his *Memoir*:

I began, with a heavy heart, to look over the pieces I had received, and lost all hope of the success of my project. They were, indeed, all very well; but I did not see that they possessed such merit as could give celebrity to any work; and after considering them well, I fancied that I could write a better poem than any that had been sent or would be sent to me, and this so completely in the style of each poet, that it should not be known but for his own production. (p. 38)

Hogg had his printer and friend John Ballantyne read the proofs of the imitation/parody of Byron at a party, where it was a big success – and where, Hogg says, it was attributed to Byron.

It is easy to imagine the forces which changed collection into imitation and parody. First among them must be the air of charity which hangs over the whole enterprise; to request poetry donations from such literary businessmen as Byron and Scott is a more hopeful than realistic project. Hogg wonders, innocently, what could have made Byron withhold "Lara" from him, but we might guess that Murray's money had something to do with it. And why would Blackwood and Murray (the proposed publishers) remove, as it were, famous names from individual books sure to sell and pack their possible profits into one volume? Certainly there was precedent for a "poetical repository." Hogg had previously edited and published a collection of songs by several hands, a book called *The Forest Minstrel* (1810); the conception of this collection is exactly like those that Burns supported.[12] This kind of collection presupposes a community of writers who share a common interest. Hogg's Preface to the *Forest Minstrel* focuses on the community of singers and writers and listeners that forms about songs. The shared interest of this community, as Hogg defines it, and as Burns would have defined it, is not an economic one. It is based, instead, on the singer's delight in song, and the social value of songs as entertainment, accomplishment and group activity. This community produces the anonymity that Burns exploits. In *The Forest Minstrel*, though, as in Thomson's and Johnson's collections, an economic motive lurks at the origin; money flows to the "editor" (as it had in Walter Scott's similar, though ballad-oriented *Minstrelsy of the Scottish Border*). Hogg's pleasant sense of community is tainted by the presence of the editor, the man who will profit from the project; people like Byron and Scott know this, and so are beyond the commercial simplicity of Hogg's vision. Hogg hopes that he can skim the profit off of the various poetic performances, playing the role of manager and impresario. But Byron and Scott are not Burnsian songsters, singing purely for pleasure; they live in a world of books, not miscellanies and medleys. They produce volumes (the unitary thing Hogg attempted in *The Queen's Wake*), labelled with their names, which when sold generate huge profits. Scott may have inserted himself between the buying public and ballad singers in the *Minstrelsy*, but neither he nor Byron is a ballad singer singing to the long winter night.

Obviously Hogg's mixture of self-promotion and charity was doomed to failure; in the end, only Hogg's friends sent in anything (excepting Wordsworth: but he sent a small lyric). Hogg's need is an economic one, and in the face of his failure he still needs the book, so he writes his miscellany himself. This solution is also a songster's solution, with emphasis this time on the performative side. The work of the performing singer is not creation, but only an appropriation or borrowing. In an attempt to create a book (to help him make a living) Hogg solicits the community of poets for common property. Since he finds that such a community does not exist, in this form, he instead parrots the various voices in one book, performing the poems himself (and generating profits by the way). That the same James Hogg who imagines an idealized community of singers would then turn around and appropriate that community's voices with great skill and cynicism demonstrates clearly the great practicality of Hogg's literary motives.

Hogg's suspension between the idealized and practical conceptions of his work (his entrapment in the pastoral paradox) produces, I think, not only the collection but also the quality of the collection, for Hogg's acute sense of being both on the inside and the outside of the literary world makes for knowing and keen parody. Hogg himself affirms this for us, in retelling an anecdote well known at the time (a version of it appeared in *Blackwood's Magazine*).[13] The anecdote describes the origin of the parody of Wordsworth, which Hogg says sprung from an "affront" he received from Wordsworth during "the Triumphal Arch scene." The long and short of this story is that while visiting the lakes in the company of John Wilson and others, Hogg joins, one day, a group of the illustrious, among them Wordsworth and De Quincey. They see a rainbow, which Hogg describes as a "triumphal arch" for the gathering of the poets. On hearing this Wordsworth says to De Quincey: "Poets? Poets? – What does the fellow mean? Where are they?"[14] This statement is odd from a number of perspectives, even without considering the insult to Hogg, but it apparently stung Hogg sharply. Hogg defined himself as a local product (the Ettrick Shepherd) but was always deeply distressed when he felt he was considered as actually rather than figuratively limited and local. As Burns' example teaches, the ideal balance between local and general is hard to strike, and the poet who takes up the posture of the knowing rustic independent runs the risk of being taken at his word, as a localized, provincial rustic. The origin of

Hogg's parody is exclusion, by Wordsworth first, but also, to expand
the thought, the exclusion inherent in the failure of his collection; his
acquaintance with poets turns out to be not great enough to make
things go. At the same time, his acquaintance with the poets' voices
was enough to allow him his perfect, knowing and hilarious revenge.

All of the poems are of high quality, but the imitation of Scott and
the parodies of Wordsworth are the best. Scott claimed that Hogg's
accuracy drove him out of the poetry business. He says that

> there was no discovering the original from the imitation; and I believe that
> many who took the trouble of thinking upon the subject, were rather of
> opinion that my ingenuous friend was the true, and not the fictitious Simon
> Pure.[15]

The parodies of Wordsworth are worth looking at closely, since they
showcase Hogg's talents and capacity. Let me give a subtle example
first. This is from "The Stranger, a Further Portion of the *Recluse*, a
Poem":

> A boy came from the mountains, tripping light
> With basket on his arm – and it appeared
> That there was butter there, for the white cloth
> That over it was spread, not unobserved,
> In tiny ridges gently rose and fell,
> Like graves of children covered o'er with snow;
> And by one clumsy fold the traveller spied
> One roll of yellow treasure, all as pure
> As primrose bud reflected in the lake.   (pp. 135–6)

A less subtle example comes from "The Flying Tailor," about a
philosophic tailor with a gift for jumping:

>   A pair
> Of breeches to his philosophic eye
> Were not what unto other folks they seem,
> Mere simple breeches, but in them he saw
> The symbol of the soul – mysterious high
> Hieroglyphics! Such as Egypt's priest
> Adored upon the Holy Pyramid,
> Vainly imagined tomb of monarchs old,
> But raised by wise philosophy, that sought
> By darkness to illumine, and to spread
> Knowledge by dim concealment – process
> High of man's imaginative deathless soul.   (p. 168)

David Bromwich calls Hogg "a connoisseur of bathos, and the most appallingly subtle anthropologist of the Wordsworthian habitat who was ever put on earth."[16] I have given both of these extracts because they show in fine and in coarse how thoroughly Hogg deserves Bromwich's version of praise, and how thoroughly Hogg has entered into his project. His sense of Wordsworth's Miltonic prose poetry, its stately movement, is very keen; note the silly but entirely accurate enjambment of "high/Hieroglyphics" in the second extract. Hogg has thoroughly absorbed the "Miltonic syntax grafted onto a strangely modern vocabulary ... [and] the sanction prudery gives to an inveterate fondness for periphrasis"[17] that are the basic components of Wordsworth's style. Beyond this, Hogg reproduces with occasionally hilarious accuracy what I would call the mixed nature of Wordsworth's poetry, illustrated here by the snow-covered graves of children, or the incongruous encounter of pants and pyramids. At such moments in Wordsworth, high runs into low with a shock sometimes pleasurable, sometimes not. Wordsworth's contemporaries were more sensitive to this sort of thing than we are, I think, but Hogg had a special capacity for seeing it. Hogg's parodies are in fact fixated upon this quality, returning to it again and again. The most provoking instance, in my examples, is the mixture of breeches and soul, where Wordsworthian stylistics are reduced to their most bathetic: pants, a joke metaphor for the body (like the body only less interesting or important), lead to the depths of the soul.

In *The Poetic Mirror* Hogg had hoped, with disingenuous naiveté, to capture the voices he imagined to be sounding freely, in the naive mode of his songster's conception of the world. The plain side of this project (the disingenuous side) is that he would embody these voices in "a neat volume"[18] and collect cash as his volume entered commerce. This fails, because poetry, as a material, printable object, does not float free – or, at least, because poetry can't be captured in this way. By performing the parts himself, doing them in different voices, Hogg skims off the free part. Poems (material objects) are not free, but style or voice, the immaterial mark of identity, does float free and can be appropriated. The material or practical side of poetry sinks his original plan, and so Hogg evades the material connections of verse by becoming a pure, transmutable voice and leaving materiality behind. In doing so, however, he puts his book in the shady borderland I have described previously; in becoming a pure voice, and by exploiting the freedom of voice, he disappears himself.

His name is not on the book, since anonymity is crucial to the success of the unacknowledged imitations. The difference between original and imitation becomes hardly perceptible, and this makes the authority James Hogg, as poet, might be able to accumulate vanish. Is the poem labelled as "by James Hogg" in *The Poetic Mirror* ("The Gude Greye Katt") Hogg's own or an imitation of Hogg? Of "The Gude Greye Katt," Hogg says it "was written as a caricature of 'The Pilgrims of the Sun,' 'The Witch of Fife,' and some other of my fairy ballads. It is greatly superior to any of them."[19] Parody becomes an unusable term if there is no original. Where is Hogg's voice? In a variation on the cacophony of *The Queen's Wake*, Hogg seems to lose his voice in this literary project, rather than find it. This loss appears quite concretely; Hogg's sometime friend William Maginn later attributes "everything worth a farthing in *The Poetic Mirror*" to John Wilson.[20] Hard to argue, for markers of ownership and identity are eliminated by the work itself. Stealing and being robbed are flip sides of the same coin.

The Queen's Wake and *The Poetic Mirror* are not precisely experiments, but they are books assembled for and inspired by the pressures of a moment, the practical needs of a man who earns his living by literature. They illustrate very clearly Hogg's struggle to find a way to make books which he could sell. Writing interesting things was never Hogg's problem; his difficulty was more in making what he wrote work successfully with the realities of writing books for a buying public. This is a matter of presentation. Hogg's difficulties run deep, though; this is because presentation is not a superficial problem. I want to examine one more of Hogg's "books," a magazine called *The Spy*, in order to get at the real importance of Hogg's struggles. In crossing the border to find his fortune, James Hogg really, actually seems to put the very solidity of his identity into peril.

Though not a work of high literary quality, certainly *The Spy*, the weekly periodical Hogg conducted for one year in 1810–11, is the most surprising of Hogg's works. Arriving in Edinburgh in 1810, penniless, and almost without acquaintance, Hogg's first project is nothing less than founding a periodical. This paper does not contain farming news, or shepherd's advice, as we might expect, but instead contains a new voice, the citified Spy, who speaks in a paper modelled after *The Spectator* and its descendants. It contains essays on contemporary affairs of state, stories, poems and contributions of various sorts from the community of readers, who sign with picturesque pseudonyms. Nothing could be more surprising, and at least superficially more of a departure from the books Hogg wrote before 1810 (the rustic *Mountain Bard* [1807] and the more rustic *Shepherd's Guide* [1807]). *The Spy* ran for a year; not a tremendous success, but quite in keeping with the runs of the periodicals it was modelled after. It contains a remarkable amount of material, including the beginnings of several of Hogg's short stories. The eighteenth-century format is ideal for the games of ventriloquism Hogg loves to play, and which his contributors seem to love too. The viewpoint of the Spy himself, that of the wise outsider, looks like a cross between the *Poetic Mirror* and the knowing voice of Hogg's autobiographies. As Addison and Steele did before him, Hogg creates a persona in the first number ("I am a bachelor, about sixty years of age ... ")[21] and steps out of character (into his "own" voice) in the last, where he will "address [his readers] for once in his real character" (p. 409). The "real character" thus finally asserted is a local, rustic genius, whose ability to conduct a magazine should amaze us, considering that he is "a common shepherd, who never was at school, who went to service at seven years of age ... " (p. 411). Like the idealized (and unrealized) version of *The Poetic Mirror*, *The Spy* is a communal venture by nature; edited by Hogg, and contributed to by various interested reader-writers, who sometimes remain anonymous. In this sense it is nostalgic, hazily recalling a literary world that is shared and cozy instead of non-local and judgmental. Hogg is the impresario and an occasional performer, and the collector of the receipts: as in an anthology, money flows to the "conductor" of the magazine, who is the keeper of the voices. A good plan, like that of *The Poetic Mirror*, and a plan equally doomed to failure. In the troubles leading to the production of *The Poetic Mirror* Hogg's immaterial conceptions of the literary world encounter a sober reality; *The Spy* and its associated traumas depict Hogg's conception of the broader literary world encountering the bewildering realities of Edinburgh society.

Hogg begins by dispatching his persona into the world of the city to spy out its faults and foibles. I will not detail what the Spy sees and talks about, except to note that it almost always got Hogg in trouble. The Mr. Spectator-like ironic honesty produces, for Hogg, financial disaster. He lost a large number of subscribers when the protagonist of (what became) his short story "Basil Lee" cheerfully sleeps with his housekeeper; he lost more (he says at the end) when he produced

a zany sort of literary critic called Mr. Shuffleton. I cannot summarize
these surreal installments; I only recommend them. Hogg produces
a lot of telling description; his description of Walter Scott is especially
telling.[22] When Hogg published the Shuffleton papers, however, his
audience "tossed up their noses, and pronounced the writer an
ignorant and incorrigible barbarian" (p. 411), and for once I am
inclined to believe him to be telling the plain truth. Hogg's portrait
of Scott, for instance, quite accurately describes Scott's constant representation of an imitative "originality" to his charmed audience (a
subject to be dealt with in the next chapter) and Hogg (or Mr.
Shuffleton) is not gentle or easygoing. The very audience that Hogg
was trying to sell his magazine to – Scott was Hogg's major friend
and patron, always – is depicted here in distinctly unflattering terms.
This aggressive self-assertion was a poor calculation for a man who
would have been overjoyed for this audience to turn a little of their
avidity his way.

The difficulty Hogg encounters here, which should be familiar
from my discussion of Burns, is perfectly illustrated in an anecdote
retailed by John Gibson Lockhart (Scott's son-in-law and biographer) many years later. It has its source in the period I have been
discussing; and describes Hogg's sense of freedom, and his free
behavior, during a visit to Scott's house:

When Hogg entered the drawing room, Mrs. Scott, being at the time in a
delicate state of health, was reclining on a sofa. The Shepherd, after being
presented, and making his best bow, forthwith took possession of another
sofa placed opposite to hers, and stretched himself thereupon at all his
length; for, as he said afterwards, "I thought I could never do wrong to copy
the lady of the house." As his dress at this period was precisely that in which
any ordinary herdsman attends cattle to market, and as his hands, moreover,
bore the most legible marks of a recent sheep-smearing, the lady of the house
did not observe with perfect equanimity the novel usage to which her chintz
was exposed. The Shepherd, however, remarked nothing of all this – dined
heartily and drank freely, and, by jest, anecdote, and song, afforded
plentiful entertainment to the more civilized part of the company.[23]

This description sounds like the Hogg that will appear in *Blackwood's
Magazine* around 1820, a subject I will come to shortly; Lockhart was
also responsible for that Hogg. Here Lockhart mixes accuracy with
caricature, fondness with condescension. Is this true? One would be
hard pressed to decide, but surely that is part of the point. The
interaction between what Hogg's character might be expected to be

and what it turns out to be, between merchandising and independence, is precisely the dynamic that Hogg would need to negotiate
in order to succeed as a spy. In Lockhart's description, Hogg's
interest, the rustic ticket that gets him in the door, is precisely that
which nearly ruins him. Like Burns, Hogg would need to juggle the
image of the Shepherd and his own plain reality with great subtlety
in order to succeed. He does not really succeed, of course; the last
Shuffleton installment is in no. 10, and one assumes the rest of the year
was a long diminishing struggle. The sheep-smeared visitor strains
the rules of conduct: he is charming, though, and so no real harm is
done. But his ventures are hobbled by his image, and he is not a total
success. *The Spy* turns into what Hogg eventually calls a "literary
curiosity."[24]

One other feature of *The Spy* is worth noting. The demise of Mr.
Shuffleton, and the accompanying clamor, has a delightful effect
upon Hogg, who protects himself by splitting off another persona
from the Spy, this time a pawky shepherd named John Miller.
Lockhart's beautiful if deadly negotiation between stereotype and
truth in his description of Hogg has its precedent in Hogg's own
version of the plain country visitor, which hangs in the same way
between self-portrait and "Shepherd":

he was equipt with a grey plaid, and staff, like a Nithsdale shepherd, and
appeared extremely bashful and simple ... [he offered] me his rough hand,
dyed over with tar and reddle, for he had just come from the bughts in the
West Port. (p. 90)

John Miller's distinctive feature is dialect Scots, and the "honesty"
associated (in the pastoral model) with it. He is put into the front
office, where he runs interference for the more vulnerably urbane spy.
It is as if Hogg had tried to leave the Ettrick Shepherd behind when
he marched off to Edinburgh, and then realized that he could not do
without his pastoral self. If he is to succeed in Edinburgh, it will not
be through blending in with the sophisticated populace. The
Shuffleton episode demonstrates not only that Edinburgh would not
let him blend in, but also that Hogg (like Burns) could not act so as
to blend in. The Spy represents the desire to blend in, and Miller
appears when Hogg realizes that it is impossible. Hogg puts Miller's
qualities to work immediately, in very specific ways. Editors of
magazines whose readers sent in unsolicited material often used some
space, either at the end or the beginning, to communicate with these

people, telling them of the fate of their contributions. Hogg does this at the end of many numbers. At the end of Miller's inaugural number, Hogg replies to someone who sent an "essay" entitled "Donald M'Donald". Hogg's (that is, the Spy's) message runs, in part: "I showed his essay to John Miller, who says, 'It'll no do lad; it's far ower queer, the Latin's terrible.'" Or rather later, in no. 25: "John Miller has examined the *Verses to Many*, but he says, they are entirely useless" (p. 200). Miller's voice is not urbane, but it is solid and direct. Dialect Scots is the natural medium for blunt "honesty." Hogg's invention of Miller is clever, transparent and desperate all at once. Following in the footsteps of Burns, Hogg must decide how to present himself to the higher world. Burns' sensitivity prevented him from turning his whole life into a series of postures, but in this regard Hogg is quite shameless. His works record a long series of experiments in self-presentation, and the virtue of looking at *The Spy* is that it indicates the personal nature of this experimentation. Burns cut the struggle short by withdrawing and assuming the songster's voice, but Hogg cannot define himself this clearly. The pastoral "Ettrick Shepherd" is his most obvious possibility, but *The Spy* never considers the pastoral persona to be the only possibility. Taking up the activity of writing poetry (as opposed to singing his songs to the rural audience) as a job, a substitute for shepherding, Hogg takes up his voice in the same way.

This is the source of his bewilderingly various work; he cannot seem to find a voice that suits him. He needs John Miller's voice because in so many ways it is manifestly his own voice, but the Spy's voice is his too. When confronted with the social intricacies of Edinburgh literary life, Hogg's confusion produces this dissonant division of the self. Whether we call them legitimate, unavoidable or simple snobbery, the social pitfalls of literary life in Edinburgh are complex and have a deep source. The adoption of rustic bluntness – the decision to simply stretch out and make oneself comfortable, and damn the chintz – pushes such problems aside, but it does not solve them. Introducing Miller into *The Spy* delightfully insulates the Spy from the consequences of the direct observation he adopts as the magazine's mission. The ruse does not protect Hogg himself, since, of course, his character's freedom is as fictional as the character himself. Such fictional freedom suffices in the case of *The Queen's Wake*, but the business of *The Spy* is highly personal. He has to sell his magazine to the same people he talks about in the magazine. Hogg is not free: his magazine is a commercial venture, and his sense of freedom from his audience's rules spells failure. Hogg can feel insulated, and his feelings can be protected from exposure, but both the Spy and Miller belong to him. Hogg can try to send his voice away through such carriers, but they are manifestly his creatures, and the consequences of their behavior return to him along with the payments of the subscribers.

As the ventriloquism of *The Spy* fades into a real problem of identity, my focus shifts from James Hogg the author to James Hogg the (possible) person, the bodily foundation of the many personas his works present. Looking for the person that assumes the mask turns out to be an Ossianically difficult project: we may look for James Hogg, but we will be baffled much as the people who looked for the remains of Ossian were. I have been arguing that questions of voice, style and form are deep ones, and Hogg demonstrates this truth in a compellingly personal way. Figurative and literal shepherd, managed by the literary man, blend together quite thoroughly. This confusion is either the source of Hogg's multiple voice, or a consequence of those voices. In any case, I want to look for James Hogg, because that name was quite well-known in the nineteenth century. James Hogg had his measure of fame, but this fame went awry: it derived from and attached to a fiction, and curiously bypassed its creator and object. Since it involves tracking several versions, this next section will be an extended one. The purpose, though, is single: to describe the process of self-presentation and personal mimicry that shakes James Hogg into several competing selves. In doing so, I will also describe, again, the ways in which the literary self and the bodily self are utterly intertwined, and the ways in which writing and the world step together.

James Hogg was the author of the works I have been discussing, but that, I hope, does not help very much. Perhaps because of his indecisive variety of voice, the simple question of identity was a large part of Hogg's career. That is, identity is a part of his career as a distinctly posed question, a question he answered willingly and often with copious self-description. For the first ten years or so of his published history his identity is very tenuous, since he begins by calling in, anonymously, from the provinces. His first publication appears about the same time as those of his contemporaries – Wordsworth, Scott, Coleridge and Southey – in 1794. He sent the poem called "Mistakes of a Night," the Burnsian low-comic ballad

I referred to earlier, to *The Scots Magazine*. The magazine published
the poem with a note:

We are disposed to give the above a place to encourage a young poet. We
hope he will improve, for which end we advise him to be at more pains to
make his rhymes answer, and to attend more to grammatical accuracy.[25]

Hogg continued to contribute things to the *Scots Magazine* for many
years; he supplemented these by putting a few together in a book,
called *Scottish Pastorals*, published in 1801 (at his own expense). After
an especially productive period, when he had published eight poems
and an account of some travels in the Highlands in the course of
about a year and a half, Hogg's activity produces the following
"Inquiry Concerning the Ettrick Shepherd," in *The Scots Magazine*
for August 1804:

Now sir, you give us such and such ballads, or poems *written by James Hogg*,
as if the bare mention of his name were sufficient, not only to confirm the
value of the pieces, but to make the author perfectly known; whereas,
notwithstanding every inquiry I have been able to make amongst literary
men, I can hear nothing of such a person ... Is such a person alive?[26]

This letter, written from the "Banks of the Nith" by someone
named Welch, furthers Hogg's ambition by calling for a further
embodiment of his voice: "There is a curiosity inherent in almost
every man who reads the works of an author, to know something
about the writer ... " (p. 572). Unpaid, except for acknowledgement
and self-gratification, Hogg begins his climb here, when he is asked to
become something other than a pure voice echoing from the forests of
Ettrick and Yarrow. Among the readers that would see this request
would of course be James Hogg; indeed, I suspect him of writing it
himself, though there is no proof for such an assertion. In the absence
of other answers, one supposes, and in dim but typical prefiguration
of *The Poetic Mirror*, Hogg in fact does write the answer to this request
himself. The letter he writes, and two others that follow it (in response
to another request), are composed in the third person and sent from
"the Banks of Ettrick." The fact that they were written by Hogg has
been curiously resisted by some Hogg scholars, but there is no doubt
that they were; besides basic verbal parallels to the *Memoir* (the first
version of which appears a few years later, in 1807), Hogg says as
much in the *Memoir*.[27] With this fact admitted, these letters of self-
assertion look like typical Hogg, full of close personal detail and high

personal praise. Here is an example, written in praise of one of the stanzas in his poem "Willie an' Keatie":

The last verse, for grandeur and sublimity of sentiment, has seldom been equalled, and could have been no disgrace to the classic muse of a Pope or a Dryden.

This sort of self-assertion is followed by another, a change of key:

What then are its merits when uttered by an illiterate shepherd, that got barely as much education as to enable him to read his Bible![28]

The letter is unsigned. The next two, written within the year, are signed "Z." These are rather more reasonable in tone, with the delight in Hogg's rustic illiteracy reduced to a quiet pride. More interestingly, the assertions of exceptional quality are replaced by a new conceit, one of muted and inconsequential modesty, where the early works are described as "thrown off" and incidental. In particular, he describes the book that "Willie an' Keatie" appeared in, *Scottish Pastorals*, as an entirely spontaneous project. Having been forced to lay over in Edinburgh while there to sell some sheep,

he took it into his head that his time could not be better employed till the next market day, than in writing a few poems, to get them printed. The thought thus hastily conceived, was instantly put into execution. (p. 822)

This story of spontaneity has caused quiet dispute amongst (the few) Hogg scholars, who have wondered about its truth; in at least one place Hogg refers to a manuscript for the various poems, which had been critiqued by friends.[29] Hogg's various tellings of the story are just confused enough to render the posturing in this letter visible. The posture is one of unpremeditation, of songster's gay spontaneity, entering into print with cheerful innocence. The earlier posture adopted by Hogg proclaimed talent by contrast, by context, in its victories over circumstance; this one pretends to be unambitious by virtue of a kind of country simplicity. The happy songster, being below it, does not see and cannot care about the world of print and literary accomplishment: this, of course, was the posture adopted so thoroughly by Burns. This kind of poet enters the literary world incidentally, by the way.

These two postures, the one proud and ambitious, the other modest and incidental, naturally offer themselves to the unknown rustic as methods of self-presentation. They take different tacks, but they are both trying to make use of ignorance, trying to transform it into something usable in the process of career-making. The proud posture tells a story of ignorance overcome, of natural and un- quenchable genius. The modest posture presents natural genius too, but presents it as quiet and unassuming: we may listen in on it. The modest method, with its unimposing presentation of pastoral convention, and its lack of aggression, is the more sophisticated of the two. We might in fact be tempted to call the transition in these letters an increase in sophistication, but Hogg, who will lapse frequently into the more aggressive and proud vein, prevents us. At the beginning, Hogg is already simply speaking in the voice of the moment. The special interest here is the purely interior nature of this series of strategies. Hogg requests information about himself, and then offers various fictions in the form of a third-person, objective description. This is a kind of marketing, but it also looks like a real if mild self-division, a small struggle to define the self. It is funny that Hogg writes in answer to queries about himself, in the guise of "Z," but I think it is also a legitimate sort of work for him to engage in. The voice of "The Ettrick Shepherd," a signature Hogg uses from the beginning, requires embodiment in a shepherd's person, as "Mr. Welch" affirms so plainly. Since this voice offers itself as a Real Rustic, it naturally raises the possibility of Ossianic imposture. It is true, as Mr. Welch says, that any pure voice calls out for body, and always has, but for a poet like Hogg, who is using his locality, his class, his origins, as the essentials of his poetic self-presentation, the presence of an actual shepherd is essential. Just as Burns was called in to witness his talent, and obligingly produced, for a time, the poetic ploughman, Hogg produces, for the furthering of his career, James Hogg, the Real Ettrick Shepherd. Hogg, of course, does this by letter, in a magazine, so that here "embodiment" amounts to a change in voice (from poetry to prose).

Hogg projects himself very aggressively into a purely textual space. As a result, he is not subject, for the moment, to the problems Burns encountered because of his carnality, but he subjects himself to other problems. Hogg's sort of self-marketing makes "him" subject to dispute; strategy undermines the firmness of the person it is supposed to benefit. The self he (pseudonymously) projects in these letters circulates in print, in the reading community associated with *The Scots Magazine*. Here he does it on the sly, under the mysterious "Z," but, beginning in 1807, Hogg will periodically issue autobiographical accounts as riders on and introductions to his poetry and stories. A printed context has the advantage of being textual; Hogg can live in his voice, circulate in his words, and this is preparatory to a career much more thoroughly literary than that of Burns. Unfortunately, he also sets himself up for manipulation and confusion, since in posturing rather too clearly, he cheerfully becomes a kind of being of print. For those willing to let it go, he remains the singing Shepherd. He may look silly, but in presenting himself, in his naiveté, Hogg displays a remarkable if destructive clarity of purpose. He does not have, as Burns had, people like Hugh Blair and Henry MacKenzie to promote him (Scott, a hard-headed man, was more circumspect than they), and his is a smaller talent than that of Burns. So he sees that he must do the work himself, and does it plainly, aggressively. Since he is trying to ride both sides of the pastoral paradox (printed ambition mixed with oral spontaneity), he cannot help but expose himself, and so of course his plans only sort of work: but he is going about his business, the business of the rustic poet. In some ways he does this quite successfully; again, "James Hogg" was a well-known name. But (again) in finding "James Hogg" James Hogg seems to lose himself.

Hogg's literary success was in the end slight, and this inevitably conflicts with the fact that in the nineteenth century James Hogg was a famous man. The noun is important here, because Hogg was not, in a narrow sense, a famous writer, but rather a famous character. The primary source of his fame is "James Hogg, The Ettrick Shepherd," a periodical character who was a mainstay of the shenanigans of that most popular of higher-quality magazines, *Blackwood's Edinburgh Magazine*, or "The Maga." This Shepherd appears in many places, but his real home was the famous tavern dialogues called the *Noctes Ambrosianae*. The *Noctes* were one of *Blackwood's* most popular features. These delightfully well-written sketches appeared regularly in the magazine during this period (beginning in March of 1822, with precursors dating from around 1820), and chronicled, very often, the literary business: who published what, what the rival magazines were up to, and so on. They are frequently described as written by John Wilson, but in the period I will be discussing, from 1819 to 1825, they were almost always the product of collaboration between (some combination of) John Wilson, J. G. Lockhart, William Maginn and, to a lesser extent, James Hogg himself.[30] These pieces have a kind of precocious modernity about them; in the end, they are most often, in some way,

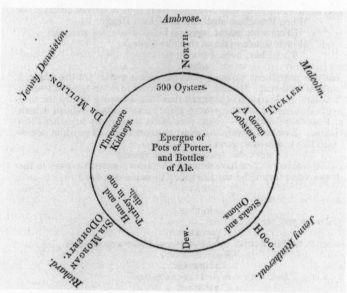

Illustration from *Blackwood's Edinburgh Magazine*, January 1825

about writing *Blackwood's*. The dramatic scene is usually a tavern in Edinburgh called "Ambrose's." Was it a real place? readers would often ask. There was, at the time, a tavern in Edinburgh called "Ambrose's," and *Blackwood's* writers did go there.[31] The characters in the sketches (Christopher North, Timothy Tickler, Adjutant Odoherty, James Hogg, among others) also have a sort of physical reality. I will come back to this, but suffice it to say that these names frequently appeared as authors in the magazine, whatever that is worth as a test of the real. The supporting dramatic action, which creates opportunities for all the crabby and opinionated talk these sketches were famous for, is an overwhelming, unbelievable carnality, in the form of eating and drinking.[32] The characters eat and drink prodigiously and constantly, mixing their beverages dangerously and indulging in vast amounts of cloying food, usually including some roast meat and oysters. The illustration reproduced above, which appeared in the installment for January 1825 (no. 17), is representative.

It is obvious, but worth mentioning, that these characters can live this life because they are fictional. They can pour whiskey through themselves all night and never feel the worse for it; the *Noctes* assert the primacy of a kind of gross physicality, but this assertion is made possible by the immateriality of the scene. The Shepherd is the spirit of plain flesh in this very fleshly fictional world, and so these consumptive details are crucial to understanding the present case. Like John Miller of *The Spy*, the *Blackwood's* Hogg speaks in a heavy Scots dialect, for the same reasons Miller does. The *Blackwood's* Hogg (and the speaker of Scots generally) speaks directly – never flinching at low subject matter, always honest and straight to the point. So the character James Hogg, in the *Noctes*, not only eats and drinks (especially drinks) with enormity, but he is independent of sophistication, sticking close to his original self, his body and natal surroundings, Ettrick Forest. The point of his character is a pastoral one; his country origin makes him simply more real, more physically present, than his Edinburgh colleagues. A typical example: in *Noctes* no. 8, Hogg has come into the city from Ettrick to see a hanging.[33] Challenged about the dignity of his amusements by one of the other characters, he responds:

Pleasure here, pleasure there, I canna bide away from a hangin' – I will tell you plainly that I thinks it's worth a' the tragedy plays that ever were acted – I like to be garred to grue [made to cry].

This is followed shortly by a discussion of whether the victim (an old woman) kicked when she went down, how black her face was, and so on. Hogg's character can be counted on to push aside city sophistication, and to speak a sort of brutal (sometimes self-serving) truth. He can also be counted on to lighten the mood by humorously referring to himself and his works in glowing terms.

Is this character actually James Hogg? The clearest answer is no: why would it be? This is a fictional character in a fictional world. The *Noctes* sketches were interesting, widely read and hence powerful fictions, but they were fictions nonetheless; they insisted upon the primacy of the "real" physical world, but they did so in a fictional setting. Hogg's actual person contradicted these fictions for at least one observer, who saw the older Hogg:

Such was my own impression, derived from this source [the *Noctes*], of Hogg, and from prints of him, with open mouth and huge straggling teeth, in full roars of drunken laughter, that, on meeting him in London, I was quite amazed to find him so smooth, so well-looking and gentlemanly sort of person.[34]

At the same time, the surprise this person feels indicates how far the *Blackwood's* Hogg had circulated beyond his original: he got to

London, for instance, before the bodily Hogg. The anecdote supports physical reality, though, and in a way that is entirely familiar in our media-saturated modern world, the person encounters the persona and proves the persona false. But in Hogg's case, he proves the persona false only in a manner of speaking, since one of the primary collaborators in the formation of this persona was James Hogg himself. It is worth being careful here, since definitions of the self that can discriminate between true self and self-created self are of the subtlest kind, and prone to error. The mechanism of production itself, in *Blackwood's*, is also far more subtle than this picture would admit, and so a brief diversion into the details of that magazine is necessary to the project of understanding who this periodical James Hogg was.

The psychological thrill of the *Noctes*, and to some extent of *Blackwood's* in general, derives from manipulations and confusions of voice. Each character in the *Noctes* has a distinct voice, and contributes that voice to the discussions – discussions are built up from these constant features, as from building blocks. In this way the early *Noctes* maintain a continuity of character, even though they were collaborative efforts. As is well known, *Blackwood's* used, in general, a bewildering array of pseudonyms and created characters as authorial by-lines; "Christopher North," eventually attached to John Wilson, being the most famous of these. Frequently these "authors" appeared as full-fledged characters – "people" – in the *Noctes*. Since the identities of the real authors and editors of the magazine, and their precise responsibilities, were kept a profound secret, the confusion and interest provoked by these strategies was real and strong. The characters of the magazine have all the written marks of real bodily people; that is, there is no certain way to tell the difference while simply reading the magazine. Most importantly, they have distinctive voices, distinctive styles. I don't wish to seem to exaggerate; their reality is simply fictional, and all well-drawn fictional characters have distinctive voices. But since *Blackwood's* made no distinction between fictional writers and real ones in the magazine itself, the net effect is that the fictional characters poach reality from the real ones. The characters speak with constancy and regularity and represent, often, the real voices (the real styles) of actual people. Fit in amongst these many voices were two that sounded more steadily real than the others: those of James Hogg, the Ettrick Shepherd, and James Scott, the Odontist.

John Gibson Lockhart's creation of the Odontist illustrates

perfectly the brutally hilarious, imperially familiar method of the magazine, and I introduce him not only for explanation's sake but also to show that Hogg's case was not unique. Dr. James Scott was a respectably successful dentist in Edinburgh and Glasgow; Lockhart had encountered him briefly in the latter city. Lockhart begins the *Blackwood's* Scott's career by attributing occasional poems and songs to "James Scott, the Odontist," and eventually turns him into a full-fledged character in the *Noctes*. Scott thought himself a wit, and so his appearance in the *Noctes* made reasonable sense. Scott apparently also capitalized on his notoriety to become a fashionable dinner companion, and was pleased with his reputation as a social poet of no mean skill. Hogg describes him in his inimitable way:

For ignorance of everything literary, he was not to be matched among a dozen street-porters with ropes around their necks. This droll old tippling sinner was a joker in his way, and to Lockhart and his friends a subject of constant mystifications and quizzes, which he partly saw through; but his uncommon vanity made him like the notice, and when at last the wags began to publish songs and ballads in his name, O then he could not resist going into delusion! and though he had a horrid bad voice, and hardly any ear, he would roar and sing the songs in every company as his own.

Ignorant and uneducated as he was, Lockhart sucked his brains so cleverly, and crammed "The Odontist's" songs with so many of the creatures own peculiar phrases, and the names and histories of his obscure associates, that, though I believe the man could scarce spell a note of three lines, even his intimate acquaintances were obliged to swallow the hoax, and by degrees "The Odontist" passed for a first rate convivial bard ... [35]

One of the wonderful things about this description is that it sounds very much like the conventional picture of Hogg, roaring out his songs with quaint egotism. It also depicts vividly the absorption of James Scott's identity by the created voice of *Blackwood's*, an absorbtion so thorough that the bodily Scott begins to act out the part written for him. Who was the real James Scott? Lockhart's accomplishment (if it can be called that) is to make this question interestingly difficult to answer. After a while, it may have been true that Scott found this question rather hard to answer too. The dark part of this fun is in the appropriation of voice, paradoxically brought about by the attribution of voice. In giving his own cleverness over to Scott, and denying his (Lockhart's) real voice the credit of its capacity, Lockhart attributes himself to Scott and ends by creating Scott in his own image: owning him as his creature. [36] Lockhart's special cleverness is in "sucking the brains" of his target, and so forcing a kind of collaboration from the victim. Dr. Scott can act up to his image, because it is in some ways himself, but that image has also left him behind and taken up a career of its own. The independence of its career is aided by the fact that the Odontist is not a simple parody of James Scott. Lockhart's Scott is also an imitation, or a parody that is concealed quite thoroughly behind a faithful presentation of character. The bald way of putting it, a way that marks the theft of self clearly, is that Dr. Scott received no money for his contributions to the magazine, while Lockhart and his cronies did. Of course, this plainness ignores the fascinating confusion resulting from the credit Scott did receive, in notoriety and reputation: in some ways, his character is augmented by its absorption, and, at least by Hogg's description, James Scott would have (or should have) admitted that himself.

Hogg's case is just like Scott's only more complicated and confusing. In Scott's case, we find the bodily Scott (call him the real one) roaring out a tuneless version of the created voice, and the body's tunelessness tags reality by its contrast with the fictional Scott's abilities. In Hogg's case, we cannot so easily split these two versions apart; Hogg and the *Blackwood's* Hogg share their voice in an intimate way. In *Noctes* no. 8, already referred to above, the Shepherd sings a song, beginning "Come all ye jolly shepherds that whistle thro' the glen" (p. 598). It is a fairly high quality song, with much of the beauty attaching to the simple chorus:

> When the kye come home
> When the kye come home
> 'Tween the gloaming an' the mirk,
>   When the kye come home.

James Hogg, the Ettrick Shepherd, the country songster of *Blackwood's* and the *Noctes*, sings this song – but so does the bodily James Hogg, the author of books. This is one of the real Hogg's songs, present in several versions, but first published as a musical interlude in his zany novel, *The Three Perils of Man*.

I do not wish to derive cheap drama from the verbal confusions possible here; I want to derive real drama from the real confusion here. We can see the possibilities that arise from Hogg's associations with and appropriation by the *Blackwood's* gang. He, the real Hogg, derives credit from this song, and that credit properly belongs to him

– the song is his. I would be surprised if Hogg was paid for this use of his song, but it is followed by a discussion of his novel, so that the commerce of publishing is carried forward by the advertising the real Hogg receives. At the same time, the fun of the *Noctes* is carried forward too, for this homely, conventionally pastoral song sounds appropriate in the Shepherd's mouth, because that character is so much like James Hogg, the person who composed songs.

The context in which this song appears forces the question of identity and voice further. In this *Noctes* the Ettrick Shepherd uses the song to trap Odoherty (another *Noctes* voice; an Irishman) into a quasi-admission that he had not read *The Three Perils* before reviewing it (Odoherty's review does not exist, as far as I can tell). Odoherty is saved from a full admission of his guilt by the intervention of Timothy Tickler, who claims that the song just sung was different from the version that appeared in the novel. The Shepherd then confesses that he has no memory of having written it anyway:

I'll gang before the Baillies the morn, and tak' my affidavy that I had no more mind of *when* I wrote it, or *how* I wrote it, or anything whatever concerning it – no more than if it had been a screed of heathen Greek... I declare I had to learn the words or I could sing the sang, as if they had been Southey's, or Tam Muir's [Tom Moore's], or some other body's and no my ain. (p. 599)

Since the implication is that he was drunk when he wrote it, this is part of the roaring character of the earthy Ettrick Shepherd. Strangely enough, though, we find that this admission is merely the echo of Hogg himself:

When *The Three Perils of Man* came first to my hand, and I saw this song put into the mouth of a drunken poet, and mangled in the singing, I had no recollection of it whatever. I had written it off-hand along with the prose and forgotten it.[37]

Who is the real James Hogg? what does he sound like? Moments earlier in the autobiographical account, this apparently actual Hogg seems unreal when he claims that this song was "first sung at" the *Noctes*. Does this mean that the *Noctes* penned by Lockhart is the shadow of some real gathering at Ambrose's where (the real) James Hogg sang this song? Or does it simply use "sung" as a metaphor for "published"? If the latter, then Hogg has forgotten his own publishing history, as well as the content of this *Noctes*, since the song actually first appeared in his novel, "sung" by one of the characters. Since the autobiographical note quoted above appears in 1831, eight years after *Noctes* no. 8, the discussion of the song's composition in *Noctes* no. 8 takes precedence, and the real Hogg might be seen as echoing his periodical double. The resulting double echo proves the effectiveness of Lockhart's brain-sucking operation, where the subject becomes enslaved to his absorbing Master. Perhaps Hogg said this to Lockhart in 1823; perhaps he says it in 1831 because Lockhart says it in the *Noctes* (in 1823). In any case, the Hogg of the *Noctes* suddenly looks oddly like the real Hogg. Lockhart's imitation proves so energetic that it ends by obscuring its own category through sheer force. Hogg's originality, copied out, predicted or preempted by Lockhart, looks as if it has been stolen away from him; imitation takes on the force of originality. What we find, instead of these undermined categories, is an interesting middle ground where public identity is a venture, a production. The *Noctes* show that he who wins the force of the original gets the most credit; the credit, that is, that may be used to provide a livelihood. The odd truth is that it is usually not James Hogg who wins. Many "James Hoggs" have been put into play, most of them by Hogg himself, and his identity becomes a bone of contention between them. Hogg's experiments with self-presentation become a way of life: writing and everyday life cross, rendering both unclear. Contest over voice, as I have argued again and again, is not superficial, not purely "formal."

Just how he fails to win, and who does win, can be discovered by pursuing more thoroughly James Hogg the song-writer, and I want to turn towards concluding by doing so. Burns gave his songs away, but Hogg could not do this, having no other job. For Hogg, the wandering ways of song were deeply upsetting. In tracing his internal conflict over song, I will end on Hogg's last and most basic complaint: he pictures himself as a writer from whom opportunity and profit have been stolen away. Interestingly, the dramatic context of "When the Kye... " reproduces (or originates) the confusion over voice. It has a different title in the novel ("The Sweetest Thing the Best Thing"), and there is no indication of tune.[38] The Poet also claims to have had sixteen verses, only seven of which he can remember. The verses given largely correspond to the *Blackwood's* version, though the first (as Tickler points out in Odoherty's defense) is substantially different. These two versions (from the novel and from the *Noctes*) are also slightly different, it should be noted, from the version eventually collected by Hogg in his edition of the songs. It is sung in a mad way by a poet who, in an exact parallel to "Hogg himself," says that he has lost control of the song he himself made up.[39] As I discussed at length in reference to Burns, songs traditionally tend to escape their makers: it is their nature. Their tendency to escape renders the determination of ownership, which governs who shall profit from them, quite problematic. All of the interesting forgetting and singing of the novel and the *Noctes* has its roots in this quality of song, a quality which springs in turn from the cultural place of song. Song is a verse form, but a performative form too, so credit is inevitably shared between maker and performer, or utterly absorbed by the latter. Hogg dramatizes the independent nature of song in the episode from *The Three Perils of Man*, where the Poet wrestles with the product of his own mind as if it were a foreign thing, with a life of its own. The Poet performs his own song, absorbing both roles, but finds that in fact they will remain distinct. Performance has its own demands, its own context, and having made the song provides no final advantage in performing it.

The singer's trouble looks like paradox, but it is not; it is only the difference between the voice of the poet, which is a literary, historical and written voice, and the voice of the singer, which is a social, entertaining, and above all enacted, physical, hear-able voice. These are different things. The fact is that song does indeed have a life of its own, and is enacted in culture in a way that the poet, the maker, simply cannot control, oversee or even foresee. The characters of the *Noctes* live in the world of performance; the Shepherd and the Odontist are performed versions of the bodily people, appropriated by the virtuosos of the magazine. This kind of performance looks like imitation, but it is distinguished from imitation by the retention of the real names. The Ettrick Shepherd of *Blackwood's* is James Hogg as performed (for profit) by John Gibson Lockhart. In our own age this sort of theft would instantly be the source of lawsuits, but the published world of the early nineteenth century is less able to supervise itself. The brain-sucking operation contributes the special *Blackwood's* touch, where imitation and ventriloquism are presented under a smoke-screen of originality and honest, direct talk. The *Noctes* are finely performed, and the performance, by its compelling quality, covers over the real authors by replacing reality with fiction. Songs fit snugly into *Blackwood's* schemes because they are so fickle by nature; Hogg's song needs performance in order to live as a song. The performance in the *Noctes*, "singing" (writing) instead of singing, performs Hogg's song but captures it too, since the words do not actually sound out into the air.

The ownership of song is an open subject of *Noctes* no. 8: "When the Kye Come Home" is presented along with a brief and interesting rumination upon or exploration of song. The Ettrick Shepherd sings his song in response to Odoherty's performance of a song (in French) by Pierre de Beranger, called "L'Ombre d'Anacreon." The Shepherd does not understand this song – it is about Greece and it's modern subjugation, as far as I can tell – and the following dialogue ensues:

HOGG A bonny tune, and, I daursay, a bonny sang too. What was't aboot, sirs?

TICKLER Love and country, and so forth. The shade of –

HOGG I daursay it's just plunder't out of my *Perils*. – Does it mention onything aboot a bonny lassie, and the flowers, and the gloaming?

TICKLER These are all alluded to, Mr. Hogg.

HOGG And the birds singing?

TICKLER Yes, that too, I think.

ODOHERTY (singing.) "Du Rossignol les chants sont toujours tendres, Toi, peuple Grec! – "

HOGG Na, na – time about's fair play, Captain. Ye've gien us the copy – I think I may be allood to gie you the original; for I'm sure the French thief has just been taking every idea I had frae me – I mean –

ODOHERTY Ha! a new light! – Beranger, too, robbing Hogg! – But, begin, dear Jamie.

Hogg then sings his song, the "original" of Beranger's. Odoherty says "Beranger, too" because the real Hogg was relatively well-known for claiming that various authors stole his ideas; the most famous example was his accusing Scott of taking *Old Mortality* from the manuscript of *The Brownie of Bodsbeck*. The clever, hard edge of the *Noctes* (James Hogg would feel the edge) is well represented in this extract, but more than mockery of Hogg's egotism is involved in making up this discussion of song. The Shepherd's argument that Beranger has stolen his song from *The Three Perils* is based on an analysis of subject matter: flowers, "a bonny lassie," birds singing, the evening. This is foolish, instead of proof of theft, because it is a list of clichés, the conventional items of song. Any song, in this sense (any song of this type) is part of a chorus, part of a larger, less well-defined cultural production. The voice of the singer rises briefly above the general din, but this voice is already recognizable, singing what the other voices sing. In this kind of milieu (as I have said in relation to Burns) original and imitation are useless categories, conceptual or otherwise. There are in fact two edges to Lockhart's sharp humor here: one edge cuts Hogg, who is represented as egotistically believing that he owns the common inheritance of all songsters, and the other cuts Beranger, whose pretentious, overblown song about Greek independence is shown up to be just a conventional song after all. Ownership is at issue, and the fact that drives the joke is that the content of these songs is not ownable; they are made from common property, and return to common ownership when they are put into circulation. The Shepherd may not agree, but his assertions to the contrary are funny instead of convincing. Lockhart commands the high ground, by virtue of a superior, un-songsterish sort of knowledge, and his perspective, resting on top of the mountain of convention, turns the whole rumination into a joke, where the naiveté of the Shepherd is prodded and exploited.

The *Noctes* and its associated materials are fun, and are created out of an easy tolerance for confusion. Hogg's accusations of theft, though, occasionally made with great seriousness, indicate the depth and seriousness of his confusion. Having ventured himself, Hogg grows panicky when he can't seem to find himself. And so the bodily Hogg is continually accusing others of literary theft or being accused of it himself. A good example of Hogg's tendency to characterize his career as marked by theft appears early on, in the first *Memoir* of 1807. He is discussing the (anonymous) publication of his popular early song, "Donald M'Donald":

There was at that period, and a number of years afterwards, a General M'Donald, who commanded the northern division of the British Army. The song was sung at his mess every week-day, and sometimes twice and thrice. The old man was proud of, and delighted in it, and was wont to his dying day to snap his thumbs and join in the chorus. He believed, to his dying day, that it was made upon himself; yet neither he nor one of his officers ever knew or inquired who was the author – so thankless is the poet's trade! (pp. 14–15)

The theft here is of pleasure. General M'Donald gets his pleasures free, and in fact garners credit for the song (as its subject) in addition. The maker is left out of this circle, his fickle song having left him, or having been taken away.

I will admit that this passage is more complicated than my formulation indicates; there is a quiet vanity whispering here, the

vanity of a person claiming modesty as a personal virtue, given away
by the conventional lament at the end. But I think the thought of
thievery is real too. Let me emphasize this by giving two more
anecdotes, which together modulate to the pathetic. The first
describes Hogg hearing "Donald M'Donald" performed, in England, with a new last verse added by the singer. Hogg, in his
enthusiasm, tries to claim the song as his. The fellow to whom he
makes his claim "laughed excessively at my assumption, and told the
landlady he took me for a half-crazed Scots pedlar." The second has
Hogg watching a Scots soldier walking down a road, singing Hogg's
song. The story ends this way:

In the height of his enthusiasm, he hoisted his cap on the end of his staff, and
danced it about triumphantly. I stood ensconced behind a tree, and heard
and saw all without being observed.[40]

Hogg, silent, unobserved, hears his voice in a country lane, coming
from another, working its pleasures for another. His voice has gone
out from him, and there is a moody pleasure in that, but this sort of
auto-voyeurism (what shall one call it?) will not make a career, at
least not a remunerative one. So Burns knew: he got satisfaction from
the aggressive anonymity possible in song, and he used this
anonymity for his own psychological ends. Hogg wants more. He was
influenced, perhaps, by the close presence of the meteoric and
incredibly profitable career of his friend Walter Scott, and in some
ways the theft Hogg laments in these anecdotes is a purely commercial
one. If he had published "Donald M'Donald" in a book, with his
name on it, he could with more authority claim it as his own.[41]
Hogg's sense of loss is also vaguely broader than this, though, and he
has an unfocused desire to capture, make use of, the energy he
somehow created in writing "Donald M'Donald." In these anecdotes
he insists on his originality, on his place at the source, and also
acknowledges that he cannot get a hold on the profit his effort
produced.

   Hogg's efforts to claim originality and its profits are also hampered
by the song itself. Here is the first stanza:

> My name is Donald M'Donald,
> I leeve in the Heelands sae grand;
> I hae follow'd our banner, and will do,
> Wherever my Maker has land.
> When rankit amang the blue bonnets,

Nae danger can fear me ava;
I ken that my brethren around me
Are either to conquer or fa'.

Hogg says that he wrote the song while feeling indignant over the impending Napoleonic invasion of Britain, and there is a later stanza that challenges Napoleon specifically. We might call the voice in this song the Voice of Britain. The sentiments are utterly conventional, but the special patriotic appeal makes this a virtue. The song circulated widely because it could; it could be sung by anyone in the British Isles and still retain a sense of local application. Hogg has lost his voice in the stronger, more general voice of patriotism. This is hardly a flaw: it is the source of the song's popularity, since patriotism depends upon submerging the sense of private interest and of a discrete self; the pleasure of a song like "Donald M'Donald" is that any singer can lose himself in the swelling chorus of British voices. Clearly, though, the genre of patriotic song is hardly the place to try to profit from song. Hogg's song takes wing because it is a good patriotic song, and by disappearing Hogg makes himself a good patriotic song-writer, singing in chorus with the multiple voices of Britain. Hogg knows this, and hence the quiet vanity of his complaints; but he is also bothered by his hypothetical loss. He can't quite disappear entirely: or he tries to reappear after the fact. Hogg presents himself, often, as the overheard pastoral singer, and his songs as the natural product of inspiration, but he can never fully naturalize his voice. He cannot do so because he does not wish to give up the credit, monetary or personal, that comes from singing with a purpose.

The world of song was changing at this period, and indeed some song-writers managed their output for a healthy profit. One such case was Thomas Moore, and it is quite possible that Lockhart introduced the discussion of the ownership of songs into *Noctes* no. 8 because he knew that around 1822 (when Hogg was publishing his first collected edition) Hogg had been involved in a curious song-dispute concerning Moore with his London publishers, Longman and Co. In this dispute Longman's had refused to include in Hogg's collection several songs that they said bore an uncomfortable resemblance to some well-known songs of Moore's, out of *Irish Melodies*. Hogg's songs do indeed bear a close resemblance to Moore's: they should, since they are quite consciously reworkings of Moore's songs. The *Blackwood's* Hogg says that he had to learn "When the Kye Come Home" as if it had been Moore's or Southey's. The corollary would be that he would have been happy to sing it, and even claim it, even if it had been "Tam Muir's." This, as I have said, is a songster's attitude. The real Hogg had a lot of this Burnsian strain in him, and he frequently reworked old tunes; he reworked some of Burns' songs (such as "Charlie He's my Darling"). In this same spirit he reworked some of the *Irish Melodies*.[42] The sole evidence for the whole episode comes from the notes Hogg attached to the songs involved when he finally published them in 1831; there is no evidence that Moore ever knew anything about it. One of the songs is "Go Home to Your Rest," which is related to Moore's "The Young May Moon." Here is the first stanza of Moore's song:

> The young May moon is beaming, love,
> The glow-worm's lamp is gleaming, love,
>   How sweet to rove
>   Through Morna's grove,
> When the drowsy world is dreaming, love!
> Then awake! – the heavens look bright, my dear,
> 'Tis never too late for delight, my dear,
>   And the best of all ways
>   To lengthen our days
> Is to steal a few hours from the night, my love!

This is Hogg's version:

> Go home, go home to your rest, young man,
> The sky looks cold in the west, young man,
>   For should we rove
>   Through Morna's grove,
> A noontide walk is the best, young man.
> Go sleep, the heavens look pale, young man,
> And sighs are heard in the gale, young man:
>   A walk in the night,
>   By the dim moonlight,
> A maiden might chance to bewail, young man![43]

As E. C. Batho says, it is hard to say exactly what relationship Hogg's song has to Moore's. It is not parody; it is not, obviously, imitation, since it contains a kind of commentary on the original. Perhaps it is best just to call it a reworking. The irregular stanza looks like one of the closest ties, and in a way it is; but both songs derive it from the tune they share, and the tune ("The Dandy O") is an old one and hence communal property. The reference to "Morna's grove" is another place of close contact, but, ironically, Moore says in a note to the poem that he owes this image to a older Irish poem translated by a friend. Whatever genre we say Hogg's Moore-songs belong to, they are typical of Hogg; they actually look quite a bit like some of the quieter parody/imitations of *The Poetic Mirror*. The realist commentary on Moore's blithe lovers' sentiments is not parody, but like the imitation of Byron in *The Poetic Mirror* ("The Guerilla") it has a parodic feel, as if it could become parody if done differently. Hogg and Moore share a subject, but take different views of that subject. In the songster's world, such a relationship is common, and variation is one of the most basic of song-writing methods.

Hogg calls his songs "proscribed M'Gregors" and seems annoyed and slightly baffled at their suppression. His notes to the songs set up a running commentary about the suppression; the most extensive complaint is in the note to "The Maid of the Sea," a complaint that applies equally well to "Go Home to Your Rest":

It is quite natural and reasonable that an author should claim a copyright of a sentiment; but it never struck me that it could be so exclusively his, as that another had not a right to contradict it. This, however, seems to be the case in London law ... I have neither forgot nor forgiven it; and I have a great mind to force [Moore] to cancel Lalla Rookh for stealing it wholly from the Queen's Wake, which is so apparent in the plan, that every London judge will give it in my favour ... [44]

Hogg has discovered the song-world of 1822 to be less convivial than he had hoped: he had, of course, discovered this before and forgotten it. Moore's *Irish Melodies* represented a very solid money-maker for Longmans, and one supposes that they were loth to endanger or interfere with this solidity. Hogg's actual problem, of course, is that he was publishing with Moore's publisher. The 1831 edition was published by Cadell, and there the proscribed M'Gregors were accepted. Still, the point is that Moore has arrived first, and claims priority over the "sentiments," and even over their contradiction.

Hogg is joking and also serious, it seems, when he threaten's Moore's immensely successful *Lalla Rookh*. His vision is contracted by annoyance, and so he can't see the *Arabian Nights*, or Boccaccio, or the rest of the numerous antecedents to the miscellaneous plan of *The Queen's Wake*. Hogg's threat, like all such defensive threats, undermines his argument, since he marshalls the same overly-exclusive literary history against Moore that he objects to in Longman's treatment of him. Hogg is wavering between the forgiving song-writer and the literary businessman, who keeps his eye on copyright and profits. In some ways, it turns out, a song can be owned, especially when it is written by a person who very successfully presents himself as the author of the song. This is becoming more and more the case during Hogg's lifetime, as the freer practice of the eighteenth century is left behind along with the smaller profits of that era. Hogg knows this, and sees that if he could tap into this commercializing of literature he could become wealthy, perhaps as wealthy as his great patron, Walter Scott. At the same time he continues to write in the older pastoral mode, portraying himself as the spontaneous singer who doesn't care about reputation, who thinks all voices float freely on the wind of inspiration, and who lets his voice float free too. In a commercial setting, such an attitude has its consequences, most especially that of lost profits. Burns wanted this consequence, but Hogg had no such independence. It is hard to see how the pastoral singer can be both spontaneous and profitable; Hogg could not see how, and so his career is a confused one.

Hogg's naively righteous complaints about the Moore episode are a symptom of a broader malaise. He is kicking here at the confines of written literary history, that most encouragingly discouraging of forces. For an ambitious poet like Hogg, history is the greatest thief of all. "When I first knew him," Walter Scott says of Hogg, in a letter to Byron, "he used to send me his poetry, and was both indignant and horrified when I pointed out to him parallel passages in authors whom he had never read, but whom all the world would have sworn he had copied."[45] Though it is typical of Hogg, we might grant him his indignation here, where a pre-emptive but unknown literary history beats him to his own thoughts. How can history do this? Part of the answer lies in the poetry Hogg was writing. Here is part of the last stanza of an early song:

> Flow, my Ettrick, it was thee
> Into life wha first did drap me:
> Thee I've sung, an when I dee
> Thou wilt lend a sod to hap me.
> Passing swains shall say, and weep,
> Here our shepherd lies asleep.[46]

Scott, one would suppose, could pick on "Thee I've sung" and "passing swains," in addition to the conventionalities of the pastoral theme; and he would of course be right to do so. These clichéd instances are mixed up here with curiously, almost hilariously homespun phrases, reminiscent of Hogg's parodies of Wordsworth.

Since Hogg was a real shepherd, he quite naturally speaks of himself as a singing shepherd. But though he was a real shepherd, in poetry his reality has clearly been anticipated and undermined by other singers. His very identity is already a convention, and so Hogg has both a place ready-made for him, and a place that will render him invisible.

We might grant Hogg his indignation, but our sympathy is tested by the obvious presence of reading in his poetry; swains pass only in literature. It is hard to say what exactly Hogg was reading at this time, but he has at least picked up a selection of the tired diction of the eighteenth century.[47] These "references" are beyond allusion; they have passed into cliché. Hogg has absorbed poetry from the air, from the voices that have carried out to the forest. Lines like his occur elsewhere because they occur everywhere. Such is the nature of cliché, an inheritance no one can (or wants to) own. In the end, we have to say that the "imitations" Hogg inflicts on Scott may have been inflicted on Hogg by literary culture, but only with his collusion. That is, Hogg's poetry is ambitious – he is ambitious, and wants his poetry to appear in magazines – and so, like Burns before him, he is artificially trying to insert his voice into a culture with a burdensome history attached to it. He must try to sing his small songs amidst the noise of thousands of other voices he has no real inkling of. This din calls for loud singing, but it also enforces conformity by defining what singing is and can be. The ambitious poet, trying to be heard, must somehow produce conformity and distinction at the same time. The immediate problem for Hogg here is that he is sending his poetry to Scott, a virtual epitome of the wider world of the culture of verse. Silent, or by his own fireside, his poetry might remain his own; as soon as Hogg sings out loud, his voice must take its place in the chorus. Hogg sees this with indignation, but we can see it more clearly. Hogg loses his poetry to history because in fact he has almost nothing to steal; his voice seems purloined, to him, because he has already taken it from others. And, again, the only reason this matters is because Hogg is trying to make a career, trying to steal into the world of letters. His ambition makes discerning and keeping his voice a pressing matter.

Can voice be stolen, as Hogg perpetually denies and asserts? In written culture, what belongs to the self, and what to others? For a poet from the forest of Ettrick (the braes of Yarrow), these questions have not only their inherent difficulty, but also a sort of urgency. If fame and fortune are to be made, if credit is to be gathered, some solution must be worked out. Part of this solution has to be a practical one, such as the world works out all the time. Hogg needs to make a living, either by generating cash, or by generating the sort of "notice" that might lead to cash, the route taken by MacPherson and Burns.[48] One of the interests of Hogg's career is that it tends to illustrate the somewhat mixed nature of Romantic literary property; his career does so because he is so relentlessly obtuse about such matters. That is, the answer to the question "Can voice be stolen?" is a disappointing "yes, and no." It depends upon the degree of materiality attributed to the voice, and upon the materiality of the written thing: it depends on what purpose and motive lies behind the exertion of voice. During the Romantic period, older conceptions of writing and its material value (such as I have detailed in discussing song as a genre) are mixed with more modern, highly supervised conceptions. In the older world, voices carry far, and the printed self drifts easily away from the bodily self. In this world the written voice is less individualized, more easily conventional, but accusations of theft (accusations of the sort Hogg makes when accusing Moore of stealing *Lalla Rookh*) are rare because such incidents do not appear to qualify as theft. In the modern world the written self may appear to become more capricious and free, but that self is sutured ever closer to the bodily self, since its career generates profits that the bodily self wants, and which culture becomes ever more capable of overseeing and collecting. Hogg hesitates between these two worlds, never sure which one he is in. He often sends his voice away, as Burns did, and just as often suddenly scrambles to get it back, lamenting its loss or accusing someone of stealing it. Sometimes Hogg's hesitation looks like opportunism, as when he quasi-naively solicits contributions to *The Poetic Mirror*, or when he aggressively (and under a pseudonym) presents himself as a spontaneously overheard singer, but I think in fact that he is an example of genuine confusion and mixed motives.

A commercial solution is not the same as a literary solution, but these two types are closely related. As in my previous discussions, literary history presents itself to Hogg in a mixed way, offering him a context that is both expressive and purely practical. Writing poetry is a possible occupation, and that occupation is defined, for the apprentice, by what has been written. Literary history is more than precedent, less than absolute law. The challenge for Hogg, for any publishing poet, is to find some way of using the contexts offered by literary history to create an expressive and practical career. Unable to formulate a steady place of reference, a firm voice, Hogg feels as if poetic possibilities have been stolen away. So they have been, so they always are. The challenge is stealing them back, and this theft is always carried out by stealth, by strategy, and by assuming a voice that will serve. This is conventional wisdom: all poets travel incognito. Hogg's career emphasizes the purely figurative nature of voice and poetic identity because his is always disappearing or changing.

Part shepherd, part literary man, part city-dweller and part country cousin, "James Hogg" is perpetually being sold off as some new combination. Because this sale is always self-dramatizing and self-conscious, it looks crazy to his audience, crazy instead of compelling. Hogg's confusion rendered him vulnerable to the brain-sucking operations of *Blackwood's Magazine*, and the buffoonish, self-aggrandizing Shepherd is the result. The periodical Shepherd is an endearing buffoon, but a buffoon nonetheless, constantly and openly giving himself away, claiming credit for anything, and enjoying himself enormously. He is who he is, untouched by consciousness or concern. He never suffers from a hangover after the bacchanals at Ambrose's; he never needs a loan, since he has no bodily needs, but he keeps in character by always asking for them. His accusations of theft are simply funny, since he has no material to lose. No wonder this performance of "James Hogg" put such pressure on the original, and no wonder it was so much more convincing than what Hogg himself kept producing. Hogg the person tried very hard to create himself, and to steal into the literary world, but he seems always only on the border of success.

CHAPTER 4

Walter Scott

Above the writers I have discussed so far, indeed above all the writers of his era, towers the figure of Walter Scott. His enormous stature, as measured by the student of sales, is, of course, of a peculiar sort. It combines with his reduced presence in the current canon to make up a confusing image; an image that at once commands respect and provokes critique. His accomplishment remains, I think, almost unparalleled, even in our era of smash hits and giant blockbusters. In the first thirty years of the nineteenth century, he published roughly thirty popular books: books whose sale was markedly profitable for those involved. This number does not include the ten or so books that either were not terribly successful or which were designed for a small audience. As far as I know, no one ever lost money publishing a book written by Walter Scott.[1]

Scott's only possible rival is Byron, whose poetry eclipsed Scott's, and whose commercial stature is imposing. Not, I think, equally imposing, as Byron would have been the first to admit. Byron's whole career fits neatly within the middle-to-late period of Scott's. When Byron eclipsed him in the poetry market, Scott simply wrote novels instead; and when Byron expired, romantically, on the fields of Greece, Scott remained to mourn him, and to write successfully after him. He was, as Carlyle said, a markedly healthy man, perhaps the healthiest poet that ever lived. His writing, both in itself and in its composition, is remarkably free of the angst that would become the rule in the world of letters. He went about his writing like a person who liked to write. Literature was his trade. He went to work every day for thirty years, and what he made there was, time after time after time, just what his audience wanted. In our age, when high literature has lapsed from public consciousness, we expect dramatic popularity to be self-punishing, and we would point to Scott's eventual shrinkage in the canon as his just deserts. His more critical contemporaries (our ancestors) thought this way too, and expected, every minute, for his popularity to vanish like the meteor they assumed it was. It never did; it outlasted Scott and his critics too. In essence, this bewildering capacity to repeat himself is my subject. How did he do it?

Coleridge, painfully leafing through the first two cantos of *The Lady of the Lake*, offered a crude method:

What I felt in *Marmion*, I feel still more in *The Lady of the Lake* – viz. that a man accustomed to cast words in metre and familiar with descriptive Poets & Tourists, and himself a Picturesque Tourist, must be troubled with a mental Strangury, if he could not lift up his leg six different times at six different corners, and each time p— a canto.[2]

Coleridge goes on to concoct a recipe for popular poetry, and to claim that Scott wrote by recipe (a charge I don't think Scott would have been interested in denying). We remember immediately, though, that Coleridge was, quite specifically, afflicted by a mental strangury, and that no poet could have been less capable of peeing cantos than himself, even though he could very well have been described as a "Picturesque Tourist." Recipe is not sufficient; poetry such as Scott writes may be whipped up by ingredient, but this formulation at least acknowledges the presence of a cook, whose skills may be greater or lesser. Coleridge was a finicky, unproductive but enormously gifted gourmet: Scott was a generous, enormously successful restauranteur, a man who liked to eat and to watch others eat. What bothered Coleridge, and what bothers, I suppose, many of Scott's hypothetical twentieth-century readers, is that he seems to have served up the same dish for every meal. Coleridge was writing in 1810, and his reading of *The Lady of the Lake* was troubled by the fact that it was a sort of *déjà lu*; it offered the same plot, the same characters and roughly the same poetry as the previous two poems (*The Lay of the Last Minstrel* and *Marmion*), disguised by a change of scenery. And yet it was the most popular poem of the three.

In the context of this book, Scott looks most like James Mac-Pherson. They are both successful literary opportunists. They are both easy, too; they both negotiate places of tension with apparent ease. In pursuing the magic ingredient in Scott's recipe, I will, because of this similarity, follow a method similar to that of the MacPherson chapter. I want first to look at Scott as a calculator, and try to understand the mechanism of his worldly success. Such descriptions demonstrate success, but do not explain it, and so the second part of this chapter (as with MacPherson) will turn to the poems themselves, since their achievement is their enactment of Scott's strategies. This too is a point of similarity between Scott and MacPherson, but I finally want to keep these two writers apart. MacPherson's success was a one-time shot, and the outburst of condemnation and conflict that his writings generated helped him gain "notice," but foreclosed on further literary activity. Scott wins over everybody, and leaves a bad taste nowhere: so he returns over and over to the same readers, who receive him happily. If anything, Scott mobilizes the energies of revival more thoroughly than MacPherson. Scott's use of his schemes, which I will describe in detail, has none of the brutality of MacPherson's methods, though, and if (as I have said) the tonic of earliness is an impossibly paradoxical drink, then in any case Scott somehow makes the impossibility nearly undetectable. My task is to understand how he was able to do so; with every poem, Scott would seem to be approaching the natural limits of his success, and then he easily, naturally and inoffensively walks by this limit to find yet greater success.

Enormous, unprecedented sales are the hallmark of Scott's poetic career. The description of sales is a brutal affair, with its hard technicalities, but it was the breath of life to Scott, and can be made illuminating. J. G. Lockhart, editor of the *Quarterly Review*, Scott's son-in-law, author of *The Life of Scott*, and familiar from the career of James Hogg, took care to record the details of Scott's commercial success, in anticipation that any information about such a phenomenon would have permanent interest.[3] All of Scott's poems were first published in what Lockhart calls a "splendid quarto," an expensive edition designed to ensure profit. Reviewers complained about this practice from the start; to be fair, these editions were always followed quickly by an octavo, in larger numbers. *The Lady of the Lake* (1810) was the most popular of Scott's poems, with sales figures rising to meet it and then falling off after. Scott's publishing career begins in earnest with the *Minstrelsy of the Scottish Border*, in 1803, a book of antiquarian appeal which sold about 4,500 copies in the first three years. This is followed by *The Lay of the Last Minstrel*, which established the scale on which the Scott phenomenon was to be played out: published in 1805, it sold its quarto out instantly, and went on to sell 12,500 copies in the first two years. One of the impressive things about Scott's sales is that they went on and on; thus, in the years 1809–11, when *The Lay of the Last Minstrel* was competing with two other Scott poems, it went through two editions of 3,000 copies apiece. *Marmion* did the same and better, in 1808. Its quarto edition numbered 2,000, and was followed a month later by an octavo edition of 3,000. In two years it had sold 16,000 copies: after two more, 25,000. *The Lady of the Lake* (1810) sold out a quarto edition of 2,050 in days, and the octavos of 1810 alone totalled 18,250, for total sales of 20,000 in its first year. *Rokeby*, published in 1813 (a year before *Waverly*) looked to Scott like a failure, and Lockhart decently leaves off his usual detailing of sales, indicating only that it had the disappointing sale of some 10,000 in three months.

To put these figures in perspective, Wordsworth's *Lyrical Ballads*, considered by him and the trade to have been a moderately successful book, went through four editions in eight years; it sold about 1,500 copies in its first three years. Wordsworth's collected edition of 1820 took four years to sell 500 copies. Somewhere in between would lie such authors as Moore, Rogers and Campbell; Byron would post numbers like those of Scott for many of the years between 1811 and 1820. Perhaps the best way to sense Scott's status as a sort of industry is to amalgamate the sales for the years 1809 through 1811, when he had four books of verse on the market. The editions of those years alone total a breathtaking 50,500 copies; this does not count the sales of other books and articles, such as his contributions to the *Quarterly Review* (just started) and his various editing projects. Thus when he began to write novels in 1813 he was already a most famous and wealthy man. His novels would take up where the poems left off, typically selling about 10,000 copies in their first year (frequently Scott would publish more than one novel a year).

This plain history of sales is authorized by Scott himself. In 1829 he wrote a large number of prefatory pieces for a complete edition of his writings. The prefatory remarks attached to the poems, including the "Essay on Imitations of the Ancient Ballads," make up a literary autobiography of sorts. Their downright style and almost shocking frankness about sales and money make them especially entertaining, or at least give them an air of revelation, of "secret history," as Scott calls it. All of the discussions in these introductions are liberally spiced with money talk; how much he made from being sheriff, how much his copyrights were worth, and so on. Scott's story of his own writing is largely a commercial history. Partly this emphasis can be explained by noting that when this history was written he was deeply mired in the troubles issuing from his bankruptcy in 1825, and writing had become, more than ever, a financial labor. Still, Scott's descriptions of how his poems came to be (as distinguished from their commercial fates once written) are astonishingly concrete: I ring no changes when I describe him a strategist. These descriptions of his practical plans and abilities are not final explanations, but they are the first layer to be gotten through on our way to the mechanism of his poetic success.

For Scott, writing is work, and in the introduction to *The Lay of the Last Minstrel*, Scott begins by describing his worldly fortunes in detail: his career in the courts, his desire to be a famous author, his office of Sheriff ("about 300 pounds a year in value"), and his various early decisions on how to proceed as an author. After a long discussion of his various anxieties and thoughts about the law, and about his worries about trying to be both an author and a lawyer, he eventually reaches the point where he has convinced himself that it would be all right to let the active practice of law lapse and to become primarily an author.[4] There is no divine wind rushing to fill him:

Thus far all was well, and the Author had been guilty, perhaps, of no great imprudence, when he relinquished his forensic practice with the hope of making a figure in the field of literature. But an established character with the public, in my new capacity, still remained to be acquired.[5]

He has arrived at a point where everything is set except for the writing. He has his paper, his pens, and the time to write; he lacks only something to write. He decides that the business of ballad writing was failing, that

Ballad writing was for the present out of fashion, and that any attempt to revive it, or to found a poetical character upon it, would certainly fail of success. The ballad measure, which was once listened to as an enchanting melody, had become hackneyed and sickening, from its being the accompaniment of every grinding hand-organ.(p. 16)

He gets an authorized subject, the story of Gilpin Horner, from an aristocratic admirer, who gives it to him as a charge. After what he depicts as a long progress of searching through available meters and forms, a congenial verse-form is authorized for him by the example of "Christabel," recited by an acquaintance (presumably, Scott would also say that he and Coleridge have a common source in older verse). The machine is primed: "I was now furnished with a subject, and with a structure of verse which might have the effect of novelty to the public ear" (p. 22). From here it was simply a matter of production and profits. Again, this bare way of describing poetry no doubt lives to some extent in the atmosphere of 1830. But Scott always regards poetry as a sort of work, and so it is not an untruthful description. In letters written at the time, his literary labors always mix, on equal footing, with other business. Here is a typical sentence:

As for my country amusements, I have finished the Lay, with which and its accompanying notes the press now groans; but I have started nothing except some scores of hares, many of which my gallant greyhounds brought to the ground.[6]

In its plain practicality, Scott's career is a successful version of James Hogg's. Like Hogg, Scott approaches publishing as calculated self-presentation. Thus, above, he looks through the various measures available to him like a person looking at fabric samples. He searches for the form that will suit him best, and which will present his project most effectively. As a defense against a sense of mediocrity, Scott has exaggerated his detachment, but his retrospective narrative of the self-presentation involved in the production of the *Lay* compresses and figures the progress of his early career very neatly. More than any author in this book, Scott's career is planned, and his early works form a series, expressive of a sort of apprenticeship. The end of this series (the *Lay*) marks the emergence of the journeyman, a full-fledged author named Walter Scott.

Scott's poems before the *Lay* are grouped under the banner of the ballad stanza. They follow in the footsteps of William Taylor's translations of Bürger (first published in 1796), some of them being translations of Bürger themselves, others being spectacular, supernatural stories in ballad form. His work on the *Minstrelsy* straddles this period (roughly 1798–1803), and in fact much of this work is published in a special section of the *Minstrelsy* devoted to imitations. This is the strain that Scott speaks of as tired out by the time of the plotting of *The Lay of the Last Minstrel*. Compared to the dramatics of Hogg's and MacPherson's careers, Scott's looks notably more orderly, but it does work off of some of the same logics. A translator has a barely perceptible identity as an author; to use Scott's vocabulary, the translator's speculation in the market of literature is underwritten by another, already successful hand. An editor (one step up in tangibility) has a voice, but that voice is subordinated, ceding true authority to the writer being edited. Like any impresario, an editor takes on some of the shine of authorship by being near authors. MacPherson exploited these two methods of presentation masterfully; Hogg tied himself in knots trying to do so. The next step on the way to incarnating a full-scale author is imitation, where an author makes his or her own product, signed with his or her own name, but still covers the nakedness of publication with things openly and loudly borrowed from others. Scott began as a translator of Bürger, and soon moved on to editing and writing imitations. *The Minstrelsy of the Scottish Border* (1803), which the title page declares to be a book by Walter Scott, collects together the various modes of apprenticeship into a kind of anthology of practice self-presentation. In that book Scott speaks with an authoritative editorial voice, presenting the works of other authors; his authority is increased by the fact that the authors of ballads are invisible, and will not contest with him for precedence. The third volume of the *Minstrelsy* contains imitations of the ancient ballad, some of which are Scott's.

So *The Lay of the Last Minstrel* appears at the end of a progress from translator to editor to imitator to author. It appears in its own volume with its own title. Unlike the *Minstrelsy*, the covers of the book are not openly a container for the writing of others, but present (ostensibly) matter wholly his: a poem "by Walter Scott." The original introductory paragraph to the poem describes the status of the poem neatly:

As the description of scenery and manners was more the object of the author than a combined and regular narrative, the plan of the Ancient Metrical Romance was adopted, which allows more latitude in this respect than would be consistent with the dignity of a regular Poem. The same model offered other facilities, as it permits an occasional alteration of measure, which, in some degree, authorises the change of rhythm in the text. The machinery, also, adopted from popular belief, would have seemed puerile in a poem which did not partake of the rudeness of the old Ballad, or Metrical Romance. For these reasons, the poem was put into the mouth of an ancient Minstrel, the last of the race, who, as he is supposed to have survived the Revolution, might have caught somewhat the refinement of modern poetry, without losing the simplicity of his ancient model. (pp. 31–3)

I want to use this as a manifesto of Scott's poetic project, so it is certainly in my own interest to declare it to be one. But this is Scott's first personal appearance as a poet, and it is also the first appearance of his characteristic measured step, which will remain his favorite mode throughout the coming successes. He will not feel the need again to so formally declare the conceptual underpinning of his project; here, at the inauguration, it needs explaining.

The overall air of calculation accords well with the retrospective version given in the Preface of 1830. This is a description not of inspiration, or even expression, but of the making or construction of a poem. The matter of the poem needs a suit of clothes, and the choice seems to be one of expedience: what fits. So the "plan" of the metrical romance is "adopted"; this form has "facilities" that "authorize" irregular rhythms; finally, the poem is "put into the mouth" of a borderline modern Minstrel, as a way of justifying the modern look of the imitation. "Regular" and "authorize" are the key words, and crucial for understanding Scott's practice. Like all the authors in this book, Scott wishes to sell the vigor of simplicity, and, as always, his audience loves this simplicity so intensely that they are dangerously close to being disgusted by it. The "simple" feature here is the (neo-)primitive irregularity of the poem, and because his readers both love and are made uncomfortable by this feature, Scott's poem needs some way to justify it. The roughness of the metrical romance is used to accomplish this; the metrical romance is irregular both in plot and in meter, and Scott wants us to accept both in his poem. Literary history (again) is Scott's ally and also his foe here. His modernity makes his irregular poetry look rough, "unsophisticated," delicious but in need of justification, in the same way that the Ossian poems needed justification for their extravagances. At the same time, precedent (history turned to rule, a list of permissibles) rescues him by providing a "model," a form that is not solely Scott's responsibility. Imitation is retained, in this pale form, for its usual purpose: to reduce the amount of author in the author. Scott is an author, but he is also authorized.

The irregularities of Scott's poem (I will give examples later) do not arise naively or naturally; they are calculated irregularities, regular irregularities. Scott does not offer his irregularity as such; he offers us a quality which looks like irregularity (looks like the hoary old romance) but which is also modern, acceptable and unintimidating. In this way, Scott's capacity for careful calculation keeps him out of the trap that caught Robert Burns and James Hogg. He can give the reader irregularity and remain regular himself.

Authorized as he is, Scott stands easily in that place so often described in previous chapters, between the ancient and the modern, or between the oral and the written. His intermediary is the Minstrel, who stands, in the poem, on the border between ancient and modern, convincingly handing the one to the other.[7] I will not make the whole argument here, but I will assert, finally, that Scott's ability to find this voice, and to ventriloquize it, is part of a larger pattern, unseen so far in my previous authors. Scott labors in the same fields, and the position between the ancient and the modern or (in the case of ballads) between oral and written should be, as it has been for my other authors, fraught with tensions. Scott's accomplishment is to stand there easily, apparently unconcerned and at ease, continually taking profit from his unique stability.

The Lay of the Last Minstrel is presented by Scott as the result of a scheme, a scheme whose end result is a subtle diminishment of Scott's exposure as the author of the work. Even in the description of 1830, the subject matter and the form come from elsewhere, from without instead of within. This kind of quiet evasion will be a constant feature of Scott's career; the plainest example being the odd and rigorously maintained anonymity of the "Waverly Novels." The diminishment of Scott's exposure arises from a combination of imitation and originality, which produces a work that is new (freshly published, capable of becoming a "sensation") and yet not riskily unprecedented. This sort of poem is different from a purely conventional poem, written in a popular mode, like the elegies MacPherson was confronted with in the *Scots Magazine*. It represents an incremental advance in the progress of history, the increment being small enough to seem acceptable and large enough to be perceptible.

Scott's strategies have very specific aims and results. For instance: in several ways, the stanza of the *Lay* is new. It sometimes changes its rhyme scheme, sometimes changes its meter, and constantly changes its length to fit the progress of the story. Metrical romances can rhyme roughly, and the rhythm can also be rocky or totally plain; but such changeability is not in them. If the irregularity of the old romance is in his poem, Scott has cleverly transmuted it into a more clearly perceptible yet more easily accepted form. For instance, in Canto II of *The Lay of the Last Minstrel*, a stanza (19) of fourteen lines, consisting of three couplets, a quatrain of the form abba, and two more couplets, is followed by a stanza of twelve lines, in the sequence aaabccbddeee. Irregular this is, yet it does not produce the rude or stupid effect that the occasionally uncaring versification of a routine metrical romance produces. The effect of the verse, or much of it, is as in the following:

> Sir William of Deloraine, good at need,
> Mount thee on the wightest steed;
> Spare not to spur, nor stint to ride,
> Until thou come to fair Tweedside.
> And in Melrose's holy pile
> Seek thou the Monk of Saint Mary's Aisle.
>
> (Canto I, stanza 21)

Much of the verse rolls through its story as the first four lines do here; the rocky intrusion of such halting lines as the last two is equally frequent.[8] This kind of irregularity exploits the difficulty in defining the difference between a calculated or imitation irregularity and a genuine one (that is, a trick from a mistake). If irregularity is part of the scheme – if it is authorized – then mistakes become literally invisible, absorbed by the calculations of the purposefully irregular poet. As in the case of Burns, the difficulty is to be Rude without being rude, to be Simple without being simple, to present the artless pleasures of the popular (or the ancient) in an artful way. This adjustment is no easy task. Readers may be interested in modern verse that looks like naive verse, which is full of mistakes (deviations from rules that are clearly in force generally), but they do not want verse that is actually naive and full of mistakes. Francis Jeffrey, of whom much more later, is as good a voice for Scott as in his writing on Burns. Here he is discussing the higher-order irregularity mentioned briefly above, that of plot:

It was [Scott's] duty, therefore, to reform the rambling, obscure and interminable narratives of the ancient Romances – to moderate their digressions ... and to expunge altogether those feeble and prosaic passages, the rude stupidity of which is so apt to excite the derision of a modern reader: at the same time he was to rival, if he could, the force and vivacity of their minute and varied descriptions – the characteristic simplicity of their pictures of manners ...[9]

Jeffrey describes Scott's challenge well: to advance and look back at once. This is a difficult trick, but Scott performs it with great success and apparent ease. His key perception is that irregularity can be turned into a sort of free agent, an ingredient to be added in. Unlike Burns' use of the forms of song, Scott's use of the forms of metrical romance is not a genuine investment in the consequences of that form. He is not repeating the form of the metrical romance: he is not, precisely, imitating it either. He is authoring a new-old romance, where he asserts his authorial self and diffuses it at the same time.[10]

Scott's metrical constructions are very successful, very clever. The narrative irregularity described by Jeffrey above presents exactly the same challenge, and Scott uses exactly the same scheme of authorized imitation. Narrative mistakes (bad plotting) thus become invisible to the critical eye of rule, but they are not so invisible to the eye in search of the pleasures of story. Imitation slides into the real thing, and from the reader's perspective Scott's story often simply wanders from regular narrative. The problem, of course, is that Scott has nothing with which to represent narrative irregularity; he has to include the thing itself. At one point in his review Jeffrey complains that Scott's narrative has the faults that I quote him attributing to romance: excessive description, lack of connection and redundancy.[11] He concludes that these faults are not serious, though, for if the story is episodic, it is protected – as Scott calculated – by the presence of the Minstrel, the buffer through which the story is told. Scott cannot represent narrative irregularity, but he can dramatize it, and so protect it and diffuse responsibility. The Minstrel is irregular, not Scott; the inset narrative of the poem is a dramatic event. By putting the poem into the mouth of the Minstrel, Scott takes it out of his own.

Scott claimed, at the beginning of the original preface, to have an ornamental aim, "the description of scenery and manners." *The Lay of the Last Minstrel* is indeed full of ornaments, parts of the machinery that are not important to the motivations of the story. The Goblin Page (claimed as the source of the story) ends up as one of these features; Scott calls him an "excrescence" (Jeffrey calls him an "ungraceful intruder").[12] "Ornament" characterizes very well these features of the poem; the largest of them is in fact the entire sixth canto, which, as critics complained, is completely exterior to the plot. Yet I think that Scott is (again) making a calculated diversion from the central plot of the poem, which involves marrying a Scottish Border heiress to an English lord. He is in fact very interested in telling this story, a version of what will become *the* story for him. I will deal with this plot later; here I want only to notice that the story is also crusted over and around with a typical (for Scott) profusion of stuff: clothing, anecdotes, historical and scenic tidbits. Ventrilo-quized through the Minstrel, Scott's mixture of spendthrift ways and true "regular" narrative interests becomes a corollary to the metric mixtures I have already discussed. The modern increment is a story with a beginning, middle and end; the wandering constitutes the authorized old ingredient, a deliciously intentional mimicry of unintentional "rudeness."[13]

Scott manufactures the form of the *Lay* in a highly self-conscious historical way, skillfully blending features of modernity with those of older things. This manufacture has a broader context, a context worth delineating, since it underlies not only Scott but all similar projects of the period. Speaking broadly, the *Lay* is the concrete product of a generation's worth of literary-historical speculation, speculation which focused on the history of the metrical romance, a genre reintroduced to Romantic readers with the publication of Percy's *Reliques of Ancient Poetry* in 1765.[14] As envisioned by Scott and his contemporaries, the history of the romance reproduced in small the progress from bold original to weak imitation which is the hallmark of all general Romantic literary histories (the history exploited by MacPherson in marketing the Ossian poems). I will discuss this bigger history shortly; here I want the specific history of romance, which produces the ballad. Scott looked at the history of romance from the perspective of the ballad collector. For the collectors of ballads, among whom Scott was the greatest, the metrical romance was a place of origin. Ballad collecting was an act not of anthropology but of literary history; ballads (considered to be "old" rather than contemporary by Romantic collectors) are seen as the degraded descendants of Middle English romance. Almost every Romantic collection of ballads contains a preface that works out a literary history which begins with the romance. Ballads, in this history, lose their dignity, becoming a sort of dirty lens through which we can glimpse the glories of the past:

We must often expect to find the remains of Minstrel poetry, composed originally for the courts of Princes and the halls of nobles, disguised in the more modern and vulgar dialect in which they have been of late sung to the frequenters of the rustic ale-bench.[15]

The specifics of this history are charged with the judgmental energies of the nostalgic collector. And so (in Scott, and in other authors) descriptions of the origins of ballads must be drawn out from sad stories of destruction. Here is one of Scott's versions, again from the "Remarks":

Another cause of the flatness and insipidity, which is the great defect of ballad poetry, is to be ascribed less to the compositions in their original state, when rehearsed by their *authors*, than to the ignorance and errors of the reciters or transcribers, by whom they have been transmitted to us. The more popular the composition of an ancient poet, or *Maker*, became, the greater chance there was of its being corrupted; for a poem transmitted through a number of reciters, like a book reprinted in a multitude of editions, incurs the risk of impertinent interpolations from the conceit of one rehearser, unintelligible blunders from the stupidity of another, and omissions equally to be regretted, from the want of memory in a third. (pp. 9–10)

Ballads, as they are "found," have no authors; thus the dynamics of their history are very similar (though in reverse) to the progress towards authorship that Scott worked in his own career. The authored work (the romance) turns into an authorless collectible through a series of imitations which gradually drift away from their source.

In this scheme, ballads are what the *Lay* is not: ballads are unauthorized imitations, full of stupidity and errors. It is essential to see the figurative nature of this history. By and large, we know nothing about the authors of Middle English metrical romances; Scott is not thinking of the more sophisticated, authored French romances like those of Chretienne de Troyes. Scott's "author" is an entirely conjectured point of origin. Romances such as those found in the famous Auchinleck MS, a source Scott knew well (it is in the Advocates Library in Edinburgh), clearly rise out of a complicated process of authorship and transmission in which the identity – or indeed the existence – of an author is completely lost. Scott's story of degradation could equally well be applied to the "original state" of his sources, whose stability he refers to with such confidence.[16] This mixture of blindness and faith should be familiar from the reception of the Ossian poems: the lack of ballad authors causes a kind of disorientation that ends in condemnation of the unauthored poem. That Scott should feel this way is especially interesting, given the strategies that I have attributed to him. His descriptions of the degraded ballad could equally well be qualified descriptions of the *Lay*:

The Ballad has been gradually molded into a composition ... expressing the same events in much smoother language, and more flowing and easy versification; but losing in poetical fire and energy, and in the vigor and pithiness of the expression, a great deal more than it has gained in suavity of diction. ("Remarks," pp. 12–13)

This should not be surprising, since the process of imitation and repetition that creates ballads out of romances resembles the process which creates the *Lay* very closely.

Given this similarity, the most charged part of the history of ballads, for Scott, is the role popularity (the central aim of his ambition) plays in producing the degraded imitation. When the metrical romances are rendered obsolete by the appearance of print and the consequent prose romances, only the most popular stories descend to the "popular mind," where they undergo their degrading alchemy. The very quality of the original, the quality that causes it to be noticed and remembered, causes the decline.

Nay, we are authorised to conclude, that in proportion to the care bestowed by the author on any poem, to attain what his age might suppose to be the highest graces of poetry, the greater was the damage which it sustained by the inaccuracy of reciters, or their desire to humble both the sense and diction of the poem to their powers of recollection, and the comprehension of a vulgar audience. (p. 10)

It may seem unlikely that Scott should endorse a history in which repetition (imitation) and popularity are the evil protagonists; it looks, indeed, like the symptom of conflict. But his attitude is simply the source of energy that allows him to write the new-old romance, and, as in his specific schemes for *The Lay of the Last Minstrel*, Scott's ability to stand in a place of tension without feeling strained is the source of his fortune. This is not, in the end, a subtle point, but the description of a fact easily discerned from the writing Scott produced; it is clearly visible in the features of *The Lay of the Last Minstrel* that I have already discussed.

The sadly downsloping history of the ballad is a subset of a larger literary history, so generally distributed during the period as to be *the* Romantic literary history. I have noted its details in my discussion of Ossian: a fascination with oxymoronic origins, where we find old, "early" and hence young and vital poetry. It is, at heart, an anthropomorphic history. Cultural youths speak forthrightly, and the anxious cultural elder of the eighteenth century makes him or herself feel younger by listening to these ancient young outbursts. Hugh Blair, quoted in reference to Ossian, is perhaps the most serene exponent of this history: its most familiar source for us is, I think,

Wordsworth's "Appendix on Diction." This is Wordsworth's description of the beginning:

The earliest poets of all nations generally wrote from passion, excited by real events; they wrote naturally, and as men: feeling powerfully as they did, their language was daring, and figurative.[17]

Like the cries of the children they resemble, the passionate outbursts of early men are quickly tamed by the accumulation of history, of previous cries:

In succeeding times, poets, and men ambitious of the fame of poets, perceiving the influence of such [passionate] language, and desirous of producing the same effect without being animated by the same passion, set themselves to a mechanical adoption of these figures of speech ... [18]

This is the end; the story is divided into pre-history and history, and as soon as history begins, modernity (in some form) begins. Decline connects the present to the past, and so the late writer must not only look back but also up. The enrichment that history brings takes away as it gives; the restraint of passion turns, somehow, into the constraint of poetry. Repetition is the result and cause of all this, for history imposes repetition on the later poet.

I have been arguing all along that conceptions of literary history have very practical effects, and here the history of the ballad produces, most specifically, the Romantic method for editing ballads. This method begins with Percy, and though Scott laments Percy's freedoms, he is a free editor himself.[19] Unlike Percy, he usually did not simply make up passages, but instead created a better ballad by combining several versions together. This is Scott's description of his method:

No liberties have been taken, either with the recited or written copies of these ballads, farther than that, where they disagreed, which is by no means unusual, the editor, in justice to the author, has uniformly preserved what seemed to him the best or most poetical reading of the passage. Such discrepancies must very frequently occur, whenever poetry is preserved by oral tradition.[20]

Scott's published ballad is an ideal, created by gauging the vectors of history through a comparison of versions, and then projecting the text back along these vectors (in the imagination). This is done "in justice to the author," for Scott always imagines a process that involves a perfect original consumed and transformed by history. As we have seen, he cannot imagine a poem without an author; or rather, he cannot regard a poem which has seen many hands as valuable in itself.[21] Again, we must see clearly the figurative turn of this history. We know, from modern scholarship, that the ballad survives in robust health into the twentieth century, and that in fact the eighteenth century constitutes a sort of high point in the history of the ballad.[22] Rendered worried and blind by the pressures of history, the Romantic collector feels pressure, and insists that he is working against time. He is also Ossianically surrounded by things he considers to be fragments, and so the process of publication is profoundly nostalgic, having as its goal the production of the original, or a more original copy. Scott's doctored ballads are the result of this curious and mystified sort of imitation, which makes a new-old poem that above all confidently claims to revivify the dead. The "ballad revival" is thus a particularly apt name for this Romantic movement, since its practitioners literally try to revivify the past, return it to us through their special imitation. It is crucial to see that Scott simply does not want to publish ballads as "found." Romantic collectors and readers feel that the thing itself will not do, and their conjectural ballad history justifies this feeling. Again, with some changes, this new invention of the old is precisely the scheme behind *The Lay of the Last Minstrel*.

As in the case of the Ossian poems, at the center of this balance between imitation and originality is the appearance of writing, the moment when the ballad, floating on the breath of the people, is fixed and made into an object (which may be sold). Scott's famous "raids" into Liddesdale, where he met James Hogg, are appropriately called raids, for booty is carried out, in the form of recorded oral culture (some of it, for the moment, recorded in Scott's head – he had a remarkable memory). This sort of appropriation, for the purposes of literary and economic advancement, was lamented by Hogg's mother, who claimed that printing spoiled everything.[23] Partly, she means by this that Scott had gotten them wrong, that he hadn't printed her versions; but certainly she also means the breaking up of the charmed circle of recitation and appreciation, which is described by Hogg like this:

Many indeed are not aware of the manners of this place; it is but lately emerged from barbarity, and till this present age the poor illiterate people in these glens knew of no entertainment in the long winter nights than in repeating and listening to those feats of their ancestors which I believe to be handed down inviolable from father to son for many generations.[24]

"Inviolable" is no doubt an exaggerated counter-claim, but the content of this scene, which evades history by repeating, is accurate enough. Seen from the inside, the action of Scott's history of degradation looks like its opposite; to Hogg, the endless repetition of popular oral culture is entirely resistant to change. The truth, as far as we can see it, lies somewhere in between, but very likely inclines substantially more to the side of conservative retention. In any case, where there is no writing, "history" means memory; the past may be retained, but its progress cannot be spelled out. The repetition of ballad texts may, in oral culture, "degrade" ballads, but that repetition cannot be part of a *history* of degradation. For the repeating singer and the listeners, repetition in oral culture is in itself innocent and conservative, a sign of vitality rather than imaginative exhaustion. In other words, in oral culture, repetition and imitation split apart. Where history is not a narrative but instead retained and repeated facts, imitation makes no sense; there is no place for such a concept. Appreciation of a tale is not dimmed or oppressed by a picture of one's ancestors appreciating the same tale, for they are dead. Stumbling into the light (the firelight) of the oral circle, bringing with him the pressure of written history, the collector mistakes listening and repeating for a gradually fading echo, and he mistakenly parallels the decrepitude of the old tellers with the decrepitude of the tradition. These mistakes generate the anxiety with which the collector grasps the tales and fixes them in writing.

Life and death meet (again) at the site of the creation of poetry, here the poetry created by the publishing ballad collector out of the "fragments" of history. In a precise parallel to the Ossianic strategy, life is granted, retrieved, by the collector out of the jaws of death. This action is both a victory over history and a writing of it (the "ballad revival"). The ballad collector inverts the relationship within oral poetry, itself a meeting of life and death. In oral culture, repetition is life, and anything else is death. Originality means loss (of a possible inheritance, now changed and gone), and repetition victory. Though the ballad collector refuses oral culture its vitality, the popularity of the ballad text belies his claim. The "vitality" Romantic culture attributed to ballad texts (and to Ossian) may be cast back into history, but it is the vitality of oral culture made comprehensible to a written audience. This (again) is the lesson of the Ossianic controversy. Written culture has a hard time admitting its thirst for the regeneration oral culture offers, and, sadly, always destroys the oral collectible in the very process of savoring it.[25] Writing catches the vital oral poem as it floats freely by, and thus preserves it from possible dissolution by giving it form outside of a memory: memory is subject to mortality. But writing saves by killing, and Romantic collectors feel but do not know this; hence, their sad insistence on the expiration of the item they find in such abundance. This oxymoronic combination of escape from and capture by time is the context for Scott's achievement as a writer (rather than collector) of poetry. The schemes of the ballad collector are crude by comparison. Written culture wants oral freedom but cannot actually get it; Scott provides an accessible parallel path. His poetry, oral and written at once (imitation, edited text and original composition), miraculously reproduces the freedom of orality in a written world. Like the stories told around the fire, Scott's poetry also escapes an always-imminent mortality; in spite of always being the same, it is always popular, and in this way imitates the vitality of popular (traditional) forms. His poetry (looks like it) escapes from the very history of degradation he so feelingly rehearses.

The keenest description of the way that Scott escapes from the consequences of repeating is given by Francis Jeffrey, in a review of *The Lady of the Lake* in 1810. Jeffrey arrives at his conclusions after five years of dealing with the Scott phenomenon, and his arrival in 1810 is a story in itself: his reviews of the first three great poems (*The Lay of the Last Minstrel, Marmion,* and *The Lady of the Lake*) form a progressive engagement with Scott's strategies, and they also demonstrate what kind of power Scott developed through his freedom from constraint. The review of *The Lay of the Last Minstrel,* which I have referred to already, is moderately positive, and contains the compliments and the complaints that were to be the staple of all criticisms of Scott, both of his poetry and his prose. Jeffrey begins plainly and accurately:

We consider this poem as an attempt to transfer the refinements of modern poetry to the matter and manner of the antient metrical Romance ... This is a Romance, therefore, written by a minstrel of the present day; or such a Romance as we may suppose would have been written in modern times, if that style of composition had continued to be cultivated, and partaken consequently of the improvements which every branch of literature has received since the time of its desertion. (p. 1)

Jeffrey goes on to criticize the conduct of the story (as not "regular"), and he particularly criticizes what he sees as the sloppiness of the poem. As in descriptions of the romance, however, these criticisms come along with compliments:

He writes throughout with the spirit and force of a poet; and though he occasionally discovers a little too much of the "brave neglect," and is frequently inattentive to the delicate propriety and scrupulous correctness of his diction, he compensates for those defects by the fire and animation of his whole composition, and the brilliant colouring and prominent features of the figures with which he has enlivened it. (pp. 6–7)

Though characteristically fastidious, this review is positive enough. It is not a complex piece, and the approval given is of a plain sort. Jeffrey says that Scott really did give us the romance in modern form, and admits that Scott's calculations have proved accurate: his wandering tale and desultory verse are accepted under the cover of the old romance. Jeffrey has not particularly exerted himself here, though, and so severe criticism lays visible but dormant. In particular, we note that all of the features he attributes (negatively) to the metrical romance – sloppy verse, interminable description, and loose narrative – are also, in some measure, attributed to Scott. That is, imitation lies perilously close to repetition, but Jeffrey seems willing to let it go. He grants Scott his case, on the basis of the negotiation between ancient and modern, and accepts things as they are.

His review of *Marmion* begins on an entirely different note. The critic is exerting himself here, and he has judgment to pronounce:

There is a kind of primogeniture among books, as well as among men; and it is difficult for an author, who has obtained great fame by a first publication, not to appear to fall off in a second – especially if his original success could be imputed, in any degree, to the novelty of his plan of composition. The public is always indulgent to untried talents; and is even apt to exaggerate a little the value of what it receives without any previous expectation. But, for this advance of kindness, it usually extracts a most usurious return in the end.[26]

Jeffrey presents these thoughts as natural fact. The phrase "as well as among men" indicates that we are again in the midst of an anthropomorphic history, here (again) a miniature of the history of poetry in general. Jeffrey makes the life of an author's works – a history just the size of a person's life – mirror the institutions of human life, and draws dire lessons for Scott from the resulting picture. Scott will suffer greater ills because he has added to the natural progress of authorship the sin of repetition:

Where a first work, containing considerable blemishes, has been favorably received, the public always expects this indulgence to be repaid by an improvement that ought not always be expected. If a second performance appear, therefore, with the same faults, they will no longer meet with the same toleration... For these, and for other reasons, we are inclined to suspect, that the success of the work now before us will be less brilliant than that of the author's former publication. (p. 2)

This is a historical lesson: the *Lay* has not vanished, and so *Marmion* is late, part of a story of degradation.[27] The weight that *Marmion* has added to Scott's poetic pretensions pushes Jeffrey out into the open, and the calculations of irregularity are no longer enough to restrain him. He goes on to detail much harsh criticism, mixed with some strong praise; the general tone is one of censure. Near the end he surmises that what he thinks of as sloppiness comes not from calculation but from over-hasty composition, and admonishes Scott in this way:

He who writes for immortality should not be sparing of time; and if it be true, that in every thing which has a principle of life, the period of gestation and growth bears some proportion to that of the whole future existence, the author now before us should tremble when he looks back on the miracles of his own facility. (p. 34)

The long and short of it is that Jeffrey considers *The Lay of the Last Minstrel* and *Marmion* to be almost exactly the same poem, and asserts that the history that they make up (the one imitating or repeating the other) will doom *Marmion*, the late-born. These are conclusions from the degenerative history: the quality of the original makes for the inferiority of the copy, and the burden of precedent constrains the steps of the late author. To be first is more important than being (in this case) interesting. Imagine Jeffrey's theoretical surprise when *Marmion* not only repeated the sensation of *The Lay of the Last Minstrel*, but extended it. Initially, Scott rather agreed with Jeffrey; he certainly vowed to write future poems more slowly.[28] That is, for the anthropomorphic historian (a group that includes Scott), all indications point towards failure for *Marmion*. What went wrong? Or rather, from Scott's point of view, what went right? By demonstrating a profound change of mind, Jeffrey's response to *The Lady of the Lake* answers this question.

From *Marmion* Jeffrey learns that the opinions of the reading public, in regard to Scott, cannot be serenely anticipated. So he delays his review of *The Lady of the Lake* for four months after the publication of the poem, and then writes (in several ways) from fact instead of theory. This review begins by acknowledging the extent of the Scott phenomenon:

> Mr. Scott, though living in an age unusually prolific of original poetry, has manifestly outstripped all his competitors in the race of popularity ... We doubt, indeed, whether any English poet *ever* had so many of his books sold, or so many of his verses read and admired by such a multitude of persons, in so short a time.[29]

The second paragraph begins with this impressive and arch admission:

> A popularity so universal is a pretty sure proof of extraordinary merit, – a far surer one, we readily admit, than would be afforded by praises of ours: and therefore, though we pretend to be privileged, in ordinary cases, to foretell the ultimate reception of claims on public admiration, our function may be thought to cease, where the event is already so certain and conspicuous.

There are many things going on here; not the least among them is the puzzlement of an essentially eighteenth-century critic facing the distinctly nineteenth-century event of the best-seller, and the consequent evaporation of critical power. But Jeffrey has also gone over, dramatically, to the other side, and now cheers Scott on from a position below and behind him. Near the end he even brings repetition around as a sort compliment:

> That he may injure his popularity by the mere profusion of his publications, is no doubt possible; though many of the most celebrated poets have been among the most voluminous: but, that the public must gain by his liberality, does not admit of any question. If our poetical treasures were increased by the publication of Marmion and the Lady of the Lake, notwithstanding the existence of great faults in both these works, it is evident we should be still richer if we possessed fifty poems of the same merit. (p. 293)

None of the above is written with intentional irony; but there is, I admit, the taste of irony about the review, a bitterness. This bitterness comes from Jeffrey's disbelief, and indeed his anger, at having been superseded by readers he considers to be less well equipped to judge than himself: "ordinary readers of poetry have not a very refined taste; and they are often insensible to many of its highest beauties, while they still more frequently mistake its imperfections for excellence" (p. 264).[30] On the other hand (trying to be generous), Jeffrey insists that the unsophisticated reader and the critic enjoy the same things in poetry. The difference between them is what Jeffrey brought to his reading of *Marmion*: memory, the ability to refer to things other than those immediately before the reader's eyes. "The one [the forgetful reader] attends only to the intrinsic qualities of the *work*, while the other refers more immediately to the merit of the *author*" (p. 264). Jeffrey is trying hard to be tolerant of the potent force that the reading public represents, since they buy his magazine too, but he can't keep it up, and his accusation that they lack memory (which he mentioned briefly in his review of *Marmion*) turns into real disgust:

The most popular passages in popular poetry, are in fact, for the most part, very beautiful and striking ... yet they are trite and hackneyed, – they have been repeated until they have lost all grace and propriety, – and, instead of exalting the imagination with the impression of original genius or creative fancy, they only nauseate and offend, by their association of paltry plagiarism and impudent vanity. To the ignorant and careless, the twentieth imitation has all the charm of the original; and that which oppresses the more experienced reader with weariness and disgust, rouses them with all the force and vivacity of novelty. (p. 266)

In other words: the popular work, in the ecstatic mind of the hypothetically ecstatic popular reader, is out of history. In the sadder but wiser mind of the critic, history presents itself in small and in large. In small, in the repetitions of the same author's previous works, and in large, in the accumulation of the broader sweep of literary history that the popular passage represents. In the popular world, imitation does not exist, and repetition is simple: each instance is as fresh as the next. Since history does not exist, degeneration and improvement do not exist either. The anthropomorphic history, to which he turns at this point, elaborating it in highly orthodox fashion, is being put to very specific use:

The justice of these remarks will probably be at once admitted by all who have attended to the history and effects of what may be called *poetic diction* in general, or even of such particular phrases and epithets as have been indebted to their beauty for too great a notoriety. Our associations with all this class of expressions, which have become trite only in consequence of their intrinsic excellence, now suggest to us no ideas but those of schoolboy imbecility and childish affectation.(p. 267)

The beauty of the original is responsible for the ugliness of the copy. Jeffrey uses this part of the history to attribute both virtue and offense to the popular work, especially the popular work of his friend Walter Scott, whom he respects and does not want to personally offend. Paradox informs the very being of the diction of the popular poem, which is alive to the dead ear and dead to the sensitive. Tired popular phrases are good when they are invented; they are only killed off by history, by the accumulation of repetitions, an accumulation which can only take place when some structure exists to catch them (personal memory, or the written memory of history).

There are two strains of feeling in Jeffrey's picture of popular poetry. One is simple disgust for the ignorant, with their loud and coarse opinions. The other is the nostalgia of the anthropomorphic historian, who is growing old himself, whose memory makes him unable to enter into simple pleasures, and for whom spontaneous fun has been buried under the weight of history. Listen to this sentence: "Most of these phrases ... are in themselves beautiful and expressive, and no doubt, retain much of their native grace in those ears that have not been alienated by their repetition" (pp. 268–9). How can a reader like Jeffrey get at these phrases in their natural state, as they are "in themselves"? That pleasant interior is lost to him, and the Scott phenomenon has rendered what he has gotten in return – the critical eye – less important than he would like. Just when we begin to wonder how he will rescue Scott's popular poem, which he likes, from being caught by his weary disgust, Jeffrey cleverly turns this impasse into a tricky solution to his theoretical woes.

Jeffrey knows Scott to be anything but ignorant, and knows him to be virtually immersed in history, a firm believer in the progress and degeneration that time brings. First, Jeffrey compliments Scott by noting his capacity for calculation: "that he has actually made use of all our recipes for popularity, we think very evident" (p. 269). He goes on to give to Scott the skillful, energetic freedom that I have asserted for him, above:

Few things are more curious than the singular skill, or good fortune with which he has reconciled his claims on the favour of the multitude, with his pretensions to more select admiration. Confident in the force and originality of his own genius, he has not been afraid to avail himself of common-places both of diction and sentiment, whenever they appeared to be beautiful or impressive, – using them, however, at all times, with the skill and spirit of an inventor; and quite certain that he could not be mistaken for a plagiarist or imitator, he has made free use of that great treasury ... he was a borrower from anything but poverty, and took only what he could have given if he had been born in an earlier generation. (pp. 269–70)

These fascinating compliments are the flip side of sad nostalgia. Jeffrey is grateful for Scott's lack of constraint, because Scott has returned the past to him, revivified the beautiful dead. Scott's singular skill is his ability to be both inside and outside of history, to use the already invented with the skill of an inventor. In his poetry the reader perpetually discovers the already discovered, because Scott has refused to be oppressed by the past. According to Jeffrey, Scott has not defeated his precursors by Bloomian originality, but through its opposite. He has simply refused to accept that history means death. History is alive, recovered and revived by him. Scott doesn't need his own real originality, since he can make such skillful and enthusiastic use of the originality he has inherited.

I think Jeffrey's solution to his theoretical problems is quite impressive. For one thing, it is a brilliant accommodation of theory to experience. He has managed to hold on to his anthropomorphic history of repetition and degeneration in the midst of his enjoyment of Scott's poetry. He has acknowledged Scott's poetry as popular and repetitive (which it is), but he has made it special too, married originality to repetition and so allowed room for critical appreciation. Jeffrey's solution contains, of course, paradox at its center. The very logic is paradoxical, and Jeffrey knows it; he has argued, more or less, that Scott's poetry is always the same but different. His contemporaries always said that there was nobody better before a jury than Francis Jeffrey: his courtroom arguments were said to be carried by his vivacity of expression, his personal energy. This supplemental energy – supplemental to logic – is the same energy that he attributes to Scott, and the same that he hopes to use here. He wants us to glide over his paradox, because Scott himself does. By allowing himself the paradox of the unrepetitive imitation, Jeffrey allows himself to be conquered by the fire of Scott's poetry. And so he ends his review by saying that if one Scott poem is good, fifty would be better.

Thus the skeptical and jaded Francis Jeffrey, scourge of Wordsworth and many other aspiring authors, himself affirms the potent accuracy of Scott's calculations. The practice of revival carries him away on its tide of pleasantly present memories. As jury-rigged as his argument appears, I think Jeffrey is entirely correct. Scott did indeed have a singular skill for freedom, for being unconstrained. As Jeffrey's need to twist around makes clear, this is not the same as being an original writer. It is instead a calculated substitution for originality, an imitation of it, that serves Scott well. He makes his tired readers feel energized by making them forget that they are in history, and he does this by presenting history itself: by offering a beautiful imitation of the dead as a figure for life. Scott's practice is an extremely successful practice of revival, since (in telling old, romance tales) it not only erases the time that separates the tired present from the vigorous past, but also because its "vigor" allows the reader to live in a semi-eternal present where (sitting around an imitation hearth) the old stories are told and retold, with no decrease in pleasure. Scott's poetry is not destructive in the way that MacPherson's is, because it makes no pretense to originality: he gives us *imitations* of the dead. As Jeffrey expresses it, Scott acknowledges the pastness of the past, and also makes the past seem present. The Ossianic method offers imitation as the original, and so supersedes the original; Scott openly imitates and repeats, and so does not need to supersede. He is a scholar, and the original, as figurative a place as it must be, is acknowledged in the footnotes. Scott's openness, his honest, above-board negotiation, is the source of his strength.

Scott's poetry did not in fact show a capacity for infinite repetition. The sales of *Rokeby* (1813) disappointed Scott, and that of *The Lord of the Isles* (1814) disappointed him again, though it must be said that both of those poems were very successful, commercially speaking. We cannot test things further, since Scott stopped writing poetry. There is an interesting conversation recorded about the reception of *The Lord of the Isles*. It is between Scott and James Ballantyne, his friend, printer and literary confidant. "Well James," Scott said, "what are people saying about *The Lord of the Isles*?" Ballantyne then delivers the disappointing news. Scott looks "blank" momentarily, and then, as Ballantyne describes it, "he said with perfect cheerfulness, 'Well, well, James, so be it – but you know we must not droop, for we can't afford to give over. Since one line has failed, we must just stick to something else.'"[31] The Scott power does not fail, and the public does not tire of his story; it merely stops buying his new poetry in such great numbers. His older poems, especially the big three, continue to sell well until after his death. Scott attributed the faltering of his new poetry to the appearance of Byron, and no doubt this is partly true. But Byron, especially in his oriental romances, represents (at least partly) an imitation of Scott, so the eclipse is not as thorough as it seems. As Scott's career goes on, and he writes long work after similar work, year after year, and enjoys success without diminution, his skill looks more and more like what Wordsworth was to call it: a spell, a charm that defeated the accumulating history of his own career, and which allowed him to escape the mortality that always seemed about to visit him.

I have been looking at Scott's poetry as a scheme, aimed at an audience, and Jeffrey has appeared as a figure for that audience. His descriptions of Scott's poetry are worked up for the occasion (necessity being the mother of invention), and my descriptions of Scott's freedom have shared this characteristic. As I have said, I think Jeffrey's description of Scott's methods, as self-interested as it is, points to the heart of Scott's success, but he need not bear as much weight as I have thrust upon him. Scott achieved his success; his calculations are not merely exterior. His poetry, in its verse and in the stories it tells, enacts his calculations beautifully. Scott's form and historical machinery establish his mode of operation, and so I have used them for this purpose too. His stories, the inside of his poems, are equally subject to his skill, and the practice that appears there is subtle, balanced, and extremely successful. In his stories, as in his calculated exterior features, the consequences of history are evaded while the pleasures of history are presented. This neat trick is accomplished in two steps. The first is a negotiation of the consequences of progress, the second an imitation of Romance structure. I will explore the first by looking at the *Lay*, and the second by looking at *The Lady of the Lake*.

In many ways the center of *The Lay of the Last Minstrel* is a good old-style comedy plot; members of rival families want to get married, and are prevented from doing so by the prejudices of the older generation. Specifically, a Border lord named Cranstoun wants to marry the daughter of a Border chieftain, Margaret of Buccleuch, and she wants to marry him; but the Cranstouns and the Scotts of Buccleuch are feuding, in good Border style. In an interesting variation, the "blocking force" here is not a father but a mother, the Lady Buccleuch, who also happens to be a sorceress. The poem sort of ends with a marriage; that is, the plot resolves in the marriage, but that marriage happens at the end of Canto v, and so the action of Canto vi must make its way without this narrative support. The marriage is accomplished through a death (a knight named Musgrave dies in a joust), and so even though the plot is comedic in form, the poem is not a comedy in the more usual sense of the term. It claims serious themes in addition to a happy ending. The names of the Border family (formally Buccleuch, informally Scott) are not an idle feature. Walter Scott claimed descent from this family (though from another branch, the Scotts of Harden), and thought of the current Duke of Buccleuch as his "chieftain." The subject of the poem – that is, the other subject, the Goblin Page – was given to him, in the form of a charge, by the current Duchess.

It is important to call the comedic plot the center of the story, because there are important outlying features. The Goblin Page and his attendants (the machinery of magic and supernatural mayhem) function almost entirely outside of this plot, as many contemporary reviewers noted; yet the Page's part of the story cannot with accuracy be called a minor feature, since so much time is spent on it. I put in the Page's category the magic book of Michael Scott, which we spend all of Canto I fetching, as well as the magical skills of Lady Buccleuch herself. Outside of this part, a sort of concentric ring, is the plot of the aged Minstrel and his recitation of the poem. As Nancy Goslee has insisted, these settings are never incidental in Scott, and in particular the Minstrel is far from incidental here. Scott never apologized for the Minstrel; as I have noted, he knew full well how important he was to the calculations of irregularity. He did, however, grow sensitive to the solitary and apparently unnecessary character of the Page's role. I have already quoted him calling the Page an "excrescence"; here is some more of that description:

I began a few verses to be called the Goblin Page; and they lay long by me, till the applause of some friends whose judgement I value induced me to resume the poem; so on I wrote, knowing no more than the man in the moon how I was to end ... In the process of the Romance, the page, intended to be a principal person in the work, contrived (from the baseness of his natural propensities I suppose) to slink downstairs into the kitchen, and now must e'en abide there ... The sixth canto is altogether redundant; for the poem should certainly have closed with the union of the lovers, when the interest, if any, was at an end. But what could I do? I had my book and my page still on my hands, and must get rid of them at all events.[32]

As we have seen, Scott was in the habit of referring to his writing off-hand. He was also in the habit of writing without knowing how he was to end, and so he would make a lot of apologies of this sort during his career. Clearly, one way of getting rid of the Goblin Page problem would be to rewrite the story, with him either in or out. Scott will not do that; I think he won't because in fact he wants and needs the Page exactly were he is, as an excrescence. As Scott notes in the original preface, he persistently adds to his interest in regular plots an extra interest, an interest in the extra or the ornamental. He is at heart an antiquary, fond of the right illustration or the quaint detail, interested in the odds and ends of history. He persistently says he is embarrassed about this, as in the letter just quoted, and yet he never makes his stories strictly regular.

A wandering interest in things along the way is indeed a characteristic of romance, a characteristic which waylays both Wordsworth and Scott (though this ambush takes very different forms in their two cases).[33] Since Scott's sharp friends (like Francis Jeffrey) referred to this part of the romance in such derogatory terms, he would have a hard time admitting his fondness for it, but we need not be embarrassed in this way. Scott's inability or unwillingness to concentrate on the regularities of plotting, the inability which places the marriage at the end of Canto v instead of Canto vi, shapes all of his writing. More than that: he wanders with a purpose, and his ability to repeat success after success depends upon his wandering.

All levels of both form and content in *The Lay of the Last Minstrel* show signs of the conflict or division between narrative direction, which drives from beginning to end with purpose, and narrative decoration, which interrupts and turns direction aside. In his commentaries, Scott's description of this conflict begins at the level of the verse form itself, so I will return briefly to this feature, with an eye towards practice. When describing his shopping for a proper measure, Scott complained of the ballad stanza, which had gone out of style anyway:

A long work in quatrains, whether those of the common ballad, or such as are termed elegiac, has an effect upon the mind like that of the bed of Procrustes upon the human body; for, as it must be both awkward and difficult to carry on a long sentence from one stanza to another, it follows, that the meaning of each period must be comprehended within four lines, and equally so that it must be extended so as to fill that space. The alternate dilation and contraction thus rendered necessary is singularly unfavorable to narrative composition.[34]

Here again Scott insults his naughty favorites, popular ballads, narrative poems that tell their stories in a measure "singularly unfavorable" to their project. I will have much more to say about the way ballads tell their stories in the next chapter; it is enough for present purposes to note that they manage to do so while stopping and starting constantly. Certainly Scott is correct to point out that any story told in ballad measure must adapt to its continual opening and closing. This kind of regularity, where each morsel of poetry is the same size, no matter what the content of the morsel, is not free enough for Scott's purposes. His criticism of it comes from the department of narrative direction. He declares that a story, which wants to move along always, will be unhappy if the demands of form impose detours and tiresomely frequent stops.

He goes on to describe looking over the octo-syllabic "measured short line" of the metrical romance. Oddly enough, this measure fails on the other side. It is too easy:

The extreme facility of the short couplet, which seems congenial to our language, and was, doubtless for that reason, so popular with our old minstrels, is, for the same reason, apt to prove a snare to the composer who uses it in more modern days, by encouraging him in a habit of slovenly composition. (p. 18)

The short couplet does not, in other words, offer enough pauses, enough stops and starts; "occasional pauses" help the author keep on course as the tail does a kite. This is criticism from the department of narrative indirection. From this side, stops are positive; they provide checks on the momentum of the story, whose desire for direction threatens the pleasures of tourism and decoration. So Scott settles on the measure of "Christabel" (much adapted, certainly) as offering a sort of in between. It contains the possibility of couplets, and the possibility of not rhyming in couplets; it does not end every four lines, but does end sometimes.[35] Scott finds rest in a measure that offers a compromise between overly-facile progress and the halting, arresting ballad stanza. In particular, Scott takes advantage of the stanzal divisions his measure retains to quarantine his smaller diversions from narrative progress. At the beginning of Canto II, for instance, the first stanza presents a beautiful (and "picturesque") view of the ruins of Melrose Abbey. This description (along with the division between cantos) has interrupted the headlong progress of a knight, William of Deloraine, who is on his way to the Abbey. The second stanza takes advantage of the pause and shakes off the description with a kind of shiver: "Short halt did Deloraine make there;/ Little reck'd he of the scene so fair." Grammar never spills over stanzal boundaries; only extremely rarely does a stanza mix descriptive and narrative modes.

How easily formal, how formally easy is Scott's relationship to form. Scott is not ruthlessly insensitive like MacPherson, nor painfully sensitive like Burns. The formal pressure exerted by the forms of old romance, the tradition of narrative poetry, is contained and controlled by an easy-going negotiation over formal consequence. The divisions and control poetry insists on are placated, but balanced against narrative progress. "Poetry" itself looks here like another old thing modernized, present but tamed and civilized. To use language similar to the vocabulary recent writers have applied to Scott's novels, his poetry is a poetry of compromise. Or, to put it another way: Scott's poetry is working poetry, poetry put to a task with professional clarity. What looks like incapacitating pressure in other writers looks, in Scott's career, like simple opportunity, the presentation of choice. This is a light-sounding claim, but such perfect accommodation to history and current taste is quite rare. In Scott's poetry, this perfection is most noticeable in the fit between poetic container and the story contained.

Turning to the story of the *Lay*, I would redescribe the balance that Scott strikes between stopping and going on as a balance between history and progress: history, that is, as a backward look, a posture which values that which has been over that which is to come. As in the formal conception of the poem, a calculated proportion is also at the center of its comedic plot. Lord Cranstoun, the hopeful lover, had before the poem begins been allied with the Carrs, the family responsible for Walter of Buccleuch's (his lover's father) death. Thus his marriage to Walter of Buccleuch's heir implies a forgetting: progress. At the beginning of the poem, "The Ladye" (as she is called) puts her opposition this way, addressing the hills and streams from her tower:

> Your Mountains shall bend,
> And your streams ascend,
> Ere Margaret be our foeman's bride! (Canto 1, stanza 18)

In order for the marriage to take place, the wheels of time must turn, and Walter's death must take its place in history, properly subordinated to the needs of present and future. Again, this poem has noncomedic themes, and for Lady Buccleuch to forget the slaying of her husband is no small matter. Progress is not portrayed as easy or light.

The past turns into the future through the violent encounter of two knights, each of whom carries the burden of his respective side. The future is present quite literally, since the prize in the joust is the next Lord of Buccleuch, a boy who has been taken captive by the other side (the families allied with the Carrs). William of Deloraine, the Ladye's favorite, is supposed to take her side in the joust, but after Deloraine is wounded Lord Cranstoun covertly steps in, and so wins the day and the bride. He accomplishes his victory by killing Richard Musgrave, his ostensible ally and mortal enemy of the house of Buccleuch. The sacrifice of Musgrave, a character we do not know or care about, illustrates part of what Scott has done to the interests of the romance, a part I will deal with in talking about *The Lady of the Lake*. Here I am interested in Scott's balance between past and future, and for my purposes the climax of the poem is not the death of Musgrave, but a song sung after his death by William of Deloraine, who finds his way to the battlefield just after Musgrave dies. What he says over Musgrave's body is said in the place of elegy. It is not a song about loss (though it has that elegiac element); it is mostly about a kind of balance, which is asserted in the face of the loss the death presents. Deloraine starts by listing the reasons he has to hate Musgrave, and then goes on:

> And thou wert now alive, as I,
> No mortal man should us divide,
> Till one, or both of us, did die:
> Yet rest thee God! for well I know
> I ne'er shall find a nobler foe.
> In all the northern counties here,
> Whose word is snaffle, spur and spear,
> Thou wert the best to follow gear!
> 'Twas pleasure, as we looked behind,
> To see how thou the chase could'st wind,
> Cheer the dark bloodhound on his way,
> And with the bugle rouse the fray!
> I'd give the lands of Deloraine,
> Dark Musgrave were alive again.   (Canto v, stanza 29)

All Scott stories contain this moment, which Scott puts in the category of "chivalry." Progress comes at the cost of a life, and the necessity of this sacrifice sets off a kind of existential panic in Scott: in all his works, he always commemorates this kind of moment in this way. Here a past full of hatred and stagnant conflict is sutured to a future which progresses beyond that past. It is hard to pin down the content of this counter-intuitive death song, but it tries to erase the moment of rupture that has turned the future loose. Deloraine wants both Musgrave's death and his life; he wants to kill him and he wants to have Musgrave around to kill. Conflict, which arrests life, is portrayed as a beautiful equilibrium, now lost and mourned. At the same time, that conflict, carried on by a desire to win, is always pressing for the future to arrive, and is predicated on a future in which Musgrave does not exist, and peace (and marriage, and growth) reigns instead of conflict. Scott wants to make peace with the necessity for stopping short; he knows that resolution demands progress, and the loss of beautiful equilibrium. He is unwilling, though, to give up anything central, and Musgrave is the result of his negotiation with loss. Musgrave's sacrifice allows Scott to briskly step by the moment of destructive creation, where progress appears, like a tourist enjoying the view but also making no investment in it. In practical terms, Scott's method allows the poem a curious sort of freedom from its own plot; it is a Romantic poem about loss, but that loss does not burden the story. Conflict is used for the purpose of narrative energy, as a thing to be gotten beyond, and yet that conflict is also naturalized, beautified, and admired. Deloraine insists that his admiration for Musgrave (a progressive feeling) lives on equal terms with his hatred, and so he and Scott can literally exult and mourn at the same time. In Deloraine's song, past and future sit balanced, motionless, for the moment, in perfect equipoise. In striking this balance, Scott deftly turns a moment of destruction into a moment of exchange, where past is handed to future with a satisfactory feeling of mutual profit. The rest of the story, since it has this perfect balance at its center, can relax and take it easy. It need not push any of its characters in the direction of tragedy or self-destruction. In my argument, this balance is the matched analog to the easy stop and start of his stanzas, stanzas which so easily exchange formal constraint for poetic profit.

Scott's careful containment of rupture takes place, of course, within the larger box of the Minstrel's song. In Scott's typical style (familiar especially from the novels) the container mimics what it contains, spelling out in small (repeating?) themes what the stories work out in large. Here the Minstrel's song is a drama of starting and stopping, of recovery and forgetting, and this drama continues through the whole of the poem. His song is sung in a castle on the

shores of that most elegiac of rivers, the river Yarrow; the poem ends
with the Minstrel cozily ensconced in a neat hut on its banks. On
summer evenings he sits and sings the songs of old:

> Then would he sing achievements high,
> And circumstance of Chivalry,
> Till the rapt traveller would stay,
> Forgetful of the closing day;
> And noble youths, the strain to hear,
> Forsook the hunting of the deer;
> And Yarrow, as he rolled along,
> Bore burden to the Minstrel's song.   (End of Canto vi)[36]

The same neat tying of past to future that the story accomplishes is
accomplished again here; this is not the Ossianic sublime. The
Minstrel has stepped back from the edge of history, where he is the
"Last Minstrel," and now lives happily in an imitation elegiac
setting, arresting the traveler with tales of the past, and entertaining
the future (in the form of youths) with his song. The Yarrow, a stream
that always sings of loss (as I will discuss in the next chapter), is
domesticated into a quiet harmonizer. Peace reigns. In an exact
parallel to the burden of the story, Scott gets everything he wants
here, without being forced into irrecoverables or full stops. The
Minstrel is the Last Minstrel, and so sings of an irrecoverable past:
yet he also has pulled back from the limit, and now carries on a sort
of commerce between past and future, a commerce in which the
pathos of the passing of things is quietly surrounded by a cheerful
accommodation to the regularities of life's progress.[37]

Scott's accommodation of history to progress is the center of his
stories, but his stories are never neat. The quiet peaceableness of his
central moments allows him a certain carelessness. With the center
become so stable, the rest of the structure can be ornamented at
leisure, and so his stories become messy, festooned with anecdote and
oddity. I would insist, though, that Scott's stories are always self-
contained. Messy they are, but the mess is always carefully contained
in compartments designed for the purpose. A classic moderate, Scott
is interested in orchestrating the peaceful meeting of extremes, but he
is not blind to the energies of the irregular, nor is he stupid. In fact,
he is inordinately attracted to the irregular; his condescending
hauteur about ballads, for instance, is always mixed with a real
devotion to them. They crowd his memory, and find their way into

all of his works. Including the ballad in his schemes is a challenge for Scott, since they not only stop and start formally, but also almost always tell stories of desperate loss and unmediated suffering.

In *The Lay of the Last Minstrel* Scott has a special box for them: Canto VI, the infamous extra canto. In this canto the Page is taken care of (whisked away by the dead-not-dead Michael Scott), and three ballads are sung as wedding entertainment. Two of the ballads, the first and the last, are in ballad measure; the middle one is in an "Italian" nine-line stanza whose rhymes and structure are very regular. The stories of the ballads are strikingly unrelenting, and made especially so by their context. They are sung as wedding entertainments, and at a wedding whose purpose and charge is the unification of feuding factions; the last ballad is about the needless death of a beautiful maiden, and the first two are about violently disastrous wedding plans. In the first, sung by a Border minstrel, an English lady wishes to marry a Scottish knight: her brother poisons her to prevent it, her lover murders the brother, and then departs to do penance in Palestine. The second is about Henry Howard, Earl of Surrey, and is supposed to be sung by his minstrel. This minstrel has seen the world, so his is the sophisticated nine-line stanza. His song tells of the separation of Surrey from Geraldine, his lover, and ends by describing their end,

> The gory bridal bed, the plunder'd shrine
> The murder'd Surrey's blood, the tears of Geraldine!
>
> (Canto VI, stanza 20)

The last, sung by a Highland bard, tells of a young woman who, instead of common-sensically staying on at a festive occasion, passionately and obstinately hurries home over stormy seas to tend to the parents she left behind, and drowns on the way.

Scott's careful arrangement of these songs into a sort of small Britain, with the border leading the way for the south and north, is typical. Yet the balanced occasion belies the contents of the songs, which so noticeably intrude upon the ritual of unification and progress the *Lay* has worked out. They sing of precisely the frozen incapacity for progress that Scott has taken such pains to portray and quietly thaw. Indeed, their stories founder exactly on the moment of possible progress, where the past can turn into the future, and instead of moving they explode, or fall apart: they do not look back nostalgically, but collapse in a present that goes nowhere. The first ballad, for instance, cannot forget or move beyond the fratricide, and this moment consumes the story, which circles around it. The song-singing ends with the disappearance of the Page; the hall fills with a mist, which the guests at first mistake for the sentimental mists rising from the last bard's song, and in the middle of the smoke Michael Scott comes and spirits the Page away. Previous to this, the page has been causing all kinds of trouble, trouble of a quite specific sort:

> The Goblin Page, omitting still
> No opportunity of ill,
> Strove now, while blood ran hot and high,
> To rouse debate and jealousy ...   (Canto VI, stanza 7)

Michael Scott, who lies in his crypt dead but uncorrupted, and (apparently) able to rise at need, is the proper figure to put an end to all this practice of rupture, hypothetically so destructive to the peaceful project of the poem. With his arrival we see the last canto for what it is: a sort of museum of destruction, a display case for the irregularity that could not be included within the story but which Scott retains, since the story itself generates irregular energies. The last canto contains the dangerous possibilities that the story as a whole excludes, and keeps them from contaminating the control of the rest of the poem. That is: this is not, I would insist, Byronic conflict, or a Wordsworthian eruption of antithetical energy. It is an acknowledgement of the pressures exerted by the possibility of disaster, and the calm containment of these possibilities. The Page is the patron of irregularity, and runs through the poem disrupting the sense of calm. Scott could have gotten rid of him: instead he corrals him, gives him a stage, a whole canto, and then whisks him away. Synecdochically speaking, this trick allows Scott to include the desperate and painful pathos of the ballads and also step free of them, unconstrained by their stops and starts. When the Page disappears, the guests at the wedding are all troubled, and feel the need to go on pilgrimages: but we do not. We can simply say, with Scott (in his easy-going way), that in any event the Page has been gotten rid of. Division is acknowledged and put away. *The Lay of the Last Minstrel* is kept from looking simple minded, prevented from appearing to be ignorant of the possibility that the marriage could dissolve under the pressure of its themes; but it keeps this possibility in an ornamental space, where it can be admired and contained.

Not all stories are like this. Romances, old ones, like those of

Chretienne or those presented in Malory's *Morte Arthur*, contain loss too, and they also are deeply concerned with the movement of history, but their interests are very different. In Malory, for instance, we are just barely into Book I when we are told how the story will end: Arthur has slept with his sister, and their offspring will bring an end to the glories of Arthur's reign. In his prophecy Merlin gives Arthur a whole life, with a glorious apogee and an inevitable death. And so through the whole of the story – through all of the many interleaved stories – the burden of the end is carried openly along. The story is not only told in the light of its end but also acted out, by its central character, in full knowledge of its end. This openness gives these stories a doubly sad air, since, for us, Arthur is dead already (a glory of the past) and his foreknowledge keeps the story of his glories from entirely distracting us from this fact. In romance, history moves inevitably, and with a bright cruelty. Romance heroes may laud and fight each other, but they are all caught up in a destined and inevitably disappearing, Ossianic world.

Another thing romance heroes do is suffer. They fall from grace and do actually bad things that they can never be free of: Arthur, for instance, sleeps with his sister, and even though he could not have known, he has sinned, and will be punished. This courageous handling of character makes these romance stories serious ones; that is, we may have serious doubts about the characters, and these doubts are provoked for serious ends. Our speculation about Gawaine's cowardice and falsehood in *Sir Gawaine and the Green Knight*, for instance, must be real speculation, and the difficulty is not easily dismissed. Gawaine has sinned, and his character has suffered and changed. As has so often been said, this quality is attached to the central, pagan-christian interest that romances have in the mortification and transformation of the self. Their interest in transformation demands that the integrity of their characters be put at actual risk, and the reader shares that risk.

Despite his claims to the contrary, Scott's poems are not romances, but they do very professionally mimic the romance. I have asserted that *The Lay of the Last Minstrel* evades a real investment in progress, the flow of time, even while insisting on the value of progress. In the same way, I would insist that no transformations ever take place in Scott's poetry (or in his novels, either), even though his works always look very much like stories of transformations.[38] In *The Lay of the Last Minstrel*, Lord Musgrave suffers for everyone else, and in his mortification the story is cleansed of its stagnation and moves to a happy conclusion. William of Deloraine has suffered physically, but his suffering has nothing at all to do with anything important; it is the consequence of a chance encounter. Lord Cranstoun, whom we might call the "hero" of the tale, does not suffer, and never becomes a full character anyway. There is a trial in *The Lay of the Last Minstrel*, but its rigors are expertly detached from the story, and the characters we know benefit from it without being risked themselves.

The best example for understanding Scott's deployment of this side of the romance is *The Lady of the Lake*. In that poem the plot of the romance is given serious attention, and the central character, "Fitz-James" (King James V in disguise), looks throughout very much like a knight undergoing trials. The first canto of *The Lady of the Lake* begins with an Ossianic call to the past, an invocation of the Caledonian muse:

> O wake once more! how rude so'er the hand
> That ventures o'er thy magic maze to stray;
> O wake once more! though scarce my skill command
> Some feeble echoing of thine earlier lay.   (Canto I, Introduction)

Well might Scott sound this note, for not only is the cast of characters virtually the same as in his previous poems, but the first scene is a sort of echo chamber for a very specific literary history, which I will discuss briefly in the conclusion of the next chapter. *The Lady of the Lake* does show an increase in what Jeffrey would call capacity or sophistication. The marriage, for instance, is held off until the end of the poem, and the other "catastrophes" (as Scott liked to call climaxes) are made to occur simultaneously. The versification in this poem is moving towards regularity; the rhymes are almost always couplets and the stanza length becomes relatively stable, at around 20–4 lines. Clearly Scott has paid attention to his critics, and the story here is less dark and confused than in either of the two previous poems (though the end retains Scott-ish murkiness). The opening canto is a model of clarity and direction. It begins with a stag listening to the approaching hunt:

> As Chief who hears his warder call
> "To arms! The foemen storm the wall!"
> The antlered monarch of the waste
> Sprung from his heathery couch in haste.
>
> (Canto I, stanza 2)

The social standing of the stag, as antlered monarch, is not an inconsequential detail, for the chief of the hunt is the monarch of the town, King James. The story follows the old romance and ballad plot, with James outriding the rest of the crowd, deep into the Highlands, alone except for his dogs and his horse, which is soon to expire.[39] James (or "the stranger") pursues the deer up what he thinks is a dead end, and, just when he is approaching for the "death-wound, and the death-halloo," the stag turns aside and vanishes into the secret places of the mountains, where he crouches and listens to his baffled pursuers.[40] James attempts to follow, but he has pushed too far; his horse dies from under him and he is suddenly sorry. He sings a little balance-song, a small version of Deloraine's song: "Woe worth the chase, woe worth the day,/That costs thy life, my gallant grey" (stanza 9). With this, of course, the chase is over, and James looks around him, only to find himself in a foreign country. In this hunt, the antlered monarch squares off with the Scottish monarch and escapes with dignity and life intact. He need not die spectacularly to keep his dignity, just as James need not kill the deer to be the best hunter, since he has outlasted all but his panting dogs. The hunt has no reward for anyone – it has no consequence. That is, it has no reward for anyone in the poem. The reader is rewarded with a thrilling description of the hunt, and is not confronted with the possibly unpleasant sight of the antlered monarch being subjected to King James. Strengths are balanced against each other so that nothing is left over. For James, his potentially oppressive amusement is balanced by his loss; for the stag, exhaustion is balanced by victory. If James' adventures are to be part of an allegory, we have not yet been given the materials to get started. He is deposited in the Highlands by an excess of energy, but nothing has pointed to this excess as a moral excess. If anything, we have been asked to admire James' stamina and even his feeling (in his mourning of his horse).

James meets a lot of people in the Highlands, people who, if they are not romance characters, are at least Romantic ones. The Lady of the Lake, Ellen Douglas, presides over an imitation-magical island, the hideout of a Highland chief, Roderick Dhu. Roderick is about to make war on James' forces, having mistaken James' hunting party for an invading army; a warlike man, he needs very little excuse, anyway. Ellen and her parents are in hiding because her father, called The Douglas, has been banished by James for various rather vague intrigues. Ellen wants to marry a classic, mild-mannered Scott hero, Malcolm Graeme, who, like so many Scott heroes, does very little throughout the story. Roderick is an interesting character. In the context of my discussions, he is Lord Musgrave filled out and combined with the Goblin Page. He serves as the carrier of irregularity in the story, the disruptive, hard-to-contain energy that Scott loves and hates. Roderick also wants to marry Ellen, and, as the protector of her family, he accumulates certain rights; his eventual defeat and capture, at the end of Canto v, will set the story free to conclude. Like *Marmion*, the poem contains a battle, but the battle has a wonderfully extra-narrative place. It takes place during the "time" of Canto v, but we do not see it until it is narrated by the Douglas family minstrel to the dying Roderick, in Canto vi. Neither of the leaders is present for the battle: Roderick has been captured, and James quite literally forgets about it until it is too late. The poem first describes it this way: "On both sides store of blood is lost,/ Nor much success can either boast" (Canto vi, stanza 6). None of that blood has been lost by anyone we know, and so the battle plays a scenic rather than narrative role.

The poem ends with Roderick dead, Ellen and Malcolm married, James on his throne, and The Douglas (in defiance of historical accuracy) restored to favor. In between, James has wandered through the Highlands, encountering and flirting with Ellen, and encountering and killing Roderick. He meets his adventures by himself, and without his identity as king. At some points he is in what looks like great danger. This has led one observer to say of his trials:

Beneath his disguise, the king eventually undergoes a kind of metamorphosis roughly similar to Prince Hal's – from a hunter of entertainment, playing at forester and knight-errant, through a recognition of the chaotic possibilities in romance, to a ruler testing the nature of his sovereignty.[41]

This is almost exactly right; but I would dispute every part of it. I will admit that we are in very subtle territory, and the difference between a man who changes and a man who simply changes his mind can be small, even imperceptible. But in a real metamorphosis, something, I take it, is always left behind; and that something can always be read as a previous self. So, to take the example given, when Hal changes, Falstaff is left behind. Kingship demands that he be left, yet his abandonment is not easy, and the wrench we feel marks the depth of the change in Hal, now Henry. In *The Lady of the Lake*, James leaves nothing behind. He may be in disguise, but this disguise is a subset of his regular self: he is always James Fitz-James, Knight of Snowdoun, and he is always simply pretending to not be the king. He is as playfully flirtatious at the end as he was at the beginning, and he is as powerful when alone in the Highlands as he is on his throne at the end.

As I have said, James looks like a character on the way to transformation. He has not been given any faults, so transformation would be difficult anyway, but still he has been reduced to a sort of extremity. Ellen sends him away from her island with a treacherous guide, who plans to turn him over to Roderick; Roderick has received a prophecy that claims that the side who takes the first life will be victorious, and plans to use James as that first blood. James is enamored of Ellen, and searches her out in an "elf-cave" in which she has taken refuge from the coming war. As Nancy Goslee points out, all kinds of magical atmospherics are conjured up; in particular, the Douglas minstrel, who is keeping Ellen company, sings a ballad of elves and transformations. The meeting between James and Ellen has the look of a romance meeting; Arthur, for instance, gets Excalibur by meeting with his Lady of the Lake in a very similar fashion. James hopes to carry Ellen away from this meeting, but she is true to Malcolm. True to romance form, a talisman is given, but, true to Scott's mimicry, the exchange goes the wrong way. James may be alone, and he may be exposed, but he is still king. Ellen gives James advice, but nothing more. There is no reason to do more, since James has not arrived in need; Ellen herself is in need, outcast and exposed as she is. Unknown to them both, the power that exposes her is right there in James. Appropriately, then, James gives Ellen a signet, which she may exchange for royal favor; she later uses it to ransom Malcolm, taken captive in the conflict. Ellen does not fill some need that James develops in his reduction (think, for instance, of Gawaine's acceptance of the magic belt). Quite the contrary: James has not been reduced, and power still rides with him, and sits on his fingers.

I won't follow James closely through all his adventures. He goes on, having one near-romance encounter after another. He encounters another possible "helper," a Martha Ray figure, driven mad long ago by Roderick's depredations. She warns him of the ambush Roderick is planning, and gives him a lock of hair from her murdered lover's head; but this is, again, not a proper talisman. It is a challenge, a reminder that James has sworn to avenge her; that is, it is not a source of power that might replace an evaporated knightly prowess, but a mark of that power, an affirmation of it. Soon after this James encounters Roderick, now also in disguise, and they pass the night together in soldierly comfort, enjoying the equilibrium of enemies I have described in *The Lay of the Last Minstrel*. Roderick promises to guide James out of the Highlands, and promises that no harm shall come to him while he is in Roderick's domain. In romance, knights often conceal their identity, and subsequent revelation of identity is often linked to self-revelation. And so again Scott's story is walking very close to a romance border; but again, he stays thoroughly on the nearer side.

James and Roderick spar verbally as they walk along, and eventually James brags Roderick into frustration. Roderick then reveals not only his identity, but also the fact that all the while he and James have walked, apparently alone, they have been shadowed by the brave soldiers of his clan; they rise up out of the bracken, "As if the yawning hill to heaven/ A subterranean host had given" (Canto v, stanza 9). Elves are in the habit of appearing in this way. They appear in this way – for instance – in the ballad Ellen hears in her cave. These, though, are not elves: they are only like elves. This is not a highland transformation story: it just looks like one. Stories of transformation, as Northrop Frye would say, often have a kind of low point, where the hero, in his descent, bottoms out and faces his crisis. Here James is alone, and exposed not only to the counter-hero, Roderick, but also to an overwhelming superiority of numbers. If his trial is one of personal exposure, an exposure which might force him to consider his self apart from his kingship, then this would be a good candidate for a moment of crisis. Even in more superficial romances, where transformation does not run very deep, such as *Guy of Warwick*, this would be a great moment.[42] Guy, in particular, would simply go at it, and would kill them all, Roderick included. James almost does this:

> Fitz-James was brave : – Though to his heart
> The life-blood thrilled with sudden start,
> He mann'd himself with dauntless air,
> And returned the Chief his haughty stare,
> His back against a rock he bore,
> And firmly placed his foot before : –
> "Come one, Come all!"   (Canto v, stanza 10)

Nothing happens here, and this proves two things. The first is that James is in no way unmanned; alone, perhaps, but still entirely himself, and still bravely radiating knightly power. The second is that James is not alone in a potentially transformative, magical world. Alone, yes, but not in a foreign world. Everything looks different, as a result of the Gaelic tinge thrown over the mountainous landscape. But there is no foreign behavior going on here. Roderick answers James:

> "Fear nought – nay, that I need not say –
> But – doubt not aught from mine array.
> Thou art my guest: – I pledged my word
> As far as Coilantogle ford:
> Nor would I call a clansman's brand
> For aid against one valiant hand,
> Though on our strife lay every vale
> Rent by Saxon from the Gael." (Canto v, stanza 11)

James is perfectly safe, surrounded by the equilibrium of chivalry, founded on his knightly agreement with Roderick but implicit, anyway, in the respect the two Brave Men have for each other. His exposure, we might say, is purely formal, for demonstration but not action. Eventually James and Roderick do fight, at the above mentioned Coilantogle ford, and Roderick is mortally wounded. This battle is carefully drawn by Scott to yield up only vague answers. Roderick dies, but not from an immediate death-wound; in fact, he subdues James and is on the verge of killing him when he misses a dagger thrust and keels over from loss of blood. He does not actually expire until much later, in Canto vi, while listening to the story of the useless battle of the armies. In affirmation of the way in which crisis is imitated but actually avoided, James does not reveal his identity to Roderick. The fight is one more Highland adventure.

My version of James' trials would be this: he is not really disguised, but has merely changed his clothes; he is not in a foreign country, but has merely witnessed a change of scenery; he has not been changed, but has merely changed his mind. It is hard to illustrate a plot feature which has been so purposefully made inconspicuous, but one place to see the smallness of James' change is in his acceptance of The Douglas, an event which takes place off-stage and is described in plain and factual terms. No change of character is required or produced. James merely corrects what he now sees as a mistake:

Yester even,
His Prince and he have much forgiven:
Wrong hath he from slanderous tongue,
I, from his rebel kinsmen wrong.   (Canto VI, stanza 27)

In other words, James' character has not been put at risk; his body
has, since he has had what Hogg would call "adventures," but
nothing inner has happened. There is no sin, no stain, no expiation,
no suffering, and hence, no essential progress. There has been
material progress of the sort detailed in *The Lay of the Last Minstrel*;
Roderick is dead, and the small world of stagnant conflict defined by
Ellen and her father can move into the broader, progressive world.
Because Roderick is so thoroughly the container of irregular energy,
the story can utterly eliminate it by eliminating him. James does not
need to change: he needs to kill Roderick.

What we have, when *The Lady of the Lake* is over, is a picture of a
sort of commerce, as we have at the end of *The Lay of the Last Minstrel*.
Everything is accounted for in scrupulous trading, figured best in the
poem by the stag hunt that I started with. James kills Roderick: but
not only did Roderick show himself a true knight, he also essentially
killed James, having been prevented from doing so by bad luck (his
blood ran out). A battle has been fought, but neither side wins;
traitors have been punished (sovereignty established) but traitors
have been forgiven, in the shape of Douglas and Malcolm. The whole
of the story has been raised up into the twilight world of chivalric
equilibrium, where blows are "traded" but character is not really at
risk (to use another economic term). All of this could be turned into
insult, but I want to turn it into compliment. Coleridge disparagingly
referred to *The Lady of the Lake* as a sort of tourism, and indeed the
poem inspired a rage for Highland travel, trips on which the visitors
would row boats on Loch Katrine and sing songs from the poem. This
is what happens to James: he tours the Highlands, as is a king's right.
This does not mean nothing happens, though nothing essential
happens. The important, and extraordinary, feature of this story is in
the way, all along, it purposefully casts the shadow of what it is not.
Especially in scenes like that of James and Ellen in the elf-cave, the
seriousness of romance is always nearly appearing, and it is nearly
appearing in a remarkably subtle and even skillful way. A true story
of transformation embroils its central character in dangers that are
more than imitations. In such stories, the forward movement of the
narrative is real, and powered by a voltage generated by the

difference between the beginning and the end. Scott does not want to work with dangerously high voltages, so he writes extraordinary imitations, which exhibit the things of romance for our pleasure, but do not risk any investment in them.

Like James Hogg, Scott hailed from the Borders, and he is a true Border poet. His stories always involve some border crossed, a limit passed. The miraculous achievement of his poems is that borders are imposed and crossed but no travel ever takes place. In *The Lady of the Lake* crossing the border means only a change of scenery. Things are the same on either side. The wealth and interest of riskier stories is displayed for us in carefully designed containers, containers which, when thrown away, demonstrate all the more clearly the unbordered serenity of Scott's world. His methods allow him to present wildly destructive energy – Napoleonic energy, say – as both attractive and destructive, without insisting on either conclusion. Primitive energies make their appearance, are admired, and disappear. Scott avoids the necessity of being either angelic or satanic, and so finds himself comfortably in middle earth.

Scott's stanzas only end when the narrative work allotted to them is finished; the other way of putting this is that their comfortable length allows for easy parcels of narrative work. Stopping and starting is made easy by the stanza's refusal to close down arbitrarily (as ballad stanzas do, every four lines). In exactly the same way Scott's stories allow for repetition, since they never invest heavily in real action. If nothing ever really starts, nothing really has to end, and so starting again is made easy. Scott's stories give themselves freedom by never investing in conflict. Scott's contemporaries noted this. It seems true enough: as a poet Scott is free of the burdens of a Romantic character. He is free in a way that his contemporary, Byron, envied and respected. Byron's stories shared the poetic marketplace with Scott's, and Scott claimed to have been superseded by them. Byron's poems display characters which closely resemble those of Scott, but with crucial difference. Byron's Romantic heroes (I say that to exempt Don Juan, the perfect adventurer) become so invested in their stories that they cannot escape without some sort of exciting cataclysm. Recalling a previous metaphor, Byron's voltages are higher than Scott's. Thus, this sort of burdened, self-destructive character, which Byron learned to create from Scott, among others, came to be called the Byronic hero instead of the Scott hero. In Byron, a character like James would have Roderick within him, and their combat would be internal and would do damage. Byron's romance stories cannot free themselves from their own energy, and so their endings are like the endings of the ballads in *The Lay of the Last Minstrel*. They cannot find progress without cataclysm because they cannot float free; they are, in my terms, heavily invested stories, risky stories. Scott's heroes are not confined by the constriction of mental space that marks the tortured Romantic soul; the walls of this cavern are not for him. If Byron's heroes could simply turn away like this, his stories would evaporate: the constriction of possibilities that drives his heroes into death would disappear. Conrad could simply go home; he could even wed Gulnare, the homicide. The quality that marks Scott's heroes, that distinguishes them as heroes (that allows them to survive until the end), is that they can leave such spaces without consequence. Roderick is confined by the Highlands, and dies immediately upon leaving them; but James is free to come and go, to cross borders at will.[43]

Scott's level-headed methods allow him to include characters like Roderick in his stories and also to have these stories remain perfectly free of irregular energies. In Byron's stories, stains always spread, coloring what they touch; in Scott, these stains are presented but never touched by anyone else. They are, as I have said earlier, in a sort of quarantine, cordoned off and then cut away to bring peace and conclusion. In the same way, the burden that history brings, the knowledge of loss, is domesticated within a commerce that refuses real investment in either the past or the future, and which, besides, carefully steps around the inevitable turning of past into future. Scott's investment is in a new-old form, and this investment pays off in stories that can always be the same, and yet always be equally compelling. Since nothing ever really starts, nothing ever really stops, and the machine can run on and on; but since irregularity is so profusely displayed, every time, the new edition escapes from simple regularity, and hence from looking like a pure repetition. Irregularity is retained as an ornament, and cleverly disguised as essential.

In this genre, revival is easy, since nothing ever dies. Compare this to Byron's romance stories, a genre he gave up after only about four years of work. They end. Every story must hasten to the same collapse, and so each new one must be revived: re-energized, re-poised on the brink. Scott's stories amble by the brink, tourists in the land of extremes and destruction. The destructive energies of irregularity are in fact essential in Byron's stories, and so Byron was faced with the dismal task of making an industry of rebellion; in that business, repetition looks like repetition, and no wonder he gave it up for the supple pleasures of *ottava-rima*. Scott's irregularities, contained and controlled, could be retailed time and again. And so Scott could sell irregularities to his regular public, and be a regular man himself; since his stories remain free, his character could too. He didn't need to travel to the East and ride, suffering internally, in a Napoleonic carriage. He could remain at home, the busy Laird of Abbotsford.

CHAPTER 5

William Wordsworth

William Wordsworth makes a good end for this study because while his career is very similar to the previous careers I have discussed, his career also modifies and extends the issues those careers bring up in important and interesting ways. He is also a high canonical poet, and so will bring to my discussion of ambition and form the context of common critical practice and canonical approval. He is also a fine and sensitive poet, as sensitive (in my context) as Burns. My discussions of Wordsworth's formal decisions and strategies will bear a strong resemblance to my discussions of Burns, because Wordsworth, like Burns, took the expressive limitations and possibilities of verse to be at least one of the most important aspects of the poetic occupation. For Wordsworth, as for Burns, the linguistic limits that define poetic practice are charged, interesting and important. Unlike Burns, though, Wordsworth did not retire from the pressure of literary history. The progress of Wordsworth's career reflects, in fact, a growing faith in the importance of precedent and continuity. In this way, too, Wordsworth will bring my discussion within the pale of canonical achievement (though I will not get to this part until the conclusion).

Wordsworth also resembles Walter Scott, in ways that have been important so far. Wordsworth is a card-carrying member of the ballad revival, interested in collecting ballads, old stories and rural anecdotes, things which he then presents to the sophisticated. His transportation of pastoral simplicity is vexed and short-circuited, though, and I will spend time demonstrating the strangely fixated nature of Wordsworth the collector of texts. Like Scott (and my other writers) Wordsworth was also profoundly interested in his readers, and profoundly interested in being a popular author. Wordsworth thought much more about success and failure than we tend to remember, and even though recent writing on Wordsworth has taken some notice of his interest in his readers, we still remember the "fit audience" of 1815 better than the anxiously solicitous Wordsworth of the Preface to the *Lyrical Ballads*.[1] Unlike Scott, though, Wordsworth's methods resist popularity: he is constantly scolding and working on his reader, emphasizing moments of discomfort rather than passing them by. As an ambitious poet who resists popularity, Wordsworth presents ambition in a new key.

He does this because a large part of his ambition is actually a poetic ambition, in high canonical style. Poetic integrity does not, however, protect Wordsworth from becoming painfully frustrated by his lack of influence over his readers, as measured by their resistance to purchasing his books. Wordsworth wants to sell books: he wants people to read his books, be changed, and make him famous. The interaction of this sort of worldly ambition with his equally intense poetic ambition creates the characteristic Wordsworthian "lyrical ballad" form, loud, didactic and obscure at once. I will begin by charting this interaction, and tracing the sources of this early but important form. After finding the basic Wordsworthian rhythm, I will then turn to Wordsworth the ballad revivalist. I take things in this order because Wordsworth's poetry of revival is the most intense and complex of the poetry I have discussed so far. It absorbs the many features of revival, as I have discussed them earlier, into a tense and difficult poetic package, and in untying this package I will need to have with me the basic energies of Wordsworthian form. Finally, I will turn to distinguishing between Wordsworth and Scott. This comparison will turn on and explicate Wordsworth's faith and investment in high literary history, a feature which distinguishes him from the other writers in this study, and which, I will argue, has much to do with his canonical status.

Wordsworth's interest in his readers, what they feel, and especially how they feel about him, has a beginning and an end. In the beginning, he is solicitous, and anxious for attention and approval. Much of the Preface to the *Lyrical Ballads* works arguments which can only be called solicitous. The tone and vocabulary of the Preface are well illustrated by the following passage, from near the end. Having spent a lot of time worrying over the reader's pleasure, he begins to conclude in this way:

But, would my limits have permitted me to point out how this pleasure is produced I might have removed many obstacles, and assisted my Reader in perceiving that the powers of language are not so limited as he may suppose;

and that it is possible that poetry may give other enjoyments, of a purer, more lasting and more exquisite nature. This part of the subject I have not altogether neglected; but ... [2]

Deeply interested in his reader, Wordsworth extends himself, insisting on the powers of (his) language, but he also draws back, held back by mysterious "limits." The end of Wordsworth's concern for his readers has a very different feel. Here is a passage from the "Essay, Supplementary to the Preface" of 1815:

Away, then, with the senseless iteration of the word, *popular,* applied to new works in poetry, as if there were no test of excellence in this the first of the fine arts but that all men should run after its productions, as if urged by an appetite, or constrained by a spell! (vol. III, p. 83)

Here the reader has become a kind of enemy, poorly behaved and senseless. Wordsworth's fretting over limits is replaced by an insistence that his potential readers pursue books with an avidity that is beyond all bounds, like the behavior of the spellbound. In this section I will move from the beginning to the end; I will do this by working out what Wordsworth means by "limits" (in the first passage), and how these limits are related to the "powers of language." The "spell" Wordsworth introduces in the later passage will turn out to be an important link: it is what Wordsworth fears, an inexplicable power to pass by limits which he cannot gather or control.

To constrain the reader with a spell is not the same thing as convincing the reader of the truth, but casting a spell over readers, charming them, is very close to what Wordsworth seems to want in many parts of the Preface to the *Lyrical Ballads.* Note, for instance, the appearance of the word "charm" in this passage:

Now, granting for a moment that whatever is interesting in these objects may be as vividly described in prose, why am I to be condemned if to such description I have endeavoured to superadd the charm which by the consent of all nations is acknowledged to exist in metrical language? (vol. III, p. 145)

Wordsworth has been discussing the difference between poetry and prose. For a poet so often accused of being prosaic, this self-attribution of charming versification is an important matter. "Charm" here is mild-mannered, exhibiting a very quiet sort of magic, but its force is, I think, magical. "Metrical language" brings with it a (mysterious) power, and that power distinguishes poetry from prose. In my terms:

"charm" describes the consequences of form. But how to explain this power?

Wordsworth both wants to convince his readers of certain things and also wants for them to find that they already agree with him, because he is simply right. The Preface to the *Lyrical Ballads* is a long struggle between these two versions of his project. This struggle produces the frequent moments of exasperation in the Preface. Here is one such moment, and an important one:

I might perhaps include all that is *necessary* to say, however, upon this subject by affirming, what few persons will deny, that, of two descriptions, either of the passions, manners, or characters, each of them equally well executed, the one in prose and the other in verse, the verse will be read a hundred times where the prose is read once.[3]

This particular moment arises from Wordsworth's incapacity to control his argument concerning the actual mechanism of the charm of verse, which I will discuss shortly. Unable to find a mechanism, Wordsworth turns to a simple assertion of pleasure. His assertion of pleasure is a counter-weight to worries over the potentially unfriendly reader. He keeps imagining readers who simply *don't like* his poems:

The reader will say that he has been pleased by [inferior] compositions; and what can I do more for him? The power of any art is limited; and he will suspect that, if I propose to furnish him with new friends, that can be only upon condition of his abandoning his old friends. (p. 157)

The basic rhythm of the Preface is created by turning from the dead-end of the reader's pleasure to the complaint about "limits." Such is the organization of the earlier quotation about "superadded charm"; it happens again here. The worry about poetic friends also continues into a passage about limits which I also quoted earlier: "But, would my limits have permitted me to point out how this pleasure is produced, many obstacles might have been removed ... " Wordsworth's assertions and discussions of poetic pleasure always run up against these limits, the limits of his power, and the limits of his argument, and these are the moments of exasperation.

The first key to unlocking "limits" is the argument about meter in the Preface, which is the final section in the general discussion of the difference between poetry and prose. Meter stands in for the formal properties of verse; and since Wordsworth has dismissed diction and subject matter as *essential* ingredients in poetry just prior to this section, we arrive at the discussion of meter ready for final formulas, and the true distinction of poetry and prose. This discussion is protean and utterly inconclusive. It has four versions, which follow one after the other, each undergoing a trial and each being dismissed or left behind as somehow unsatisfactory. These versions can be summarized quickly. The first insists, with a punning logic, that meter "regularizes" irregular and excessive passions. This claim is undermined by the fact that he also argues, shortly later, that meter can make passion-less poetry more exciting. The next version makes meter a superior mode for story-telling because it dampens reality by making events "unsubstantial."

The next version, a well-known part of the Preface, begins with one of Wordsworth's periodic disclaimers: "If I had undertaken a SYSTEMATIC defense of the theory here maintained ... " (p. 149). If he had done this he would have derived culture from a single principle, "namely the pleasure which the mind derives from the perception of similitude in dissimilitude." From this principle follow the sexual appetite, taste, moral feelings, and "ordinary conversation." He claims that meter could be shown to derive its power of producing pleasure (that is, of counteracting pain) from this principle, but, he says, "my limits will not permit me to enter upon this subject, and I must content myself with a general summary."[4] Whether we are actually given this summary is unclear; the next version does not reuse the terms of similitude. It does gather up much material that has gone before, and puts it into a list that has an air of logical desperation about it. The list adds music, the traditional handmaiden of charms, to the previous versions, and pushes everything into one category: "a complex feeling of delight, which is of the most important use in tempering the painful feelings always found intermingled with powerful descriptions of the deeper passions" (p. 151). This logical desperation leads immediately to the exasperated assertion of pleasure that I noted before: "All that is necessary to say, however ... " What bothers Wordsworth about these arguments, the feature that makes him abandon them one after the other, is that they all depend upon a mysterious principle of action which Wordsworth cannot quite capture. He desires the control of mechanism, but each explanation finds only some power that can only be asserted.

Wordsworth's use of the word "limits" is as complex as I would wish. Most simply, the limits he keeps asserting are generic: the Preface, being a minor dependent upon the poems themselves, should be short and humble. This sense of limit is used as a metaphor for more important senses. Most pointedly, the strongest limit Wordsworth encounters is a philosophical (or epistemological) one: the argument he wants to make simply can't be made. What is the charm of verse? Its charm is its ability to give a mysterious pleasure to the reader, a special pleasure that prose is incapable of. It does this because it does: that is its charm. The reader's pleasure, utterly contained within the limits of the reader's self, is beyond the reach of Wordsworth's argument; he encounters this limit as one might a rock, and it turns all prosaic argument aside. This entirely durable limit or border to the extension of Wordsworth's poetic power rules his prose into its characteristically polemical shape. In the section on meter, for instance, each argument demonstrates its own limits, its eventual dependence on some mysterious principle of action, and then stops. His argument fails, revives again, and goes on, only to fail and revive once more. In this way a book of poems gets a Preface; the Preface gets an Appendix. His arguments go on and on, and as we sense the anxiety that forces them to go on we sense that the real "limits" he complains of are the limits of his power as a writer. He is afraid that his writing won't do what he wants. In the terms I used in beginning, his poetic ambition, and his insistence on the efficacy of poetry, is brought up short by his painful worry that he is not reaching his readers. The poetic part of his project keeps looking like it depends on the success of the book as marked by the reader's desire to read it. As readers of Wordsworth have so often noted, he is afraid that the power of his writing is for him alone, and remains solipsistically within him. "The power of any art is limited." So persistent is Wordsworth in worrying about the unreachability of his readers and the parallel danger of solipsism that he drives his projects to the edge of endurance; he does this in his prose and in his poetry. They both end in the same place, circling tensely around the frustrating limits of poetry and personal knowledge. This tension, as Geoffrey Hartman taught us, is paradoxically the source of Wordsworth's greatest poems. The way in which his limits rule or compress his poetry into beauty and power is, in my argument, an analog to the process of Burns' song-writing; but Wordsworth's self-limitation is more demented, more energetic, less willing. Wordsworth's poetry is border poetry in an extreme form.

For me and for Wordsworth, the proof is in the poetry, and I will turn to the poetry by following a turn on Wordsworth's part. He moves immediately from the end of the arguments about meter to

poetic examples: "In consequence of these convictions I related in
meter the tale of 'Goody Blake and Harry Gill'... " (p. 150).[5] He
goes on to say that this "curse poem," as Hartman refers to it,[6] is
based on a popular story, which he got from Erasmus Darwin.[7] It is
aggressively subtitled "A True Story," an assertion which is repeated
in the Preface ("for it is a *fact*," p. 150). Robert Mayo notes that
"Goody Blake and Harry Gill" was reprinted more than any of the
Lyrical Ballads, and I want to add to "Goody Blake and Harry Gill"
another popular unpopular poem, "Peter Bell," which was one of
Wordsworth's best-selling publications.[8] These two poems demonstrate not only Wordsworth's interest in the powers of art, but also
the strange return of Wordsworthian limitations upon art. This
return packages the Preface into a series of limited movements, and
it has a parallel effect on the poetry.

Though aggressively plain, in Wordsworth's best *Lyrical Ballads*
style, "Goody Blake and Harry Gill" is also a plainly artful poem.
Wordsworth uses the doubled ballad stanza to effect, as in the
following:

> Young Harry was a lusty drover,
> And who so stout of limb as he?
> His cheeks were red as ruddy clover;
> His voice was like the voice of three.
> Old Goody was old and poor;
> Ill fed she was, and thinly clad;
> Any man who passed her door
> Might see how poor a life she had.   (lines 17–24)

This stanza compresses Harry and Goody together, and their
compression creates the pathos of the poem. Since the point of the
poem is that the social and psychological "space" between Harry
and Goody is artificial and unjust, this is solidly appropriate. It is this
space that Goody overcomes when she curses Harry and gains her
poetic justice. Her curse breaks down Harry's unpleasant isolation,
his refusal to see how close he is to Goody; all people, in the *Lyrical
Ballads*, are "naturally" close. The perception of this closeness, the
inescapable sympathy that breaks down Harry's selfish limits, arrives
with disastrous totality. Goody's triumphant leap into Harry's inside
is the subject of the climactic stanza of the poem:

> She prayed, her withered hand uprearing,
> While Harry held her by the arm –
> "God! who art never out of hearing,

"O may he never more be warm!"
The cold, cold moon above her head,
Thus on her knees did Goody pray,
Young Harry heard what she had said,
And icy-cold he turned away.   (lines 97–104)[9]

The simple human story of the poem is that Harry becomes entangled with Goody; grasping her by the arm, he finds that he can no longer hold her life apart from his own, and her suffering becomes his. This story is repeated quietly and artfully in the loss of parallel between the half-stanzas.

This poem is thus quite plainly about power, and fits snugly within the interest in affecting others that grips the Preface. It depicts the space between selves in an active, socially charged way, and by doing so makes the extension of power between selves all the more important. But how does Goody do it? This question must occur to any reader of the poem who has not read the Preface, and it is a precise version of the questions about the charm of verse that create the Preface. All readers of the 1798 edition of the *Lyrical Ballads* would have been without the Preface, and the baffling refusal to name the exact agency by which Goody makes Harry cold would have looked like just that: a refusal. The blank spot where the "how" of Goody's power lies is to be filled in by the speculative and imaginative reader. Here is one such reader (Wordsworth's friend Robert Southey), speculating about this blank in 1798: "is the author certain that [the story] is *well-authenticated*? and does not such an assertion promote the popular superstition of witchcraft?"[10] That is, Southey thinks that Goody's power is the crude power of spells and charms. It could well be, with the poem as it stands alone, and so the edition of 1800 tries to forestall this reading with explanations about imagination, presented in the Preface:

I wished to draw attention to the truth, that the power of the human imagination is sufficient to produce such changes even in our physical nature as might almost appear miraculous. The truth is an important one; the fact (for it is a *fact*) a valuable illustration of it. And I have the satisfaction of knowing that it has been communicated to many hundreds of people who would never have heard of it, had it not been related in a Ballad, and in a more impressive meter than is usual in Ballads. (p. 150)

The reader who ascribes witchcraft to Goody understands that the poem is about power, but misunderstands the sort of power it depicts (or wants to depict).

The poem itself could easily have made the argument about imagination, but for Wordsworth this business is beyond the limits of poetry, and so he does it in prose. Wordsworth's reading of his poem gives power to the poet, and to utterance and feelings. This power is bound tightly within the poem, which Wordsworth hopes will have a certain sort of power. The poem contains a lesson and it disseminates that lesson through the power of its verse. In other words, power is doubled here, depicted (in Goody) and enacted, in a powerful poem. The distance Goody overcomes, when she bridges over the physical, social and psychological difference between herself and Harry, corresponds to the distance Wordsworth wishes to overcome between himself and his reader, the limits of the self. The nature of the power in the poem (Goody's power) is left curiously, willfully isolated, and, in typically Wordsworthian fashion, this willfulness makes for a flaw that creates (in turn) the interest of the poem. The anxiety that produces the prose addendum is an indication of the flaw within the poem, and yet Wordsworth refuses to correct the poem itself; he liked his poems to be problematic, and it is important to remember the pains he took to make them that way. His addition of prose is thus a version of the (pained) humility of the Preface: "the power of any art is limited." In keeping with the argument of previous chapters, I would modify this slightly: the power of Wordsworth's art is in his limitations. In "Goody Blake and Harry Gill," the limitations Wordsworth apparently finds in his dramatic ballad form mean that his poem can make no space for the prosaic interruptions of explanation, and so the poem must end by obscuring the point of its lesson in its telling of the story. The dramatic effect of this limitation is that, in the poem, the explanation for Goody's power rests precisely between the imaginatively poetic and the crudely magical. Goody, a person of limited means, overcomes her limitations through her curse; Wordsworth, in a pointed parallel, claims, hopes to overcome the limits of the self through imagination, the charming power of his poem. The prose/poem package repeats the rhythm I have ascribed to the Preface; the limitations of the poem give rise to anxious repetition in a different form. This happens by design: the rhythm of limitation (of the encounter with limits) followed by repetition is what he wants, or can't help having. Wordsworth's assertion that his ballad has circulated widely because of its form helps us to see that an important force behind this rhythm is a vexed but basically plain desire for success, for readers. He has a lesson to teach (about imagination) but this interactive and didactic ambition gets tangled with his strong and even perverse sense of the limitations of poetic form. The result is that the hopeful extension of power turns into a depiction of the extension of power, and the consequent isolation of the powerful poem must be breached or supplemented by an explanation of power. The "text" made up of the poem and its prose is a tense one: the poem claims the power to move past the limits of the self, but also loiters at that very border, anxiously refusing to assert, in plain terms, that poetry has that power.

Shortly after writing "Goody Blake and Harry Gill," Wordsworth began work on "Peter Bell," a poem which would occupy him, off and on, for the next twenty years. In its final form, it has a prose dedication (to Robert Southey, appropriately enough) that also describes the (prose) project of "Goody Blake and Harry Gill" very neatly:

The Poem of Peter Bell, as the prologue will show, was composed under a belief that the Imagination not only does not require for its exercise the intervention of supernatural agency, but that, though such agency be excluded, the faculty may be called forth as imperiously, and for kindred results of pleasure, by incidents within the compass of poetic probability, in the humblest departments of human life.[11]

The whole poem looks like a careful, even very careful correction of "Goody Blake and Harry Gill." "Peter Bell" attacks mystery from the beginning, and replaces it with careful explanation and careful reasonings. In reaction to the dramatic isolation that marks "Goody Blake and Harry Gill," Wordsworth multiplies his voice in "Peter Bell" so as to allow plenty of room for explanation. Wordsworth uses his plain prose voice in the dedication (the analog of the explanations of the Preface), and a versified yet plainly prosaic voice for the "Prologue," which repeats, in a strangely airy way, the message of the dedication. This voice is succeeded by the lyrical ballad voice of the story itself, the conduct and tone of which is very much like "Goody Blake and Harry Gill." If this poem has a lesson to impart, Wordsworth is leaving nothing to chance: he says it, and then says it again, and then again, in a series that goes from pure prose on one end (the dedication), through a middle form, to plain *Lyrical Ballads* verse on the other. One could add to this list the "prophetic tones" that Hazlitt heard Wordsworth read this poem with, though I am not sure where this feature would fit in.[12] The story is scrupulous too,

again looking like a lesson learned from "Goody Blake and Harry
Gill." "Peter Bell" is full of powers, but powers of the mind, and
mysterious sights that become clear. Wordsworth pulls the reader to
the end of part I by capably producing the expectation that Peter's
hardness of heart will call forth these powers, as Harry's hardness
did; at the end of part I we do not yet know (from the poem) that
these powers will be those of the mind. Our anticipated narrative
moment turns into gothic mockery as Wordsworth gives us a few
funny stanzas of the scary images which might be in the pool Peter is
peering into, among them a coffin, a shroud, imps, idols and demons;
the best is this wonderful gothic joke: "Is it a fiend that to a stake/Of
fire his desperate self is tethering?" (lines 551-2). Looking at this
catalogue of frights, Peter looks briefly like a gothic protagonist:

> He looks, he ponders, he looks again;
> He sees a motion – hears a groan;
> His eyes will burst – his heart will break –
> He gives a loud and frightful shriek,
> And drops, a senseless weight, as if his life were flown!
>
> (lines 571-5)

Here the poem is interrupted by the end of part I. We are left
hanging, in suspense, and the (narrative) pleasure of the interruption
parallels the power that has been exerted over us by the poet, in
bringing us to this moment. But as in "Hart-Leap Well," this is not
a power Wordsworth wants; or, at any rate, it is a power he wants to
mock, and so Peter revives and goes back to work, pulling out of the
water not an imp or an idol but the real body of a drowned man. We
expect Peter's eyes to be opened – and so they are, but they are
opened on the same old world. Since we are thirstily reading
(spellbound) as Peter faints at the end of part I, we are being chastised
along with him for mistaking the charms of verse for a crude and
otherworldly power. By pressing the reader up against the end of part
I, using the energies of the gothic narrative, Wordsworth recreates in
a purposeful way the stuttering that plagues him in the Preface. The
liminal (Hoggian) pleasures of the supernatural are mocked by
balancing them on the edge of the story. The reader is chastised for
straining at the bounds of "the humblest departments of human life"
by being repeatedly returned from the edge to the plain middle earth.
As Peter encounters one (imagined) supernatural admonishment
after another (ghostly calls, bloodstains on the road, the shaking

earth), he thinks that the boundary between worlds is being continually crossed; we are reflected back from the limit to the everyday world by our privileged knowledge of the everyday explanations.[13]

Reading "Peter Bell" we know, in a way that we did not know in "Goody Blake and Harry Gill," that further underground, below the bizarrely nocturnal miners, is Wordsworth himself, arranging a poetic and humble world around Peter's nasty self. The busily corrective Wordsworth wants "Peter Bell" to stay "within the compass of poetic probability," so as to illustrate the wonders of everyday life. In spite of his attentions, though, Wordsworth runs up against his limits again here, and I think the whole of "Peter Bell" is not nearly as plain as it claims. It wants to show that imagination is a plain sort of power, and that through the imagination sympathy and wisdom (truth), what the poet has, can reach inside a person and change them. The dedication, the Prologue and the poem all make this claim. Peter himself figures one sort of susceptible reader, whose unenlightened sensibility renders him susceptible to gothic charms, and that deluded or bad reader is the target of the poem's pedagogic purpose. Reading over the dedication again, in a different key, we can note that perhaps the more important of Wordsworth's claims is that poetry does not need the supernatural to be charming, to "imperiously" call forth the imaginations of readers and bind them in front of the book, the book the poet has written (in order to prove the point). The "kindred results of pleasure" are the hypothetical pleasures of the reader of the poem. Peter is a reader, reading a "poem," and his imagination is called forth: but he does not enjoy himself, oppressed as he is by Wordsworth's imagination. These two versions – imagination's effect on Peter, and the parallel but conjecturally powerful effect on the reader – are the embodiments of Wordsworth's poetic ambition and his worldly ambition, respectively. They are compressed confusedly together in "Peter Bell," giving the reader an interesting double presence. So thoroughly, so fastidiously does Wordsworth inset voice within voice, hoping to control the various poetic powers here, that the poem ends up in a curiously impotent isolation. "Goody Blake and Harry Gill," isolated from explanation, leaves the reader on the outside, which is both what is good about the poem and what clearly bothered Wordsworth about it. In "Peter Bell," Wordsworth includes the (bad) reader in the poem itself (he is Peter), hoping by this trick to control the perspective of the real, outside reader. It is a poem about the powers of the imagination: it hopes that this is the same thing as being a powerful, imaginative poem, but the reader, so plainly addressed, knows this is not true.

"Peter Bell" is not a bad poem; it is a funny, wry poem, and a sincere poem too; it has more of the zany energies of the lyrics of 1798 than the staid proprieties of its published date, 1819. It is, however, a failed poem: it cannot fulfill its impossible desire of including the whole poetic world inside itself. It fails at the limits of poetry. We sense Wordsworth's great sincerity and conviction when he depicts Peter's conversion as a visitation not from another world but from his own imagination. Peter may figure the bad or thirsty reader, but he also figures readers as Wordsworth wants them: he is reachable, as susceptible as Harry Gill. "Peter Bell" soothes Wordsworth's deepest anxiety – that the reader is unreachable – by conducting a polemic about the susceptibility of the imagination. Like the other writings I have been discussing, though, it does not explain and control poetic power but rather shows it, returning as the Preface does to the simple assertion of the inviolable inside of poetic pleasure. Since the description of the mechanism of pleasure (of susceptibility) is impossible, Wordsworth can only show Peter "reading," and through him figure the pleasure of the reader reading "Peter Bell." Though everything is directed at us, we are left utterly outside the poem because Wordsworth has already figured and depicted the reader inside the poem. The very attempt to reach out, to grab and control the reader's imagination (as Peter's is controlled) ends in isolating the poem even further. "Peter Bell" talks to itself. It does carefully correct for the flaw in "Goody Blake and Harry Gill," but the final lesson is still that the power of art is limited. Wordsworth's poem cannot with certainty pass over the limits of his own imagination and reach that of others; it can only depict that crossing. It is easy to imagine that fateful knowledge of this fact created Wordsworth's fascination with "Peter Bell"; he kept it by him for twenty years before publishing it, reading it in "prophetic tones" to people like Hazlitt. Those tones are one more supplement, one more location of a hopeful power.

The importance that the simple ambition for moved readers plays in Wordsworth's writing both peaks and disappears in the "Essay, Supplementary to the Preface," attached to the 1815 edition of poems.[14] It peaks in the exasperation and real anger that overwhelm the discussions of popularity, and disappears in the defensive formulation Wordsworth creates in order to protect himself from his own lack of popularity. As a whole, the "Essay" is entirely driven by reflections on popularity, reflections produced by the years of disappointment following the nearly non-existent sales of *Poetry in Two Volumes* (1807). Much of it is made up of a revisionary literary history, the point of which is to prove that all great writers have been unpopular. There is a desperation about the whole argument, and no wonder, since one of its tasks is to prove Shakespeare unpopular. Difficult enough; and when confronting the equally vexing case of Thomson, Wordsworth is driven to the limits of definitional argument. Witness this hair-splitting: "The case appears to bear strongly against us: – but we must distinguish between wonder and legitimate admiration" (p. 73). The hopelessness of arguments about the reader's pleasure is total in this essay, and frustration has turned this hopelessness into polemic. Having witnessed the effects of Scott's charms and spells, Wordsworth must defend himself against such readerly passion, in any way he can.

The beginning of the literary history in the "Essay" rehearses the anthropomorphic history familiar from previous chapters; I will put this aside and skip to the end. By the time he reaches the end Wordsworth arrives at a high modernist formulation we find perfectly familiar:

Wherever life and nature are described as operated upon by the creative or abstracting virtue of the imagination; wherever the instinctive wisdom of antiquity and her heroic passions uniting, in the heart of the poet, with the meditative wisdom of later ages, have produced that accord of sublimated humanity, which is at once a history of the remote past and a prophetic enunciation of the remotest future, *there*, the poet must reconcile himself for a season to few and scattered hearers. (p. 83)

By pronouncing truths which are both ancient history and the remote future, Wordsworth escapes the pressure of the present. We have seen this strategy before, in Walter Scott. The result here is the same, a release of the tension that provides the interest of the writing I have discussed so far. Through this defensive maneuver Wordsworth lets himself off of the sharp hook of impossibility that he so compellingly struggles on in the *Lyrical Ballads*. The paragraph that this passage comes from begins with the passage about popularity I referred to at the beginning of this chapter: "Away, then, with the senseless iteration of the word, *popular* ... " Wordsworth is still in the place of a potentially interesting Border poet, situated as he is between the life of the future and the death of the past. He relaxes here, though, and in a Scottian way evacuates the tension of this position by simply accepting it and refusing to struggle. This is an end point: worldly ambition disappears into a vague sense of literary history, and with it disappears the energy productive of poetry of quality.

Wordsworth's encounter with limits produces his repetition; as his ambition encounters the limits of poetic form, that form comes alive, nervously insisting and withdrawing; it also dies and needs to be supplemented by repetition. As he himself encounters his limits, the limits of his power, his ambition (his poetic project) dies, only to revive again in repetition. In the end, in Wordsworth, repetition is a complex and troubled figure for revival. The intensity of his poetic ambition ensures that the energies of revival penetrate his poetry entirely: this makes for poetry of great complexity and nearly demented energy. Focusing on repetition as the basic Wordsworthian figure and rhythm, I want to explore Wordsworthian complexity, and in doing so will redraw and re-present the energies of revival that constitute this book, for they are all gathered and put to work by Wordsworth's desperate but ultimately hopeless faith in repetition as expression instead of failure, life instead of death, revival instead of loss.

I have previously extended metaphors and descriptions of limits, the lines between different parts of the world, to the world of pastoral and revival that governed earlier chapters, and I want to reassert that extension here as a way of finding the promised complication of Wordsworth's poetry. The figure that presides over these limits or borders is that of the collector/editor, discerner of texts, and importer of literary material (MacPherson, Burns, Hogg and Scott all fit this description). This figure is familiar to us, in our self-consciously anthropological era, but in the Romantic period he was relatively new. Scott does much to define collecting as an activity, combining erudition (old-style antiquarianism) with the democratic urges of the modern field-worker. The idea of collecting is an interesting one, if we think of it as a new and mildly eccentric activity, and especially if we think of it as a literary activity, leg-work which produces books, like *The Minstrelsy of the Scottish Border*. As such, collecting is clearly related to, perhaps even grows out of, the traditions of loco-descriptive poetry. The landscape poet strolls out of his library and looks for the materials of verse outside, where he or she will find the stuff that will then be enlisted to support the moral and personal metaphorizing of the poem. Scott's "raids" into the Border country look very much like this stroll, where the receptive and active mind puts itself in the presence of inspiration with striking formality and artificiality. The collector, of course, finds not simply materials for writing verse (though he may find that too), but also verse itself, wild and flourishing. In both traditions literature and the physical world (actual places) work together as palimpsestic text. The collector's version of this interaction is especially concrete, since he brings back literature as a tourist might bring back an artifact or a botanist the dried specimen of a rare plant.

The collector's map is both a literal and figurative one, and the collector's task is double too. He must literally move, travel, so that he can encounter the literature he seeks; this travel coincides with a social descent, out of the higher realms where a ballad (say) is an artifact, to the lower reaches, where it is functioning culture. When Scott took Hogg with him on his raids, he took him both as a geographic and a social guide. The collector's work is to use himself as a point of contact between cultures. He returns bearing things which, when put into a book, will allow others to reproduce this encounter in the comfort of their homes. The activity of the collector could be thought of as bringing cultures closer together, and from a plainly informational point of view this is may be true. But the profit of his journey, its motivation, lies in the very distance; a book like Scott's *Minstrelsy* is interesting because it is foreign, or reproduces a culture which the reader would not encounter in other ways. The collector lives on the border between two cultures, and profits from passing over it; the economy of ballad-collecting is very much like other import-export relationships, which are most profitable when the objects traded are rare. In traversing the border, the collector defines it. He defines locality, verifies it, by virtue of denying it himself, by travelling and so defeating the exclusiveness of local identity. This is, of course, a truth made truism by the experience of modern anthropologists, and I have pursued the painful side of this paradox most pointedly in discussing MacPherson's border crossings. What I want to emphasize is the relationship of the collector's verse to the tradition of the poetry of places. What counts, what makes the collector's work interesting, is that it creates a strong sense of place; it draws borders around cultures, and in doing so allows the reading culture, the higher culture, to contemplate its own place and identity by placing it in the context of others. The items the collector brings back are texts uniquely identified with place; often by subject, as with the group of Border ballads associated with the river Yarrow, but always by their source: where they were "found." Border ballads are about the Borders, but they are about the Borders because they grew there, an indigenous, inherent product of a specific locality.

Scott's trips are founded in his extremely strong sense of locality, and especially in his sense of the magic fertility of the Borders. Fertile, in their wild beauty, but especially fertile in story and song. Long after Scott, folklorists thought of the Borders as the birthplace of the ballad, and though this thought is wrong, one can understand its appeal, for Scott's local sense endows Border glens with a special vitality. Of course, ballads themselves help to make the Borders look like the true source of ballads, since they are so interested in border states of all kinds, whether political (that between England and Scotland, for instance) or more personal; the border between life and death, or the delineation of a special, haunted place around which a border is drawn. As previous chapters have shown, a trip to Scotland during this time was always a poetic trip in general, but a trip to the Borders was a poetic trip in specific. The *Minstrelsy*, published in 1803, is full of highly local anecdote, the anecdote that Scott's readers would come to crave in his novels. In his presentation of "The Dowie Dens of Yarrow," for instance, Scott deploys a whole little Border world to ground the ballad in its place. He attributes the names of real people (of his "own" clan: the Scotts) to the characters in the ballad, and locates the site of the battle fought in the ballad:

It is a low muir, on the banks of the Yarrow, lying to the west of Yarrow Kirk. Two tall unhewn masses of stone are erected, about eighty yards from each other; and the least child, that can herd a cow, will tell the passenger that there lie the two lords that were killed in single combat.[15]

I have chosen this example with a purpose, since I will be talking about Wordsworth's "Yarrow Unvisited," but here I wish only to note that the reader who reads "The Dowie Dens" in Scott's book reads a text that could literally stub one's toe during a tour of the poetic braes of Yarrow. So Scott found it, "a very great favorite among the inhabitants of Ettrick Forest" (p. 303). "The Dowie Dens of Yarrow" literally lives on the banks of the Yarrow, and may be visited there.

Wordsworth, the great ambulatory poet, has much about him that can be placed in the category of the collector. His poems are frequently either attached specifically to a place, literally, or else revolve in their content around some special place. The earlier Wordsworth also likes to describe his peculiar selection of verse as having been in some ways "collected." His diction is the diction of "real men"; the incidents of his poems are often incidents from tours and walks, encounters, or thoughts about places and inscriptions. In the very early poetry, "An Evening Walk," for instance, these Wordsworthian typicalities are also dramatized as loco-descriptive poetry, where the poem follows the "I" of the poet as he roams the world. "An Evening Walk" also contains that famous, infamous encounter with the suffering female vagrant. As Alan Liu so convincingly argues, the poem literally stumbles over this woman, and only with effort recovers the posture of easy repose.[16] The quiet of the swan-song turns to horror on the pivot of place, the poet and the vagrant having (conjecturally) shared the same vista of peace.

Though she has been shorn of her context, this woman is a ballad character. In "An Evening Walk," she serves a largely eighteenth-century function: she provides a vehicle for general thoughts about social justice, political economy and the practical results of government policy. She is out of context, though, and so this encounter is not deeply local. Unattached, the female vagrant is swept up by the poem and put to peculiar and unstable use. The poem must turn, pass on, in order to move from the swans to the woman, but the turn happens only in the highly abstract space of poetic conduct. That is, there is no narrative eye to swivel, no story to work up to the woman; the poet turns only in his mind in order to discover her forcibly coincidental presence.

> Fair swan! by all a mother's joys caressed,
> Haply some wretch has eyed, and called thee blessed;
> Who faint, and beat by summer's breathless ray,
> Hath dragged her babes along this weary way... (lines 241–4)[17]

The poet of "An Evening Walk" does not collect her from her ballad context. She has already been collected, and she is merely put to use, exploited. The collector, as a conscious, self-conscious presence, is not here. By the time we reach *The Ruined Cottage* and the *Lyrical Ballads*, the collector and his activities (the travelling poet, and the story of travelling and locality) have become a primary focus of attention. I want to take "The Thorn" as the focus of my discussion of Wordsworth's collecting not only because there the collector is present in vivid detail, but also because the poem (tangentially) encounters the traditional ballad; understanding Wordsworth's encounter with rigid ballad form is crucial to understanding the energies of his poetic practice.

Both in matter and in form "The Thorn" looks like a cousin to the ballad. But is it *influenced* by the ballad? The purely factual side to this question hinges on Wordsworth the person's knowledge of the ballad we know as "The Cruel Mother."[18] Collected early on, near the beginning of the eighteenth century, this ballad contains the female sufferer in bare and pathetic form. It is impossible to know whether Wordsworth knew this ballad, though given where Wordsworth lived (the north) and the daily place the ballad had in culture, an affirmative answer seems the most likely. As Mary Jacobus has pointed out, the closer source, and one which Wordsworth certainly knew, is Bürger's ballad, translated in 1796 as "The Lass of Fair Wone" by William Taylor of Norwich, and published in the first issue of *The Monthly Magazine* in 1796.[19] The excitement that this issue caused in Wordsworth (and Southey, and Coleridge) is well known. The interest of this biographical facet need not end here; for Bürger had read Percy's *Reliques*, and had been deeply influenced by Herder's thoughts about British literature and its relationship to popular sources. Wordsworth, it should be remembered, bought his copy of Percy's *Reliques* in Germany in 1798, after he had written "The Thorn." Percy's collection does not contain "The Cruel Mother," but it does contain ballads from the same family, like "The Jew's Daughter" (sometimes called "Little Sir Hugh") and "Lord Thomas and Fair Ellenore." The presence of a thorn tree at the scene of child murder is traditional, traditional enough that one might call "The Cruel Mother" an example rather than a cause of this association. Behind all of this is the general atmosphere of northern traditional culture (northern European, that is) and so Bürger was drawing on tales and traditions that are demonstrably and securely linked to the same sources that are illustrated by Scottish traditional ballads. The irony of balladry's influence on Wordsworth at this point in his career is that it should be directed by the literary glitter of Bürger's "ballad" style; this is true for Scott, too, surprisingly enough. But the crucial difficulty for the literate, higher-class citizen in encountering traditional ballads is the encounter itself, and

Taylor's translations of Bürger provided a spectacular and arresting conduit for finding ballads, even though they represent a sort of collection three times removed from what we today call authenticity. "The Thorn"'s context is thus a vaguely specific one. Its interests, its materials, were floating free in contemporary culture; they had already been collected, and released into various environments.

But of course the poem is highly local, in several ways. It derives from a particular and peculiar biographical encounter between Wordsworth the person and a thorn, and it is also local in that strange and Wordsworthian way, obsessed with a specific spot, reading its story out of the literal feature of that spot. It has a dramatic narrator who looks so much like a ballad collector as to be nearly a parody, in his sensational encounters with the lower-class figure. If we think of the collector as having an interestingly energetic relationship to place and the demarcation of place, then "The Thorn"'s obsessive returnings, both physical and rhetorical, make it look like either a collected text or a poem about collection. I want to discuss this formal feature more thoroughly – the structure of the poem – as it relates to ballad structure and ballad interests; but to do so requires first a diversion into ballads themselves.

One of the attractions of ballads as objects of study is that formal features are significant in plain and clear ways. Ballads are divided into stanzas because they are sung to rounded tunes; the melodic material is one stanza long, and is repeated for each stanza. They often have refrains or refrain-like lines within the stanza because the tunes have two important melodic sections separated by two very similar, non-developmental sections. Bertrand Bronson, who was one of the first to emphasize clearly enough to scholars that ballads are songs, would call this rounded structure a lyric element: one which interrupts, and indeed impedes, the progress of the narrative which the ballad develops.[20] That this is true is entertainingly indicated by the way refrain ballads (like "The Cruel Mother") are printed in Child's great collection; the first stanza gives the full complement of lines, while subsequent stanzas include only the narrative lines, omitting the refrain. This is perfectly understandable – the lines are always the same, lexically speaking – but it does remove the text even further from its identity as song, which revels in repetitions of all kinds.

Two pleasures interact to produce the characteristic form of the ballad: the pleasure of the song, which caresses its melodic line repeatedly, letting listener and singer catch it and enjoy it, and the pleasure of the story, which follows the development of a linear and progressive narrative to its conclusion. These opposed forces accrete the ballad into stanzas that advance the story by units separated from each other by the pause (of the singer) between stanzas. But like the borders between countries, these spaces are connectors too, across which the story develops. The stanzal divisions are energetic, active ones. The ballad at once protects the pleasure of the song by giving each stanza a satisfying unity, and exploits the story to energetically underwrite the repetition of the melody with new and progressive content. The space between stanzas is traversed consciously, actively, reminding us of the division, but moving past it too.

The basic beauties of the ballad arise from this interaction. By "basic beauties" I mean those features so characteristic of the eighteenth-century ballad: incremental repetition and the technique called "leaping and lingering." To illustrate these beauties, take two stanzas from "Fair Margaret and Sweet William":

> I dreamed a dream, my dear lady;
> Such dreams are never good;
> I dreamed my bower was full of red swine,
> And my bride-bed full of blood.
>
> Such dreams, such dreams, my honoured lord,
> They never do prove good,
> To dream thy bower was full of swine,
> And thy bride-bed full of blood.[21]

William has just been visited by the spirit of a Martha Ray figure, a lover jilted for a higher-class bride. The delightfully oxymoronic term "incremental repetition" is illustrated by the symmetrical way this exchange is depicted, the way the extending stanza feels forced to mirror the structure of the original statement. These sorts of stanzas earn their oxymoronic description by moving on only by reaching backward to previous material. The song leaps to the next narrative snippet, moving over the stanzal boundary, but leaping with a look backward: back to the beginning of the melodic line, but also lingering over phrasing, producing a stanza with neighborly simi-larity but narrative difference. Individual lines do this too, as in the lingering on "I dream." The ballad feels the need to repeat "dream" (in this case) while telling the story of the dream, repeating phrasing in a way called out by song but unnecessary in straightforward narration. The ballad genius is a sticky one – it does not want to let go of things it likes. "Leaping and lingering" describes the way ballads tell their stories in general. They elide context, and focus on climaxes of various sorts: so they will linger on narrative moments and then leap quickly to the next, without much concern for interconnection and other narrative proprieties.

These are sophisticated techniques. Together, they produce the beautiful way ballads have of softly and even sadly lingering over the thing they are discussing, refusing, or at least seeming to refuse, for a while, the interests of story in favor of the beauties of phrase or tune. Ballads do move, telling their often brutal and fascinating stories, but they do it in a constantly hesitating way. The paradoxical net effect of these methods is that the often sensational-seeming stories of ballads are smoothed over, the whole thrown into a dreary and blurred light that tends to erase highs and lows of narrative interest. Thus it is that ballads, though bloodthirsty and violent, rarely seem exploitive in the gaudy way that popular printed literature frequently is. Instead, they are often deeply melancholy, even oppressively dark and sad, and this feeling is intensified by the even, lingering, elegiac nature of the ballad form. Elegiac because these stories linger over their material, sadly fixated by it, sacrificing the faster pleasures of pure narrative to develop the darker beauties of the interrupted narrative.

When we think of ballads as song, we are no longer tempted to describe their formal features as a sort of poetic simplicity or naiveté. But if the form is removed from the supporting medium of song, repetitions of this sort become distinctly odder. This oddity prompted Wordsworth to justify the structure of "The Thorn," which has distinct ballad features, in the famous note to the poem:

Now every man must know that an attempt is rarely made to communicate impassioned feelings without something of an accompanying consciousness of the inadequateness of our own powers, or the deficiencies of language. During such efforts there will be a craving in the mind, and as long as it is unsatisfied the Speaker will cling to the same words, or words of the same character.[22]

Readers have long been interested in the apparently well-thought-out but deeply confusing "theory" of repetition that the "Note" to "The Thorn" offers.[23] I will connect this fascinating defense of repetitive structure to my previous thoughts shortly; here I want only to note the appropriateness of Wordsworth's vocabulary. Ballads have an appetite for their own structures, and though instead of a craving in the mind we might call this appetite a craving in the ear, or in the heart, in any case craving seems a perfect word for the possible motives behind the curiously accretive structure of ballad texts.

Perfect, too, for describing, or creating, motives for the anxious, even demented ballad structures of "The Thorn." It has many instances of what we might call incremental repetition. Think of the relationship between these two stanzas:

> Now would you see this aged thorn,
> This pond and beauteous hill of moss,
> You must take care and chuse your time,
> the mountain when to cross.
> For oft there sits, between the heap
> That's like an infants grave in size,
> And that same pond of which I spoke,
> A woman in a scarlet cloak,
> And to herself she cries,
> "Oh misery! oh misery!
> Oh woe is me! oh misery!"
>
> At all times of the day and night
> This wretched woman thither goes,
> And she is known to every star,
> And every wind that blows;
> And there beside the thorn she sits
> When blue day-lights in the skies,
> And when the whirlwinds on the hill,
> or frosty air is keen and still,
> And to herself she cries,
> "Oh misery! oh misery!
> Oh woe is me! oh misery!"   (lines 56–77)

I have described the lack of any straightforward evidence of traditional ballad influence on "The Thorn" because in fact I wish to describe the ballad features of "The Thorn" as coincidental. Not lightly coincidental, but deeply coincidental: "The Thorn" looks like a ballad because it has similar interests, it has a similar craving. In a modification and intensification of the strategy of "Peter Bell," the lyric, interrupting elements in "The Thorn" might be thought of as ideologically or polemically motivated. They interrupt the sensational plot because Wordsworth wants to teach us a lesson about sensational plots, and to cure us of our addiction to "degraded German romances." The spectacular thing about "The Thorn," what makes it so interesting, is the way it enacts its own lessons by depicting the fixated reader, in the interaction between the narrator and his listener. The listener's first interruption produces an especially interesting version of ballad features:

> Now wherefore thus, by day and night,
> In rain, in tempest, and in snow,
> Thus to the dreary mountain top
> Does this poor woman go?
> And why sits she beside the thorn
> When the blue day lights in the sky,
> Or when the whirlwinds on the hill,
> Or frosty air is keen and still,
> And wherefore does she cry? –
> Oh wherefore? wherefore? tell me why
> Does she repeat that doleful cry? (lines 78–88)

Here the poem revolves around its own phrasing because the listener has become fascinated by the fascination of the narrator, who is fascinated by Martha Ray's fascination for the spot under the old thorn tree: the listener repeats these questions because Martha repeats her cry. The story of "The Thorn" gets entangled in its own borders, helplessly lingering about the spot where the story is contained. This poem intensifies the stickiness of ballad form until the poem moves not at all; it has a past (the story of Martha Ray; Bürger's ballads; or "The Cruel Mother"), but it has no future because it is detained in contemplating its own fixation. We expect that the poem will draw a line around Martha and her story, containing them, and then sell them to us in all their sensationalism (like Bürger's ballad); but instead it draws a line or border around the whole poem, the encounter and its description. It refuses to package Martha, and unexpectedly settles on her in the same way that she settles on her "mournful cry."

"The Thorn" also refuses to cross the border between this world and the next. This is not true of its sources; "The Lass of Fair Wone" is openly ghostly, and even the non-source, "The Cruel Mother" is what is sometimes called a "revenant" ballad. This is part of Wordsworth's program, of course, as I and others have already pointed out. Martha haunts her spot (in turn a figure for the baby's haunting of her) literally, returning forever to the source of her misery, and marking it with her cry. Martha does not return to her spot from another country, across a border; her returns take place in the same oddly gray world she and the narrator (and the listener) inhabit all the time, a world which is marked out, but never placed into context by the delineation of border. Her returns are like those of a moth to a lamp – she never goes elsewhere, and yet she seems always to be depicting a return of sorts.

She is, though, very much like a ghost since Wordsworth is making his anti-ghost statement while holding onto wailing haunts and other ghostly effects. "The Thorn" does not deny the existence of a border between worlds: it simply refuses to cross it, and in fact gathers energy from this refusal. It acknowledges the border, verifies it, but does not cross. And so "The Thorn" is a border poem (if not ballad), a poem caught and detained just as it is traversing its own borders, and it is also a poem about the collection of ballads, or at least about collection. Here the collector sallies into the country, out of his element (the sea), and finds something worth bringing back. "The Thorn" becomes a border poem, instead a poem which exploits borders, when the collector cannot return with his prize. He remains in the field, helplessly observing and unable to package and transport his story. This collector's encounter with the country subject is, like the formal encounters of ballad form, a sticky one. Martha is a ballad character, encountered in her milieu, and ripe for exploitation. In "An Evening Walk," the "I" stumbles across this figure, but then just walks away; this is what makes that poem's use of the figure so much more exploitive. In "The Thorn," the encounter never ends; the collector cannot return over the border to a land of clarity or objectivity. He is trapped in a border region where his material has value, certainly, but where he cannot seem to turn a clear profit on it. The narrator insists that the listener will have to go to the thorn himself, for what the narrator has with him is inadequate.

In precisely the same way, the story itself – the product of the collector's efforts – flutters on the border of becoming a ballad. The same craving for the material of the text that interrupts the traditional ballad's progress interrupts "The Thorn"; but this is a craving of the mind, not the ear, and the craving itself is depicted in the poem, as well as enacted by it. Lyric energy interrupts both the lyrical ballad and the ballad, turning them from strict narrative purpose in order to satisfy their respective cravings. But Wordsworth substitutes lyric purpose for lyric pleasure and in doing so makes the lyric interruption of narrative part of the subject of the poem. "The Thorn"'s insistent return to its subject matter is a meditative instead of a sensory one.

The narrator of "The Thorn" repeats his story to the exasperated listener in the same way that Martha can only repeat her cry. For identical reasons, he and Martha are caught up repeating themselves. Wordsworth justifies this as a subject of poetry in his note, part of which I have already quoted:

> Now every man must know that an attempt is rarely made to communicate impassioned feelings without something of an accompanying consciousness of the inadequateness of our own powers, or the deficiencies of language. During such efforts there will be a craving in the mind, and as long as it is unsatisfied the Speaker will cling to the same words, or words of the same character. There are also various other reasons why repetition and apparent tautology are frequently beauties of the highest kind. Among the chief of these reasons is the interest which the mind attaches to words, not only as symbols of the passion, but as *things*, active and efficient, which are of themselves part of the passion. And further, from a spirit of fondness, exultation, and gratitude, the mind luxuriates in the repetition of words which appear to successfully communicate its feelings. (p. 594)

Here Wordsworth describes repetition as his natural poetic mode. The repeater in this description is one with the charmed reader, who reads and rereads because he is caught in the circles of poetic magic. As in the Preface, this argument itself feels compelled to say things over; so that, in quick succession, we get arguments asserting that repetition is not tautology but craving, that words are things ("part of the passion") and that the mind "luxuriates" in repetition as a sign of successful communication. As in the Preface the need for argumentative completion drives Wordsworth to contradict himself: repetition comes both from the inadequacy of words (and the subsequent craving) and from the speaker's exultation in their adequacy, the source of luxuriation. This kind of argument is like the fixed movements of Martha Ray; Wordsworth both sticks to his subject and seems to be forever returning to it, going and staying at once. "Craving" perfectly describes the results of the sense of inadequacy that oppresses Wordsworth in general. Craving rises out of that gap between words and people (or between people) that only power can bridge. Delightfully, in the note to "The Thorn," Wordsworth depicts both falling short and crossing over as the source of his repetitions. "The Thorn"'s inclusion of voice is like "Peter Bell," but its intensity, and its generation of a prose rider makes it

much more like "Goody Blake and Harry Gill." "The Thorn" is
different from "Goody Blake and Harry Gill," though, because
concern over power turns into lyric practice in "The Thorn";
craving becomes a formal principle. "The Thorn" practices what its
story tells: it consumes itself, doubling back, repeating, incapable of
advancing, because its story cannot tell itself.

Wordsworth's repetitive description of "The Thorn"'s repetitions
produces oxymoron as explanation. Wordsworth is of course quite
right to offer oxymoron to us. Oxymoron (listening to the singer
singing alone) governs the world of collection, and it also describes
"The Thorn" very accurately. Wordsworth luxuriates in the success
with which the repetition of "Oh misery!" communicates the
inadequacy of that phrase in painting the depths of Martha's
torment. Repetition appears as a way of expressing perpetual
shortfall. Returning to my ballad descriptions, repetition is (to
Wordsworth) elegiac at its source: elegy splits repetition off from
tautology by noting that loss always intervenes, between instances, to
make for difference. Words return to sing the loss of their own powers.
Each new instance contains within itself the admission that it needed
to appear to compensate for the hollowness left after the last. Craving
(successfully) describes the failure that keeps repetition from being
literal repeating. Words rebound from their limits, and so return,
only to rebound again. Martha's story is about loss, its perpetual
reenactment, and it takes as it's expressive mode perpetual reenactment. In the same way that ballads leave a stanza behind with a sense
of regret, and so leave by looking back, "The Thorn" leaves Martha
at her spot only by admitting that returning to the spot is the only
way to carry the story away. This is powerful poetry, an extraordinary binding of tension with strength.[24]

In his review of 1798 Southey complained of "The Thorn" that
any attempt to imitate tiresome loquacity inevitably becomes
tiresome loquacity itself. Wordsworth should have taken comfort in
this complaint, for it neatly sums up the self-referring, self-constricting
project the poem involves. Repetition (always) implies borders, and
depicts, through an inability to move over it, a limit to the material
that repeats. The largest structure of this sort in the Wordsworthian
canon is the shape of his poetic career itself. As readers have long
noted, the tiresome loquacity of the later Wordsworth, so plain in his
tone, so repetitive in his sentiment, does much to dramatize the
powers of the early, fixated, fascinatingly, untautologically repetitive

Wordsworth. His career is elegiac in structure, dramatizing loss, indicating loss by singing after the loss of power. Shelley read his career in this way, after the crucial year of 1815:

> In honoured poverty thy voice did weave
> Songs consecrate to truth and liberty, –
> Deserting these, thou leavest me to grieve,
> thus having been, that thou shouldst cease to be.[25]

So I too have already quickly interpreted Wordsworth's career, in reading over the anxieties and denials of the "Essay, Supplementary." There repetition is denied its vitality by a compensatory insistence on maturation, progress, and a concomitant insistence that the progress of literary and personal history does not necessarily entail loss. In 1815, Wordsworth insists that the endless repetitions of a (future) history will bring a progress of taste and a rise in reputation. He loses his sense of the elegiac energies of repetition. As he does this, the limits of power and of mortality are pushed back out of sight by the simple assertion of life. The encounter of life and death is the site of poetry; when Wordsworth denies or vitiates this encounter his poetry dies, and he begins to simply repeat. My larger point, though, is that this structure of repetition and loss is itself a Wordsworthian structure, and that our attraction to the great Anti-Climax is that it allows us to read over yet another tense and interesting poem, made from the structure of his life. My purpose in reading this larger poem is to find in its depiction of lapse the difference between "revival" in its easy form (as represented by Walter Scott, who will himself appear) and revival in its energized and deeply responsible Wordsworthian form. The movement from elegiac repetition to simple repetition is visible in Wordsworth's changing poetic practice, and the best examples for illustration are the curious poems about the Yarrow, along with their traditional ballad companions.

1803 not only saw the publication of Walter Scott's *Minstrelsy of the Scottish Border*, but also the first meeting of Wordsworth and Scott. In fact, it was in Scott's company that Dorothy and William did not visit the Yarrow, a river located in the Scottish Borders, in Ettrick Forest, at the tail end of their Scottish tour in the fall of that year, and so generated the subject of "Yarrow Unvisited." Since Scott was fresh from his Border ballad project, and deep in the composition of his first successful long poem, *The Lay of the Last Minstrel* (which is set in the

Borders, near the Yarrow), visiting the Borders with Scott was a poetic event. He recited much of the *Lay* to them during their brief visit, and no doubt would have recited the traditional poetry of the Yarrow if given the chance. The publication of "The Dowie Dens of Yarrow," in the *Minstrelsy*, by the way, marks the first publication of a full-length, traditional Yarrow ballad. "Yarrow Unvisited" itself recalls and refers to an imitation of the Yarrow ballads, composed in the mid-eighteenth century by William Hamilton of Bangour, called "The Braes of Yarrow." This strikingly beautiful poem was published in Percy's *Reliques of Ancient Poetry*, where Percy describes it as written "in the ancient Scots manner."

Wordsworth's poem and the Yarrow ballads express both their unity and their elegiac fixity through their interest in (and the difficulty of) rhyming on the word "Yarrow." The ballads exacerbate the difficulty by returning constantly to the word "Yarrow"; as far as I can tell, this is a relatively (or even extremely) rare ballad feature. The version that appeared in the *Minstrelsy*, for instance, contains only two stanzas (out of seventeen) that do not rhyme on Yarrow, and one of those is a fastidious stanza written by Scott himself. These ballads make their song a difficult one by insisting so on Yarrow, but they make beautiful profit from this challenge. They mobilize a relatively small group of words to do the work: narrow, thorough (a version of "through" that was archaic and poetic in 1800), marrow, tomorrow. This group helps define the story; "narrow," for instance, almost always refers to the straights of the grave, and "thorough" describes the stabbing, with sword or spear, that is the narrative climax. But the best rhyme, the favorite, is on the word "sorrow." In Scott's version, a third of the Yarrow rhymes are on "sorrow," including four of the last five. "Sorrow" makes a good rhyme, of course, because the story of the ballads is so sad. All of the poems in the Yarrow family are laments. Their story, whose climax is the leaving of a corpse on the banks of the Yarrow, turns around and around the Yarrow as it is consecrated by this event. The song itself, in its form, turns around and around the word "Yarrow" and the sorrow now fixed there. In other words, these poems demonstrate an unusually tight lyric construction; they demonstrate a beautiful unity of content and form. They draw an unusually tight formal circle around themselves, but the story itself welcomes this binding because it tells, in turn, of a tight, "Thorn"-like circle of emotion that constricts the heroine's life to the one haunted spot of her lover's death. I have no doubt that this constriction, expressing itself as it does in a circling repetition, is what caught Wordsworth's eye. As a piece of illustration, here is the end of Scott's version, very likely the traditional source that Wordsworth knew:

> As she sped down yon high hill,
> She gaed wi' dole and sorrow,
> And in the den she spyed ten slain men
> On the dowie banks of Yarrow
>
> She kissed his cheek, she kaim'd his hair,
> She searched his wounds all thorough;
> She kissed them, till her lips grew red,
> On the dowie houms of Yarrow.
>
> "Now, haud your tongue, my daughter dear!
> For a' this breeds but sorrow;
> I'll wed ye to a better lord
> Than him you lost on Yarrow."
>
> "O haud your tongue, my father dear!
> Ye mind me but of sorrow;
> A fairer rose did never bloom
> Than now lies cropped on Yarrow."[26]

The lamenting strain in this poetic material, the material that this family of poems shares, is very strong. Even "Leader Haughs," the most cosmopolitan member of the family, cannot tell its story without sounding the elegiac note. This poem (which Wordsworth describes as the source of "Yarrow Unvisited"'s meter)[27] was written by a man named Crawford, who was a member of Allan Ramsay's Edinburgh song-circle. It is largely a set descriptive piece; but its description is curiously darkened by the injection of a quick story about a hunted rabbit that dies on the Yarrow. Its final stanza expands the elegiac note, in a farewell to Border culture that sounds the "sorrow-Yarrow" chime as its last rhyme:

> But minstrel Burn cannot asswage
> His grief, while life endureth,
> To see the changes of his age,
> That fleeting time procureth;
> For mony a place stands in hard case,
> Where blyth fowk kend nae sorrow,
> With Homes that dwelt on Leader side,
> And Scots that dwelt on Yarrow.

Scott loved these lines, and was apparently in the habit of reciting them when visiting the Yarrow. Hamilton's Yarrow imitation, mentioned earlier, even intensifies the repetitive nature of the material. He retains the high proportion of Yarrow rhymes, and a high proportion, in turn, of "Yarrow-sorrow" rhymes. He also adds a unique and curious line to the beginning of each stanza. Every stanza has a repetitive first line, built along the lines of this one: "Wash, O wash his wounds, his wounds in tears."[28] Here pure sadness trips up the conduct even of a line; Wordsworth's word, craving, neatly characterizes the force behind this strangely halting rhythm.

The Yarrow ballads appear often as antiquarian's imitations and sophisticated derivatives long before the era of the ballad revival because their fixations make them unusually satisfying collectibles. In them the collector gets aggressively, highly local texts. He can get his text by going to an especially poetic place (remember Scott's note, which dwells on the topography and history of the Yarrow). Because the poems thus collected also themselves dwell on the place, the collector's trip is a sentimental one, re-creating the sad journey the heroine takes to collect her lover's corpse. This coincidence of story and form and collection creates a sort of rapture that is easy to see in Scott, or in the beautiful re-creation of Hamilton of Bangour. When printed, this effect is made generally available. The educated, non-travelling reader can sorrowfully linger over the story while also reflecting on, savoring, the delicious locality of the text, its Border flavor, since the poems produce the whole package of emotion within themselves. Speaking plainly, one could say of these texts that they travel well. To the reader of the collected texts, the border that the poems draw around Yarrow looks like an actual border, which lays between that reader and the primitive poet and his country location, between (say) Edinburgh and Ettrick forest or England and Scotland, and which the reader has the pleasure of traversing. The constriction of these poems has much in common with that of "The Thorn," but with crucial difference. "The Thorn" is uncollectible; by including the collector within it, its immobility is complete. The reader cannot gather Martha up, because another reader (the narrator) has already done so, though he is having trouble offering her to us. The Yarrow ballads, so clearly packaged, have just the opposite effect. The editor/collector may preface his poem with the details of its finding, but since that voice is outside of the poem, we, the readers, can ventriloquize it, and substitute our own.

Such is the family of texts that Wordsworth refers to in the heading attached to his poem. The title runs:

> Yarrow Unvisited
> (See the various poems the scene of which is laid upon the Banks of Yarrow; in particular, the exquisite ballad of Hamilton, beginning
> Busk ye, busk ye my bonny bonny bride
> Busk ye, busk ye my winsome marrow! –)

The poem itself begins with a list of places visited on the real, biographical tour of Dorothy and William (and Coleridge, for a while) in 1803. The "winsome marrow" ("marrow" is a Scottish word for loved one or spouse) of the poem proposes that the Yarrow should be added to that list. On the real tour, so self-consciously a tour in search of inspiration, this addition would have made perfect sense, and was in fact abandoned only because of a lack of time. The speaker in the poem responds with interesting vehemence to this proposal:

> "Let Yarrow folk, *frae* Selkirk Town,
> Who have been buying, selling,
> Go back to Yarrow, 'tis their own,
> Each maiden to her dwelling!" (lines 9–12)

"Frae," marked out by the italics, is included as a mark of Scottish locality, and furthers the half-mocking tone of the speaker. By the middle of the poem, this speaker is denying the Yarrow its delicious poignancy:

> "What's Yarrow but a river bare
> That glides the dark hills under?
> There are a thousand such elsewhere
> As worthy of your wonder." (lines 25–8)

Denied its poetic context, the place of the Yarrow becomes just a place, unbordered, unmarked. The "winsome marrow" silently objects:

> – Strange words they seemed of slight and scorn;
> My true-love sighed for sorrow;
> And looked me in the face, to think
> I thus could speak of Yarrow! (lines 29–32)

Here the "sorrow" rhyme is still elegiac, but the corpse mourned is now a curiously textual one, since the loss is not only a poetic visit to the Yarrow but also the poetic spirit that the speaker denies.

At this point the speaker abruptly changes direction, returning Yarrow's attributes, and claiming that not seeing it is the best way to enjoy it:

> "Oh! green," said I, "are Yarrow's Holms,
> And sweet is Yarrow flowing!
> Fair hangs the apple frae the rock,
> But we will leave it growing."   (lines 33–6)

"Holms" is a Scottish word from Scott's "Dowie Dens" and from "Leader Haughs"; the "frae" here, not italicized, is part of a sentence essentially quoted from Hamilton's imitation. This stanza returns not only beauty to the Yarrow but also specifically poetic beauties. The strange and unexplained tension between the two postures the speaker takes up is what makes this a lyrical ballad, Wordsworth's personal and especially tense genre. The contrast between the two halves of the poem, set up by the interruption of the winsome marrow, illustrates the unreality of the poetic pleasures of the Yarrow. The first part is defensive panic (worry that reality will destroy poetry) and the second part an artificial sort of rationalization. There is thus a quiet fun in the artificiality of the second, an irony that points out, quietly, the artificiality of collected pleasures.

In addition, though, this poem is haunted by the haunting poems it calls up. In the same way that the edge of the first part makes the second look overly artificial, the dark shadow of the Yarrow ballads makes the ease of the last part look overly easy. In all Yarrow poems, to go to the Yarrow is to die, and this sense tugs at the bright affirmation of imagination in the last stanzas of "Yarrow Unvisited." For instance, it makes the turn the "sorrow" rhyme takes look less convincing:

> "Should life be dull, and spirits low,
> 'Twill soothe us in our sorrow
> That earth has something left to show,
> The bonny Holms of Yarrow!"   (lines 61–4)

Or, at any rate, it makes this rhyme look like the poem as a whole, less like affirmation than defense from the worry that visiting a place marked by the imagination will mean the death of imagination.

The sharp edge of the Yarrow stories is that their heroine refuses compensation, refuses to be consoled. The ballads stay fixed in their sorrow. What makes "Yarrow Unvisited" so interesting is that we are pointedly shown a speaker refusing to acknowledge this fact. That is, we are asked by Wordsworth (through the medium of his headnote) to see the tension in the poem as an anxious sort of tension, a denial. The speaker in "Yarrow Unvisited" is trying overly hard not to see the bodies strewn on the banks of Yarrow (in the ballads there are often ten or eleven of them), going first in one direction and then in the other, talking overly loudly all the way. And so a poem that presents itself as extremely plain and direct in its speech turns into a sophisticated poem about what we might call an ethics and aesthetics of collection. Because it so pointedly refuses to see the deadly nature of its poetic spot, "Yarrow Unvisited" hones the sharp edge of the Yarrow elegies. It asks us to square our savoring of the Yarrow poetry with the painful story the Yarrow poetry tells; we are asked to square the idealized Yarrow with Yarrow stream and Ettrick inhabitants, singers of sad songs. Like "The Thorn" and "We Are Seven," this poem suggests that what we are after in collecting is a sort of corpse, the killed and pinned natural specimen. Like those two poems, it does so by being a disturbed poem, by depicting an artificial surface disturbed by buried and denied energies. And as in those two poems, the spot in question is a source of both imaginative life and death, so that the speaker both wants to go there and wants to get away. "Yarrow Unvisited" does not accomplish its task by depicting a traumatized collector, as "The Thorn" (and, to a lesser extent, "We Are Seven") does. It instead depicts a speaker who cannot face the possibility of trauma. The resistance of the speaker to going over the border comes from a fear of getting caught in an impossible economy, like that of "The Thorn." The solution of "Yarrow Unvisited" allows for the retention of poetic magic, the magic of the spot and its verse; the lyrical-ballad drama of the poem, its irony, acknowledges the artificiality of this solution. The speaker installs himself between two extremes. On the one side is dangerous capture by the elegiac spot; on the other is an equally frightening escape, where the energy of the Yarrow poetry leaks away, leaving the speaker with only loss. The drama of the poem keeps these two sides in tension.

In "Yarrow Unvisited," Wordsworth's lyric sensitivity irritates the simple pleasures of visiting the Yarrow and mourning over the

Yarrow poetry by keeping him aware of the corpses scattered about on the riverbank. Wordsworth's interaction with the ballad is always, I think, productive of disturbed verse. He is highly sensitive to the way ballads turn back on themselves as they tell their stories, and he connects this turning to their subjects; here, the elegiac singing of place. Unlike Scott, and especially unlike MacPherson, he cannot easily savor these elegies. For Wordsworth, the beauty of the songs is connected tightly to their origin and their violent subjects, dark energies that he reminds us of. The ballads present this energy so plainly that we might overlook it in recollection. For instance, Scott's primary version, which he obtained from James Hogg, has the heroine not only kissing her lover's wounds but drinking his blood. Her trip to Yarrow is not mourning posture, a picturesque scene, but rather a raw and fierce fixation on her loss; she is like Martha Ray, only more articulate. Such scenery is hardly subsumable into the quiet tourist's vision of "the bonny Holms of Yarrow" at the end of "Yarrow Unvisited." Indeed, such scenery is hardly subsumable in any vision of human life; it is an extreme of suffering that few forms other than the ballad dare to reach for with sincerity. Wordsworth, along with many sophisticated readers of the period, remembers and loves such moments, but Wordsworth works hard, in many places, to understand and rationalize his enjoyment. He knows that it comes at some expense of spirit. "Yarrow Unvisited" names two sources of expense; the first comes in pursuit of the heroine in the story, captured in endless sorrow; the second in our observation of the country inhabitant, turned from spontaneous, unheard singer into recorded and picturesque country singer, object of the tourist's interest.

"Lyric sensitivity" is another expression of what, especially in reference to Burns, I have called poetic integrity. It is the opposite of MacPherson's ruthless poetic sense. MacPherson, the perfect picture of the imperial and thoughtless collector, celebrates melancholy pleasures like those of overhearing the cries of Martha Ray, or the pain of the heroine of the Yarrow ballads. This celebration is enacted by crossing easily over the borders of culture and geography and language, and by slipping carelessly past the limits of form. In their drooping focus on "Yarrow," Wordsworth's poem and the ballads it derives from reinforce the lesson that form is a deep matter, and that poetry of high integrity derives from a relentless recognition of this fact. Their beauty is the result of their limitations, their refusal to blind themselves to the limits of human life and the exactly parallel limits of poetic form. Instead of crossing the border, such poems encounter their limits and turn around in contemplation of those limits.

There is no ease in Wordsworth's good poems; that is the sign of their quality. The fact that poems like "The Thorn" and "Yarrow Unvisited" are so disturbed, though, reflects the fact that Wordsworth is not a singer of ballads. He is a literate poet: he has read his Ossian, he is somewhat distracted by the beauty of the Yarrow ballads. His poems poise themselves between collection and a beautiful isolation. Through this poise they can be both Romantic poems of revival, communicating simplicity to the jaded, and also poems of integrity, refusing to claim that the unheard voice can be overheard. In Wordsworth the buried coin of the early unburdened singer is left buried; we know of it by the disturbances it causes in the world above. Simple "honesty" is not available to Wordsworth; simple "expression" is not available to any poet. Given his integrity, it is not possible that he could simply visit the Yarrow and carry his poem away. To get there, borders must be crossed, and the painfully sensitive early Wordsworth cannot do it. He knows the limits of his art. In the case of "Yarrow Unvisited," these limits are quite specific, and made the plain subject of the poem. The disturbed solution to the lyric problem (how to sing of this spot and also leave it unviolated?) is to portray the collector and also the impossibility of his project. Wordsworth's use of disturbed lyric as a way of finding expression is as much a choice as song was for Burns. It is natural to him. That "natural" means here a combination of cultural pressure, personal need and lyric form does not empty out that word; such is the nature of art as I have depicted it.

Scott's unhewn stones notwithstanding, Wordsworth need not have feared seeing any dead bodies on the banks of the Yarrow. His fears, we might say, are all in his imagination. Scott is never afraid of dead bodies anyway, never haunted by spirits, in the true antiquarian spirit. Exhumation is his business. Wordsworth eventually did go to see the Yarrow in the company of James Hogg, and once again, much later, in the company of Scott himself. I promised that investigating the Yarrow poems would illustrate the deep responsibility of the early Wordsworth's enactment of revival, and "Yarrow Unvisited" presents the responsible side. The easy side appears in the two poems that are produced by the two visits ("Yarrow Visited" and "Yarrow

Revisited"), poems quite appropriately presided over by the genius of Scott. It surpises me that Wordsworth wrote these two poems at all; "Yarrow Unvisited" depends, in many ways, on their non-existence, or upon our ignoring their existence. Wordsworth knows this too. About "Yarrow Visited" he wrote (in a letter to R. P. Gillies):

Second parts, if much inferior to the first are always disgusting, and as I had succeeded in "Yarrow Unvisited," I was anxious that there should be no falling off; but that was unavoidable, perhaps, from the subject, as imagination almost always transcends reality.[29]

In Wordsworth's early poetic logic, as I have said, there is no repetition without loss; so, in essence, formal repetition is impossible because things are never completely said anyway. The speaker in "Yarrow Unvisited" has fearful knowledge of this fact, and resists going to the Yarrow for fear of being caught there (and, I suppose, for fear of the opposite: of not being caught at all). That is the fun of the poem, the tension that justifies it. "Yarrow Visited" is not an exciting or energetic poem, but neither is it a stupid poem, so that it knows what has to have happened in order for it to come into being:

> And is this – Yarrow? – *This* the Stream
> Of which my fancy cherished,
> So faithfully, a waking dream?
> An image that hath perished!
> O that some Minstrels harp were near,
> To utter notes of gladness,
> And chase this silence from the air,
> That fills my heart with sadness!   (lines 1–8)[30]

The "Minstrel " referred to is Scott, the notes of gladness *The Lay of the Last Minstrel*. Scott's presence helps Wordsworth make his plain way out of possible total loss, beginning in the next line:

> Yet why? – a silvery current flows
> With uncontrolled meanderings;
> Nor have these eyes by greener hills
> Been soothed, in all my wanderings.   (lines 9–12)

This poem does not burst out of the magical circle of constriction that creates great Wordsworthian lyric; it simply does not sense limits. It is unbordered, unmarked, and so travel to the Yarrow is possible. Why shouldn't it be? There is nothing to fear, no chasm of imagination to cross. We see the cruel irony as Wordsworth becomes the tourist so subtly mocked in "Yarrow Unvisited":

> Where was it that the famous Flower
> Of Yarrow Vale lay bleeding?
> His bed perchance was yon smooth mound
> On which the herd is feeding...
> (lines 25–8)

As this poem evaporates lyric constriction, it loses the force of the "Yarrow-sorrow" rhyme, which sounds only twice; in fact, the poem rhymes on Yarrow only these two times. And why shouldn't this be true? Why circle uselessly about "Yarrow" when any other rhyme will do? The last rhyme is one of the two Yarrow rhymes, and it tries to do its plain work:

> The vapours linger round the Heights,
> They melt, and soon must vanish;
> One hour is theirs, nor more is mine –
> Sad thought, which I would banish,
> But that I know, where'er I go,
> Thy genuine image, Yarrow!
> Will dwell with me – to heighten joy,
> And cheer my mind in sorrow.
> (lines 81–8)

The clear chime of the "vanish-banish" rhyme is almost Mac-Phersonesque in its blithe sadness, and the final quatrain is just as untroubled. Its sentiment is unobjectionable; the speaker, who sounds like Wordsworth the person, has no objection to make. All of the bizarre worries of the early lyric mode vanish here, and "genuine image" becomes a possible category. The Yarrow can be taken along with the traveller; communication has been successful, the Yarrow has been visited. So the last rhyme inverts the classic Yarrow form (by putting Yarrow first, sorrow second) and also inverts the Yarrow elegy. "Yarrow Visited" claims confidence in compensation; if the Yarrow heroine could feel this way, she could forget her lost lover and marry the suitors who cluster about her.

In this capturing of the Yarrow, a simple, general revival becomes possible (another Yarrow poem can be written, for instance) when Wordsworth's dire sense of limitation lapses. As limits evaporate, repetition as a specific formal element vanishes (the "Yarrow-sorrow" rhyme disappears), since Wordsworth's tense repetitions mask an obsessive fear of language's limitations. In the place of Wordsworthian repetition a plainer, unelegiac sort appears, the sort that "Yarrow Visited" as a whole embodies; it is best described as revision, the great task of the older Wordsworth. In the revisionary world, things can be done again, said again, and they can be just the same; in this world, repetition can be tautology. Things can actually happen again; no loss intervenes. The memory of the Yarrow can be called up again and again, and can compensate for sorrow again and again. This is revival in its easiest form, revival without loss and anxiety, compensation without trouble. This world (where tautology is possible) is a less interesting world than that of the early Wordsworth, but it is also a less painful world, since genuine images exist there, and things can be accomplished, obtained, possessed, and enjoyed. It is the mature, later poet's world. In this world loss can be compensated, and so we get the bright, pale affirmation of the last stanza of "Yarrow Visited." This poem is not a bad poem, in itself, but it does not have the formal tightness of better (earlier) Wordsworth poems; this is parallel to its nearly total loss of tension and energy. As people we may or may not deplore this movement, but as readers of poetry we must at least note it as a loss in itself. Wordsworth's art is in his limitations.

As Wordsworth the poet trips over the borders of language's powers, he repeats himself and disturbs his lyric as he stumbles. In "Yarrow Visited" Wordsworth is no longer off-balance, and so that poem does not stumble at all. Critics, with their large view, have been interested in this lapsing of tension, the great anti-climax, because in itself it indicates a larger pattern, which is a stumble itself, and repeats the earlier tension. "Yarrow Visited" is the poetic equivalent of the endpoint of the "Essay, Supplementary." The interest of both of these endpoints is that they repeat – in a Wordsworthian way – the energy of limitation they so pointedly let go of. They show the limit of Wordsworth's powers, and they define the limits of his art. The result is that, when taken together with "Yarrow Unvisited" and viewed from on high, "Yarrow Visited" is (as I have said) ironically part of a successful and interestingly Wordsworthian poem, where the poetics of repetition are hard at work. In this larger poem, the repetition of "Yarrow Visited" is not tautology; its presence, Wordsworth's desire to say it again, marks loss, the loss of lyric vitality, lyric intensity, lyric importance. If "The Recluse" exists, it is at this level; Wordsworth's life is his longest poem, and includes all the others. Wordsworth himself, who loves elegies and epitaphs, clues us into this larger, sad poem: "I was anxious that there should be no falling off; but that was unavoidable ... " We can give him credit for this sad, keen self-appraisal, just as we can give him credit for continuing to include his youthful, anxious lyrics in the collections of his staid middle and old age.

Having survived, in some sense, the return to Yarrow, Wordsworth sees no reason why he shouldn't do it again, and so writes "Yarrow Revisited." In this poem Scott's presence grows, and the loud insistence on compensation grows too:

> And what, for this frail world, were all
> That mortals do or suffer,
> Did no responsive harp, no pen,
> Memorial tribute offer?
> Yea, what were mighty Nature's self?
> Her features, could they win us,
> Unhelped by the poetic voice
> That hourly speaks within us?
>
> Nor deem that localised Romance
> Plays false with our affections;
> Unsanctifies our tears – made sport
> For fanciful dejections:
> Ah, no! the visions of the past
> Sustain the heart in feeling
> Life as she is – our changeful Life,
> With friends and kindred dealing.   (lines 181–96)[31]

I feel cheap in scraping at the elderly calm of this sort of verse, and it would be stupidly superior to devalue the affection for Scott that this poem quietly asserts. But Wordsworth himself, through the drama of the "Yarrow" series, has produced the itch that the critic must scratch. We long for the charged energies of the unvisited Yarrow; we look back to the Wordsworth that would read over *The Lay of the Last Minstrel* with dismay, even boredom. As usual, the prosing Wordsworth disturbs things with a wonderful addendum (in a Fenwick note: perhaps I should say the shadow of the prosing Wordsworth). It seems to refer quite specifically to the second of the stanzas that I quote above:

On Tuesday morning Sir Walter Scott accompanied us and most of the party to Newark Castle on the Yarrow. When we alighted from the carriages he walked pretty stoutly, and had great pleasure in revisiting these his favorite haunts. Of that excursion the verses "Yarrow Revisited" are a memorial. Notwithstanding the romance that pervades Sir W's works and attaches to many of his habits, there is too much pressure of fact for these verses to harmonise as I could wish with the two preceding poems.[32]

The power that the poem attributes so easily to poetry is troubled here; "fanciful objections," which "Yarrow Revisited" insists sustain the heart, fade under pressure from fact and from history. Wordsworth knows this, but his poem sings loudly in the face of this fact. It should, of course; how could Wordsworth give these verses to the sick Sir Walter if they did not in some way encourage him, and tell of inevitable recovery? Yet the life of Wordsworth's lyrics is the dark inevitability of loss, of falling off, of failure. As I have said, we can feel bad, as critics, that we are so eager, like Shelley, to kill off the older Wordsworth so that we can sing elegies over his younger self. Yet Wordsworth invites us to do so, and so we must. Saying it again defines Wordsworth's project, his poetics; the fade of the echo that sounds down the Yarrow is a sad fact, yet it is one of the ways that we find our way to the original sound.

The disturbed craziness of Wordsworth's honesty is in keeping with the intensity of the ballad, the genre that stands behind the poems I have been discussing. As a way of concluding, I want to demonstrate the usefulness of the context I have developed from and applied to Wordsworth by reading a less crazy poem, and in particular a poem over which the ballad does not, at least not explicitly, brood. The poem we call "Tintern Abbey" has long been taken as an example of Wordsworth's high lyric accomplishment, and this feeling about it is supported by its strong blank verse, the very opposite of ballad energy. Still, the full title should clue us in to the fact that we are still haunting the perilous borders of Wordsworth's genius: "Lines Written a Few Miles Above Tintern Abbey; On Revisiting the Banks of the Wye During a Tour, July 13, 1798." All of the various kinds of information that this title gives us, and its status, has been extensively discussed of late, as a part of the strong historicized and contextualized readings that have characterized recent interest in Wordsworth. These readings have demystified "Tintern Abbey" quite thoroughly, and in the best instances have written mystification into the poem as part of an impassioned poetic practice.[33] Since personal and historical motive, in a sense very close to my sense, has been thus reattached to the poem, I will not work any revelation in discovering it there. Rather I want to read this most reread of poems to show that it demonstrates the Wordsworthian rhythm, and that my vocabulary of limits appears quite naturally as an explanation of the tense accomplishment of Wordsworth's best poetry. In short: in describing the poem as a memorial of a memorial tour "Tintern Abbey"'s title leads us to expect, quite correctly, a poem charged by the problems of locality, limits, recall and loss that the Yarrow poems deal in. In a highly deflected way, "Tintern Abbey" is a poem of the ballad revival, and deeply expressive of Wordsworth's version of that revival.

"Stuttering," the word I applied to the repetitions of the Preface, may seem a plain word to apply to a poem with the pretensions and high seriousness of "Tintern Abbey," but stutter this poem does. As has so often been noted, it begins with a highly connected (unbordered) world that has every appearance of being unperilous and compensatory, but this sense of connection is interrupted and disappears. The speaker then tries again; then the next version of compensation fails too, and so on in the basic Wordsworthian rhythm, the stutter of repetition engendered by the encounter of limitation. The speaker has returned to repose under a remembered sycamore, and finds his repose repeats but does not duplicate his previous repose. The second verse paragraph begins with a strong statement of Yarrow-like repeatability, of the (captured) usefulness of the Wye memories. They have given the speaker a sense of "tranquil restoration" in the midst of a later history. The tranquility of this claim grows, under the pressure of affirmation, to the swelled chorus of the end of this paragraph:

> While with an eye made quiet by the power
> Of harmony, and the deep power of joy,
> We see into the life of things. (lines 48–50)

We recognize this as a great and hopeful, intensely ambitious Wordsworthian claim, where "power" erases separation, anxiety, and the fearful gap between words and the world to produce a kind of universal interiority, where everything is inside the same space. As we have learned to expect, though, this claim deflates and breaks off: "If this/ Be but a vain belief, yet oh!... "

As in my previous examples, strong lyric form appears in encountering limits: this breakage is marked by the limiting of the verse itself, and the fearful gap between things is represented in practical form by a sudden division into stanzas. These stanzas are purely expressive; they appear not because they are forced by literary history (stanzal form) but because the voice in the poem breaks off, and the space between stanzas figures this break. In a pattern to be repeated precisely a few years later in the Preface, Wordsworth then offers us the simple facts of memory and pleasure in substitution for his rapt, impossible explanation of their power:

> How oft, in spirit, have I turned to thee
> O sylvan Wye! Thou wanderer through the woods,
> How often has my spirit turned to thee! (lines 56–8)

If he cannot rest with his explanation, if he worries we will not believe him, then he can at least offer us (to use earlier terms) the reread text in the place of the power that makes us read again.

The poem could well end here, but, having encountered the limit of the impossible, the poem must circle: fixated, Wordsworth must say it again. Instead of "Once again do I behold" we get

> And now, with gleams of half-extinguished thought,
> With many recognitions dim and faint,
> And somewhat of sad perplexity,
> The picture of the mind revives again (lines 59–62)

Expansion, ambition, failure, limitation and revival: Wordsworth's rhythm, and the rhythm of culture I have traced throughout.[34] Death (personal and cultural) threatens this poem, and the poem responds by repeating itself; the encounter of the limits of mortality produces poetry. That is, death is personal, cultural, and also specifically literary. The limits Wordsworth encounters, in their simplest sense, threaten to end the poem, make it break off before compensation is found. The poem expires, and then revives again. The picture of this next verse paragraph is paler, suffering from the earlier disappointments of the poem, but it once more asserts revival:

> While here I stand, not only with the sense
> Of present pleasure, but with pleasing thoughts
> That in this moment there is life and food
> For future years. (lines 63–6)

Connection is asserted again, and the past is joined to the future by the suture of a meditative present. After admitting the melancholy of the lost pastoral of youth ("I cannot paint/ What then I was ... "), Wordsworth rallies himself with renewed assertions of "recompense," a keyword linked to "compensation" and "revival." The poetry swells again, singing again of a kind of unity with the world, which denies the loss that threatens to be inevitable:

> And I have felt
> A presence that disturbs me with the joy
> Of elevated thoughts; a sense sublime
> Of something far more deeply interfused,
> Whose dwelling is in the light of setting suns,
> And the round ocean, and the living air,
> And the blue sky, and in the mind of man
> A motion and a spirit, that impels
> All thinking things, all objects of all thought,
> And rolls through all things. (lines 94–103)

With the passage about the senses half-creating, half-perceiving, this paragraph or stanza gives us another hopeful total inside, where the limits of the self (or of time, or of the ability to "paint") dissolve and all is available.

Universality collapses again and the poem breaks off again ("Nor perchance, if I were not thus taught"), beginning the last verse paragraph. After the expansions of the first two major paragraphs, which strive to integrate a lofty sense of self with an equally lofty sense of the universe, the turn in the last paragraph to the dear friend, a person standing next to the speaking voice, always carries with it a twinge of surprise. In parallel to the previous turn to the simple fact of the pleasure of memory, the poem here (perhaps desperately) asserts human interconnection in place of universal connection. As in the Preface, as in other Wordsworth writings, we see this desperation because, in some way, Wordsworth wants us to. He doesn't cross out the previous stanzas, even though they are palpably failures of a kind. He wants us to cross, fail and revive again (with him). Here the great assertions of Romantic creed are even cheerfully left behind, acknowledged as chancy, or overly abstract, or as ultimately personal and (hence) unconvincing. The first two arguments (for they are that) proceed outward from the self to encompass the world, trying to erase the fatal division that threatens to close the soul of the poet off from people, readers, nature, or the past from the present. Stanzal borders appear as the parallel to the failure of argument, the limit that must be survived in order to start again (in a new stanza); the revival is marked too by the abrupt retreat of the level of abstraction that distinguishes the end of one paragraph from the beginning of the next. The ends of the first two major movements stand as high-water marks, beyond which the poem, with philosophy and rhetoric, cannot go.

With great beauty, and a confused sadness, the last section steps back from such ambitions, with a sort of recognition, and turns aside to a person. This turn has plain possibilities, though it is still self-centered; the poet "reads" himself in the eyes of his companion. The poet offers his companion's memory, her soul as the great meeting place where limits vanish. Past melts into future, and nature, the natural scene, melts into "these my exhortations," this poem. Wordsworth, not modern critical taste, makes this scene into a tiny reading community, and an oddly assertive picture of successful communication. As nature "lead[s] from joy to joy," connecting past to future, and informs " the mind that is within us," connecting inside and outside, so the poet and his companion link up in a (familiar by now) attempt to defeat the limits of simple human mortality. "Exhortations," and the reading of wild eyes, are the agents of this linkage. As a contrast to the previous stanzas, this section offers us simple things, people writing and reading, instead of the machinery of metaphysics. But these things, in Wordsworth, are painfully complicated, and even, as I have argued, function as his most powerful figures for failure and isolation. They do carry with them a strong sense of sincerity and yearning, though, and because this section is so beautiful it is hard to remember that it too fails. It is cut off logically, rhetorically, by the limits of mortality:

> Nor, perchance
> If I should be, where I no more can hear
> Thy voice, nor catch from thy wild eyes these gleams
> of past existence ...
> (lines 147–50)

This part of the poem rather desperately asserts physical connection, and this assertion has its formal parallel: Wordsworth refuses to break off into another stanza. In other ways this break is precisely like the earlier ones, and so this refusal is a sad one (or a hopeless one). The limit here is that of human life; the object tripped over is a tombstone, Scott's unhewn stone.

Let me summarize my narrative of "Tintern Abbey"'s progress, which I have drawn up quickly since I prepared for it so elaborately. The speaker begins with a dreamlike continuous landscape, which interrupts itself with the uncertain notice of the hermit's fire. He then offers us, as the power of nature to interconnect things that fall apart, "the power that rolls through all things." To stretch to such distances makes the poem spring back, quickly, to a purely personal claim of purely personal memory. The poet then offers us a slightly more limited (because more personal) great claim, where nature becomes the "soul of all my moral being." Overtasked again, the poem contracts to the interpersonal, and an exchange between people that describes Wordsworth's (constant) dream of the perfect poet and his perfect reader. All interpersonal exchange, even the most intimate, is limited by the confines of the body, just as life itself is, and recognition of this limit eventually closes off the section of readerly perfection. The last section makes the simplest of all the declarations in the poem: If I am, as I must be, divided from the past, and others, by death, then in any case we did stand here, together, and we loved that and each other. Logically speaking, there is the same kind of desperation here as when, in the Preface, Wordsworth finally grasps onto the simple fact of the reread poem as his final, his only proof of the powers of poetry. The affirmations of revival, of compensation, have been made again and again, and they end here in the simple assertion of their presence.

"Tintern Abbey" contracts with measured steps from the bounds of the universe to the barest human facts. Its desperation is purely logical; emotionally, desperation has been limited through measured repetitions, the finding of an end in limitation. The epitaphic assertion of plain human renewal at the end offers itself as the poem's last hope, its place of inevitable rest. There is nothing else to say; the power of any art is limited. At the same time, the previous arguments are not lost to us; they are plainly left behind, like pearls on a string, made discrete by their spontaneous, inherent accretion into stanzas. In other words, Wordsworth would, if he could, go on talking forever, submitting version after version to us, always reaching for that final connection, the ultimate strong persuader. He would die before he got there, of course; his limits will not permit him to go on indefinitely.

I would argue for great success and great beauty in this poem, but I would not argue that this success is reached by solving problems. This is still the stuttering, strangely persistent Wordsworth. In "Tintern Abbey," though, Wordsworth knows both his tendency to go on, to say it again, and the beauties, moral and aesthetic, available through the regulation of his desperations within the lyric bounds of poetry. And so the great Romantic lyric takes beautiful shape. The weight of knowledge increases as the poem progresses (since it refuses to revise by crossing out), and the circle of limitation grows tighter and tighter. The passing from stanza to stanza sadly turns repetition into hopeful revival, argument against loss, "beauties of the highest kind."

Conclusion

Like many recent readings of Wordsworth, my reading has attempted to render him a more interactive and less imposing poetic presence. Practitioners of high literary history, like the early Geoffrey Hartman, and even deeply formal critics of the Demanian school, seem now to need correction; we feel that Wordsworth's poetry should somehow be described as (in my broad terms) poetry that a person might write. A person, that is, instead of a personification of either language or literary history itself. I have used Walter Scott's eminently worldly figure to help me pivot into an ambitious history of Wordsworth's accomplishment.

Pairing Wordsworth with Scott (pairing any writer with Scott) has the beneficial effect of insisting on an at least partly practical vocabulary. There are two important differences, though, between my discussions of these two writers, and I want to use these differences as a way of generating a concluding perspective. First: in discussing Wordsworth's writing I have talked much less about the worldly calculation and strategy that formed a major focus in all four of the other chapters. Secondly, I have implicitly described Scott's accomplishment as of a different order than that of Wordsworth. Exploration of these two subjects – making them explicit instead of implicit – turns out to be the same task, formulated by the second; it is the recovery of the distinction between Scott and Wordsworth.

When we bring Wordsworth down to earth by describing his connections to politics and contemporary events, or by describing the genesis of his writing in personal and plain terms, as I have done, we make two corrections. The first is a canonical correction, as I noted above; we bring him down from the high and highly abstracted reaches of the literary canon. The second might well be thought of as the source of the first. We correct Wordsworth himself: Wordsworth is relentlessly abstracting when discussing his own motives, relentlessly high in his vocabulary. As Marjorie Levinson has said in reference to her own reading of Wordsworth, a reading which is the very model of the corrective spirit: "It is difficult to read Wordsworth in this conscientiously contentious way because the poetry explicitly rebukes even the gentlest material interest."[1] In Wordsworth's own descriptions, his motives are high literary ones. This makes him the perfect opposite of Walter Scott, and thus Scott's usefulness as a contrast. Though I treat Wordsworth's self-descriptions with skepticism, I would also argue that such descriptions are true, in their own way, and that what they describe distinguishes Wordsworth from the other poets in this book. Wordsworth's relationship to literary history, like that of the other four poets, is plainly ambitious. He wants a place in it, in simple and more complex ways. Wordsworth's ambitions, though, are self-consciously historical themselves; this is part of the source of the projection into literary history that takes place in the "Essay, Supplementary." Wordsworth wants his place, and he also wants to define that place; he wants to be a part of the story of history, and also tell that story himself (decide its plot). He assumes the posture of a major writer. This kind of self-consciousness, the attempt to write both the material and the narrative of literary history, interacts with the ambitions of later academic or cultured readers to form the powerfully canonical Wordsworth we have been so busily demystifying recently.

This strategy (for it is that, a strategy of a high sort) can be demonstrated quite plainly. I will begin by showing Wordsworth as he is pictured in a subtle instance of high literary history, "False Themes and Gentle Minds," one of the central essays in Hartman's series of histories. In this essay the work of Wordsworth the poet is to finish history's "purification" of the symbols of romance and so present the substance of poetry to the modern, demystified, "gentle" mind. Hartman describes Wordsworth's achievement this way:

His poetry quietly revives the figure of *Natura plangens*, one of the great visionary personae of both pastoral and cosmological poetry.[2]

With its easy Latin and its simple virtuosity of knowledge and reference, this sentence describes a history in which the forces that act on Wordsworth as he creates his poetry are larger than he is; he is an active agent, but an active agent in a narrative whose scope extends beyond him. Since the size of Hartman's historical abstractions makes them ungainly companions for the simple poet, Hartman makes Wordsworth a synecdoche for something larger: "the English poetic mind."[3] This sort of critical personification is typical of relatively unsophisticated intellectual history, and it would be unfair to put Hartman in this camp. But like all histories of this scale, Hartman's history calls out "the English poetic mind" to make it more plausible that Wordsworth's poetry could do the things Hartman says it does; something as large and capable as the national poetic mind can quite conceivably sit down for two centuries and work on purifying the symbols of romance, mediating them for the modern era.

Hartman's argument itself is not overly general. Its conclusion is Wordsworth's "Hart-leap Well," and he arrives there very convincingly through its ballad-like predecessor, Bürger's "The Wild Huntsman," after preparing the literary historical ground by discussing Milton and Collins. Hartman quite wonderfully sums up the late eighteenth century's distanced and abstracted relationship to the older "superstitions" and supernatural powers, and argues that Bürger is no solution to this sterility, since he offers only non-reflective, directly exploitive versions of those powers. Wordsworth is Hartman's hero, and he rescues the themes of romance by occupying what Hartman describes as a reflective space, in which "the rights of the mind" are reestablished after Bürger's kidnapping. The reflection that runs through "Hart-Leap Well" is a "refining principle" that writes a literary history for the modern era:

Thus the poem is really a little progress of the imagination, which leads from one type of animism to another: from the martial type of the knight, to the pastoral type of the shepherd, and finally to that of the poet. And in this progress from primitive to sophisticated kinds of visionariness, poetic reflection is the refining principle: it keeps nature within nature and resists supernatural fancies ... In Wordsworth the new and milder morality grows organically from the old: there is no apocalyptic or revolutionary change, just due process of time and nature. (p. 296)

"Hart-Leap Well" is a beautiful place for Hartman to end because through it Wordsworth's accomplishment can be depicted and also enacted; the poem takes its place at the end of history and also talks about how history gets there. As in all fine critical writing, the author and the critic collaborate in making the point. Wordsworth is pictured here as not only part of literary history (a synecdoche for the Poetic Mind), but also as a literary historian himself. "Hart-Leap

Well" is both the end of the history, accomplishing a kind of purification, and also a picture of it, a progress from primitivism to modernism. Through poems like "Hart-Leap Well," the English Poetic Mind can have archaic energy and reflection too. In the terms I have used, Wordsworth works a revival (he reestablishes the pleasures of romance) by repeating himself (his poem works by putting one version of romance after another). The strong claim in Hartman's essay is its insistence on continuity or ease, which both he and Wordsworth accomplish by erasing or transcending limitations. While Hartman would insist on Wordsworth's fear of limits, he also pictures his success as a transcendence.[4] Wordsworth transcends the limits of his person by becoming literary history itself; this transcendence allows his poetry to transcend the limits of art by evading apocalypse, Hartman's large word for what I have called the encounter with borders or limits. Hartman's Wordsworth evades or passes by mortality by being identified (in the argument) with the transcendent, impersonal narrative of high literary history, in which poetry operates through but finally above the poets themselves.

High history erases mortality by creating a place where abstractions act independently of their material source; the results of this method are related to what Sylvander and Clarinda do for Burns and Mrs. M'Lehose. As Hartman describes Wordsworth, it is hard to decide to whom the credit for this victory over mortality should be given. Hartman's performance of the historical drama rescues Wordsworth (for us) by giving him up to the care of the forces of history; Wordsworth's poem is not only a small, continuous literary history in itself, but it also tells a story of continuity, where the imposition of mortality is turned to account as a lesson of the deathless "spirit," the immaterial *natura plangens*.[5] As Hartman says: purification is a process by which the frightening forces of the past are made gentle, so that they may be re-presented to the modern world. In this essay Hartman and Wordsworth are equally agents of history, and also equally above the mortal world. History is made from the actions of its agents, but, once given form, floats above them and the repetitive mortal world, full of fits and starts. Hartman is Wordsworth's ideal reader here, the collaborative partner in the writing of a purer literature, the high untainted history Wordsworth yearns for in the "Essay, Supplementary."

It has been the business of recent writing about Wordsworth to thoroughly ground this history, either directly or indirectly. To quote

Levinson again: we "refuse the transcendence until such time as we can trace its source and explain its character" (p. 57). Because Wordsworth's transcendence is and has been a critical collaboration, grounding this history is our proper critical responsibility. As I have said, however, I think something is obscured in this grounding. That something admits a poet into the high history, and links him with other poets who qualify as agents: in Hartman's version, Wordsworth is finally linked with Milton, another writer of history. I have figured our recent loss of this something as the loss of the capacity to distinguish between Wordsworth and Walter Scott. In an attempt to retain or recover this capacity without the reanimation of the personifications of high history, I want to re-step through the history Hartman uses to arrive at "Hart-Leap Well." My history will end a bit further on, though, in the first canto of *The Lady of the Lake*.

The opening canto of Walter Scott's *The Lady of The Lake* (1810), "The Chase," has a short and specific literary history behind it, identical with the facts of Hartman's depiction of the history leading up to "Hart-Leap Well." Ballads about hunting are extremely common in most northern European cultures, and during the Romantic period (as Hartman discusses) this theme gained currency through translations of Bürger's ballad "Der wilde Jäger." Scott made his own contribution to this part of the revival, publishing and translating Bürger's two most famous ballads in 1796 (under the titles "William and Helen" and "The Wild Huntsman"). These two ballads are at the center of the gothic ballad craze of the late 1790s, and their plots are good examples of what Wordsworth calls the outrageous stimulation of the ballad, and what Hartman calls an unreflecting use of Romantic energy. They work on the written, gothic (narrative) principle that extravagant and outrageous exploitation of vulgar themes is justified by the moral turn of the conclusion; in simpler form, this direct turn to lesson and punishment occurs in oral ballads too. As Hartman says, Bürger's ballads express no knowledge of their revival of romance, and they hold no space for reflection. They tell stories of immediate punishments with total immediacy. It takes no time or effort to cross over from this world to the next.

Wordsworth's version of this story (still following Hartman) is "Hart-Leap Well," first published in 1800. It begins with the hunting knight appropriating a vassal's best horse, the third of the

day. The climax of "The Wild Huntsman" appears early in
Wordsworth's poem, in the third stanza:

> Joy sparkled in the Prancing courser's eyes;
> The Horse and Horseman are a happy pair;
> But, though Sir Walter like a falcon flies,
> There is a doleful silence in the air.   (lines 9–12)[6]

As Hartman says, the silence that surrounds the appropriately
named Sir Walter here is not that of the spirit world, but that of
endurance, since he has simply outridden the rest of the hunt, even
his dogs: he is left to pursue the hart alone. The ride, unbridled as it
is, does not carry Sir Walter directly into allegory but to a scene in a
secluded dell where he finds his prey expired near a spring. If Sir
Walter's energy has taken him too far we (and he) cannot see it, for
he looks upon the dead deer with "silent joy" (line 36). The hart
retains its brute dignity by keeping its death to itself, and the hunter
participates in this dignity. The beauty of the spot, and the suicidal
passing of the prey, are to the knight a source of pleasure, and so he
erects a "pleasure-house" to commemorate the event. Part of the
motive is a boast: "till the foundations of the mountains fail/ My
mansion with its arbour will endure" (lines 73–4). The ballad
atmosphere that surrounds this poem becomes more palpable
towards the end of this first section; Wordsworth even works a nice
example of incremental repetition, the signature of the mature British
ballad:

> And in the summertime when days are long,
> I will come hither with my paramour,
> And with the dancers, and the minstrels song,
> We will make merry in that pleasant bower.   (lines 69–72)

This stanza, which is in Sir Walter's voice, becomes:

> And thither, when the summer days were long,
> Sir Walter journeyed with his paramour;
> And with the dancers and the minstrel's song
> Made merriment within that pleasant bower.   (lines 89–92)

After this stanza Wordsworth begins to tell that Sir Walter died, but
then breaks off, saying he will add a "second rhyme." If there is going
to be a ballad lesson, this is the place for it; Sir Walter has had his
brute pleasures at the cost of God's children, but he has not seen his
own exploitation. The ballad machinery is only warming up, and the
appropriate material, in ballad form, is waiting in the wings.

The pressure that the ballad material exerts here is a very specific instance of the pressure of literary history and conventional expectation. It is this pressure that causes Wordsworth to break off. Or rather, it is this pressure which Wordsworth abruptly bleeds off, in the best-known lines of the poem:

> The moving accident is not my trade,
> To freeze the blood I have no ready arts;
> 'Tis my delight, alone in summer shade,
> To pipe a simple song to thinking hearts.   (lines 97–100)

Wordsworth can ride the crest of the wave of history, but he would rather not, and this abrupt turn is a skillful drama of his peculiar abilities and interests. The rest of the poem is more recognizably Wordsworthian, with its pedestrian meter and diction, its shepherd, and its hymn to nature. It contains the lesson ("Never to blend our pleasure or our pride/ With sorrow of the meanest thing that feels" [lines 179–80]), but refuses to punish Sir Walter except in memory. Sir Walter has, if anything, failed to ride into the spirit world on his hunt, and he and his mansion crumble into dust. The shepherd believes that the curse on the spot will continue in the mansion's place, "till trees, and stones, and fountains are all gone" (line 160). In the same way, though, that it is the shepherd's voice that tells the story of the supernatural groans of the well, and the pathetic death of the hart, it is the shepherd who contributes the eternity of the curse, the ballad element. This shepherd is part of the ballad genre; Wordsworth later describes him as derived from an oral source (a "real" shepherd) from whom material has been collected.[7] Wordsworth changes the shepherd's version of the story from retribution and curse to the consolation provided by Nature:

> She leaves these objects to a slow decay
> That what we are, and have been, may be known;
> But, at the coming of the milder day,
> These monuments will be overgrown.   (lines 173–6)

As this poem is transformed from ballad to lyrical ballad in the middle, by a firm turn away from literary history, so the ballad discontinuity of the curse is transformed in this mild millennial moment, which leaves the spot free of its burden. For Hartman this moment is so mild, the turn so convincing, that he describes the poem as without break, a beautiful continuity.

Wordsworth short-circuits the natural economy of the exploitive literary ballad, which moves from exploitation to exhaustion (from which it derives its "lesson," that exploitation exhausts itself), by breaking off in the middle, in the same way that he breaks off in "Peter Bell." This break restrains the reader and the poem, turning from exploitation and exhaustion to restoration or revival. It does so by fragmenting voice; the first part is conducted in the poet's voice, which has ready arts to frame the moving accident of the hart's death, while the second part is told by the moralizing (or, in Hartman's term, the reflective) "I" and a credulous popular voice, a split like that of "The Thorn." The voice of the first part and the shepherd tell the same story from differing perspectives, one from each side of the hunt (hunter and hunted), and the "I" adds his version to these. Wordsworth replaces the shepherd's version of the story with his restorative version because the shepherd's curse repeats ballad exploitation; the "I"'s revivalist story is progressive. The lesson here is moral and literary, a double point issuing from the central exploitive theme; do not exploit the weak (reader).

Hartman is surely right to say that this poem ushers in the millennium without catastrophe. That is, the work of the poem is to try to turn the possibly double catastrophe of the two deaths into a mild progress of maturing history. In my terms, Wordsworth tries to turn the crude powers of exploitive writing into the higher powers of persuasion and truth-telling. He does this by telling the tale more than once, replacing one mode with the other. He tries to fill in the blank spot of power with rational explanation; the shepherd notes that nothing grows there now (evidence of curse) while the higher voice insists that the spot will be overgrown. This is Wordsworth, though, not Walter Scott, and so the spot is still bare even as the higher voice speaks. The bareness of the spot combines with the bareness of the voices – they compete with each other, and we must choose, ourselves, between them – to create an effect very similar to that of "Yarrow Unvisited." The poem both denies the presence of mortal energy and also shows it to us by pointing to where it is(n't) buried. Wordsworth's stumble over this spot creates the break between the "parts," the break that gives birth to the higher voice. Hartman's high literary history cannot see this break because this break gives birth to high literary history: that is, high history sees the break as simply the symptom of a higher-order continuity. The moralizing "I" that appears here marshalls cruder ballad energies into a literary and progressive history. If we call the shepherd's voice the voice of magic, then the higher voice is the voice of art. The creation of the higher voice takes effort, and a kind of restraint. By creating it Wordsworth can write a progressive and smooth, unstumbling history, in which his poem plays a part; but he can only create this progress by breaking abruptly into the accumulating ballad energies of the story.

The best way of describing Hartman's reading of Wordsworth is that he listens intently, obediently, we might say, to the higher voice. This becomes clear when we add Scott to the history of the inclusion of "archaic energy." I have discussed the opening canto of *The Lady of the Lake* previously, and so I will not go into great detail here. My previous description suffices to illustrate how closely Scott follows the small literary history behind the story of the hunt, and also how unlike that history his story is. In *The Lady of the Lake* exploitation has been left behind as a subject, but the interest of exploitation still tags along at a distance, a shadow. Scott's hunt, as I have said, has no consequences other than the sponsorship of a sort of travel, James' tour of the Highlands. James is not punished for his excesses, and no lessons are learned, no credulous stories told. No moralizing voice appears to turn his story to account, and so no literary progress, the sort that writes literary history, is made. Scott's poem is not, in other words, a moment in history, a place where past and future meet. Indeed, as I have tried to describe, Scott's primary project is to avoid the intimation of mortality that such a moment provides. Of course Scott joins the past to the future constantly, and the primary motivation in his depiction of seamlessness is the depiction of progress. So, ironically – ironic because Scott is not part of high literary history – Scott's evasion of mortality makes him figure progress and the Poetic Mind far better than Wordsworth. Scott puts the materials of history to mild use, and apocalyptic moments of all kinds are tamed and turned into gentle progress. Scott does not want to make his poem into a moment; literary history is not conjured into being. Wordsworth's poem, on the other hand, is a drama of history and its action is the drama of pushing poetry up higher. Wordsworth's poetry is designed to be consumed as dramatically progressive poetry, poetry that stages the drama of literary history. It was written with the historian in mind, and it makes a space for the historian to settle in and find history. We can find history there because Wordsworth takes the past and turns it into a future; he diverts the stream of history towards us, its scholars and product. His poem does struggle for a Hartmanian purification, but equally importantly, it contains the drama of that purification, which the scholar delights in, since it looks like the struggle of progress.

In other words, Scott's usefulness is that he shows us what "purification" actually looks like. Scott purifies the energies of form and poetry, what Hartman figures as the energies of Old Romance, into a sort of tasteless essence. He is a strategist of ease, and by making this so clear he allows us to see Wordsworth as simply another sort of strategist. Wordsworth's aims are different, but, like Scott, he wants his poetry to do something for him. The English Poetic Mind did not write "Heart-Leap Well": William Wordsworth wrote it, a person with certain aims and high talents. We no longer grant him transcendence. We depict him, instead, as wanting it. Wordsworth, too, writes from human motives and pursues his strategies, as all writers must. Wordsworth's poetry has its place in a low history, and that place is exactly the same as the place any other author might have: he wanted his readers to like and to buy his books. We have always known that the Muse did not descend for Scott; we can admit now that it did not descend for Wordsworth either.[8]

Wordsworth may not enact a seamless moment of progress, but he does do something, and his active historical presence is quite different from that of Scott. High literary history cannot see Scott, and so cannot put it in this way; but such is the implicit content of its argument. That Wordsworth and Scott do remain distinct teaches us that we should not abandon high history in favor of low history; we simply need to see high history as another kind of history: "transcendance" as description. This high history is more clearly a literary history than the low history. Its lack of interest in individual, contingent action helps it concentrate on poetic action, the forces in literary history that derive from the expressive possibilities of poetic form. High history knows (implicitly, perhaps) that form is a force whose interest and importance is partly its very detachment from the writing individual, its appearance of transcendent force (high history would object to the qualification the low history teaches us to make: "partly"; "appearance"). In high history the imposition of rule, of form, the constriction of possibility produced by the existence of previous example, is more than an annoying complication in the book-publishing business. Its constriction forms the place of art, and thus only those sensitive to the power and possibility of that limitation can participate in high history. In one sense this is a platitude: the best players of games are those for whom the rules multiply rather than restrict possibility. I have argued throughout this book, though, both implicitly and explicitly, that "form" is more than shape, more than material constraint. We like and value the low history because it is clearly a moral history, where human consequences are engaged and determined. Thus part of my description of MacPherson's writing insists that to put Ossian into prose is to strip a Highlander bare. It is a simple extension of this way of thinking to see the things typically discussed by the high history as having a moral side too: Wordsworth's incapacity to stop repeating himself in "The Thorn" (a formal decision) is the same as his incapacity to package up Martha Ray for the pleasure of the consumer. I do not mean to imply, in a vague way, that Wordsworth is somehow a better person for this incapacity: only that he understands that there are deep energies involved in the packaging. "Art," as I have defined it, is a moral world, whether we like it or not, and so we find it a distinct world and a valuable one. In my story Burns and Wordsworth recognize the consequences of form thoroughly and wholly, and because those consequences are moral ones I have called this accomplishment "integrity," and would define their accomplishment as a real, poetic accomplishment. High history, selective by definition, is an elite history (it cannot see Walter Scott), but, as Harold Bloom would insist, the truth is that the force of art is not felt in the same way by all. We need not form aggressive hierarchies in admitting that not all poets are the same, that Wordsworth is different from Scott. The high history of poetic form and accomplishment does not rise up out of and so transcend the low history of human motives. Such is half the claim of this book. The other half is to insist that the high history (the force of form apart from poets) is the necessary companion of the low history, and that a true picture of poetry cannot do without either: beauty and profit must be equal partners in our understanding of art.

Wordsworth and Burns, so hypersensitive to limitation, the circles drawn around all parts of human life, wrote poetry of high integrity and real beauty, because limitation is the breath of poetry, its source and end. This is the distinction I wished to recover: Wordsworth and Burns are poets of high integrity and sensitivity, while MacPherson, Hogg and Scott are not. Scott, though, deserves a final word. MacPherson's brutality shows Scott in his best light. Scott is easy, but cheerful and respectful; he wants the world to be better for everyone in the most heartfelt and sincere of ways. I would say of him, finally, that his evacuation of form comes not from insensitivity but from an idiosyncratic kind of sensitivity. He wants his poems to be vacations from consequence, and thus the nature of his poetry. He wants this, though, because he knows and is pained by the moral consequences of form – figured for him, always, by the always-tense border between Scotland and England – and wishes them away. They cannot be wished away, and so I have felt it necessary to critique Scott often. We can, however, value the humanity we find in Scott's cheer, in his wholly imagined relaxation of form, and in the happier world he wants for us. It is his accomplishment; not a poetic accomplishment, but one we can value on other grounds. Crossing the border always makes a difference, and the real poet shows us this truth always, but Scott would no doubt be the more simply pleasant companion on the tour. Even Wordsworth found his presence irresistible, and was able, for some moments, to relax on the banks of the Yarrow.

Notes

INTRODUCTION

1 *The Well-Wrought Urn* (New York, 1975), pp. x–xi.
2 See the delightfully clear, quick critique offered by John Guillory in "Canon," an essay in Frank Lentricchia and Thomas McLaughlin's *Critical Terms for Literary Study* (Chicago, 1990), pp. 244–8. Speaking more generally, I would also note the less quick but penetrating analysis in Jerome Christensen's "From Rhetoric to Corporate Populism: A Romantic Critique of the Academy in an Age of High Gossip," *Critical Inquiry* 16 (1990), 438–65.

1 JAMES MACPHERSON

1 MacPherson's activities on behalf of the Nabob (ruler of a southern Indian state) are detailed in George McElroy, "Ossian's Imagination and the History of India," in *Aberdeen and the Enlightenment*, ed. J. S. Carter and J. H. Pittock (Aberdeen, 1987), pp. 363–74.
2 "Elegy on the Death of his Excellency George Haldane, Esq.," *Scots Magazine* 21 (1759), 526.
3 On this question see Fiona Stafford, *The Sublime Savage* (Edinburgh, 1988), pp. 42–3. I would think that there is every reason to be suspicious that the insistence that the poem is *not* MacPherson's came from MacPherson himself, even if he did write it: it was important that he not look too much like an original poet himself, once the disputes over Ossian's authenticity began. Stafford's book is an excellent source for a picture of the current body of MacPherson scholarship, especially from the documentary point of view. For another much more general overview, see Howard Gaskill, "'Ossian' MacPherson: Towards a Rehabilitation," *Comparative Criticism* 8 (1986), 113–46.
4 From "On the Death of Marshall Keith," published in October 1758; quoted from Stafford, *Sublime Savage*, p. 47.
5 The beginning of Fragment 1. The original edition of the *Fragments of Ancient Poetry* (1760) is reprinted in facsimile by the Augustan Reprint Society, publication no. 122 (Los Angeles, 1966).
6 This is from the *Conjecture* itself, and not part of the *Scots Magazine*

excerpt; quoted from the edition of M. W. Steinkle (New York, 1917), p. 57.

7 It is worth noting that the real landmarks of sentiment (*The Man of Feeling*, *A Sentimental Journey*, *The Deserted Village*, and *The Sorrows of Young Werther*, for instance) all appear after the Ossian poems. *Werther*, a famous case, quotes Ossian for pages and pages, at the climax of the book. The sentiment that the Ossian poems present is obviously related to that found in such works as *Pamela* and *Night Thoughts*, but it is also clearly not simply like what is found there.

8 Ossianic ballads in their original Gaelic also rhyme in various ways.

9 As they were in Thomas Blacklock's collection of Edinburgh verse of 1760 (*A Collection of Original Poems*).

10 Robert Fitzgerald, in a convincing article called "The Style of Ossian," *Studies in Romanticism* 6 (1966), 22–33, claims that the "foreign" features of MacPherson's prose come from the Gaelic ballads. He discusses the inversions, as well as the constant genitives.

11 From "Mr. M— G—," June 21, 1760, contained in *Select Letters by Mr. Hull* (London, 1778), vol. II, pp. 169–70.

12 Oddly enough, the review in the *Scots Magazine* was simply a republication of the *Monthly*'s. The *Monthly*'s review begins in January 1762 (vol. 32), p. 41.

13 Blair's discussion is in his "Critical Dissertation on the Poems of Ossian" (1763), attached to most editions of the poetry after it was written; the *Critical*'s review is the lead article in the issue for December 1761. The best discussion of the force of classical precedent in arguments over epic and *Fingal* is in *The Theory of the Epic in England 1650–1800* by H. T. Swedenberg, Jr. (Berkeley, 1944), esp. chapter 4; see also the relevant discussions in Stafford, *Sublime Savage*.

14 This is still true, I think, though the winds have shifted; its associations now bring condemnation instead of praise. The constant is that the poems themselves end up playing a minor role to their atmosphere.

15 From "Carthon." There is no authoritative edition of the Ossian poems, and the first editions are not readily available. In the American edition I have (*Poems of Ossian* [Boston, 1860]), this is on p. 225. The "feeling" of this kind of passage is quite specifically discussed (in the context of manners and politeness) by Adam Potkay in "Virtue and Manners in MacPherson's *Poems of Ossian*," *PMLA* (January 1992), 120–30.

16 For ease of location, this is near the beginning of the essay, directly following the long quotation of Lodbrog.

17 Primary among the sources of information on this subject is Derick Thomson's *The Gaelic Sources of MacPherson's Ossian*, Aberdeen University Studies no. 130 (Edinburgh, 1952). Thomson is a good guide, but I will mention two others I have found useful: Ludwig Stern, *Ossianic Heroic Poetry* (translated by J. L. Robertson in *Transactions of the Gaelic Society of Inverness* 22 [1897–8], 257–325); and Neil Ross, *Heroic Poetry from the Book of the Dean of Lismore* (Edinburgh, 1939).

18 Thomson, *Gaelic Sources*, passim.
19 "Strength" here describes the fact that ballads gathered in the eighteenth century bear a close resemblance to those gathered in *The Dean's Book*; see Neil Ross, *Heroic Poetry*.
20 "Selma" is not a person but a place, a name derived from the traditional home of the Finns, often spelled "Selama."
21 Ross, *Heroic Poetry*, pp. 9–11.
22 This theme – the burden of the past – has been noticed in a very general way by Robert Folkenflik in his "MacPherson, Chatterton, Blake and the Great Age of Literary Forgery," *The Centennial Review* 18 (1974), 378–91.
23 This feature is especially interesting to Ian Haywood, in his book *The Making of History* (London, 1987), which contains a very complete discussion of the "historical" side of MacPherson's project.
24 *Ossian and Ossianic Literature* (London, 1899), p. 2.
25 MacPherson's Prefaces are always interesting; nowhere is his interest in money and reputation so apparent. The Preface to the first edition of the poems, in 1762 (actually December 1761), for instance, begins with a quite fascinating exploration of literary fame and novelty. In the course of this discussion MacPherson discusses the possibility of forgery, and of becoming famous by pretending to not have written something.
26 The sources I have found most helpful for information about the Highlands are: T. C. Smout, *A History of the Scottish People, 1560–1830* (London, 1970); R. H. Campbell, *Scotland Since 1707*, 2nd ed. (Edinburgh, 1985). A detailed look at governmental policy during the first half of the century is available in Rosalind Mitchison's "The Government in the Highlands, 1707–1745," in *Scotland in the Age of Improvement*, ed. N. T. Phillipson and R. Mitchison (Edinburgh, 1970), pp. 24–46.
27 About 250 miles of roads were constructed in the 1730s; around 800 miles were added to these after the '45. These were military roads, and not commercially important. See Campbell, *Scotland Since 1707*, pp. 53 and 84–5.
28 See Nancy C. Dorian's *Language Death: The Life Cycle of a Scottish Dialect* (Philadelphia, 1981), p.21. I found the first chapter of this book to be the best overview of the history of the linguistic divisions of Scotland and the fortunes of Gaelic.
29 *Tales of a Grandfather*, third series (London, 1923), p. 482.
30 The cultural role of Highland dress in Scotland is a confused and confusing one; Hugh Trevor-Roper describes its history after this period in "The Invention of Tradition: The Highland Tradition of Scotland" in *The Invention of Tradition*, ed. Erik Hobsbawm and Terrence Ranger (Cambridge, 1983), pp. 15–41. Throughout this essay I will use "tartan" to describe just what it means: the cloth from which traditional Highland dress was made, the distinctive pattern of which was outlawed along with the other things (this led Highlanders to dye their cloth black).

31 What happened to the clans, as well as what they were like, is wonderfully presented in R. A. Dodgshon's "'Pretense of Blude' and 'Place of Their Dwelling': the Nature of Highland Clans, 1500–1745," contained in *Scottish Society 1500–1800*, ed. R. A. Houston and I. H. Whyte (Cambridge, 1989), pp. 154–76. See also Malcolm Gray's *The Highland Economy*, 1750–1850 (Edinburgh, 1957).

32 Gray, *Highland Economy*, pp. 50–1.

33 For a good description of agricultural progress, see Campbell, *Scotland Since 1707*, pp. 18–38. A feisty account of the "clearances" in the Highlands is available in *The Highland Clearances* by John Prebble (Harmondsworth, 1969).

34 Quoted in Campbell, *Scotland Since 1707*, p. 85. A further sample of this surveyor's (named Telford) notes is available in *Source-Book of Scottish Economic and Social History*, ed. R. H. Campbell and J. B. A. Dow (Oxford, 1968).

35 This is from the fascinating deposition of Lachlan MacVuirich in the Highland and Agricultural Society of Scotland's *Report* on the Ossianic controversy, ed. Henry MacKenzie (Edinburgh, 1805), appendix pp. 277–9. Lachlan's situation is examined and substantiated in the light of modern scholarship in Derick Thompson's "The MacMhuirich Bardic Family," *Transactions of the Gaelic Society of Inverness* 43 (1966), 276–304.

36 *Report*, appendix, p. 47 (a letter from Hugh M'Donald to H. Mac-Kenzie).

37 *An Enquiry into the Authenticity of the Poems Ascribed to Ossian* (London, 1781), p. 81.

38 The editor of this edition (Edinburgh, 1870) is Archibald Clerk.

39 Hector MacLean, quoted in Thomson, *Gaelic Sources*, p. 85.

40 From *A Journey to the Hebrides and the Western Isles*, conveniently available with Boswell's *Journal of a Tour to the Hebrides*, ed. Peter Levi (Harmondsworth, 1984), p. 118.

41 This exchange can be found in George Black, "President Jefferson and MacPherson's Ossian," *Transactions of the Gaelic Society of Inverness* 33 (1925–7), 355–61.

42 See Ian Grimble, "The Reverend Alexander Pope's letter to James Hogg," *Scottish Gaelic Studies* 9, pt. 1 (1961), 102.

43 *Gaelic Sources*, p. 5.

44 *Journey*, p. 116.

45 Remember: Gaelic (or "Erse") had *become* primarily oral. A long classical and scholarly tradition had lapsed, but its written records survived.

46 *Report*, appendix, p. 14 (a letter to Hugh Blair from John MacPherson of Sleat).

47 *Report*, p. 56.

48 They are also the focus of Ian Haywood's *The Making of History*.

49 I found this book in the Osborne collection at the Beinecke Library at Yale University. The curious formality of Ritson's declaration is

heightened by the fact that the copy of Ossian had clearly never been read.

50 p. 42; also quoted in Thomson, *Gaelic Sources*, p. 4. The phrase "15th century" is an insult from Shaw, and he italicizes it throughout his work. Shaw was a friend of Johnson, who may have collaborated with Shaw on an Ossianic tract; see Thomas Curley, "Johnson's Last Word on Ossian," in *Aberdeen and the Enlightenment*, ed. Carter and Pittock, pp. 375–93.

51 Shaw is also scandalized when his informants, gradually understanding who he was and what he wanted, began asking to be paid before they divulged their Highland secrets (p. 56).

52 From his "Dissertation Concerning the Poems of Ossian," *Poems*, pp. 71–2.

53 Interestingly, modern linguistic observation insists that isolation produces tremendous linguistic variation; in the Highlands, for instance, dialectal variation could be discovered between two sections of a small village, separated by only a few hundred yards. See Dorian, *Language Death*.

54 Blair, in the "Critical Dissertation," *Poems*, p. 89.

55 This natural consequence of "collecting" is discussed more broadly, within the context of the ballad revival, by Susan Stewart in "Scandals of the Ballad," a chapter in her book *Crimes of Writing* (Oxford, 1991), pp. 102–31. Stewart's book shares many interests with this book (though they also share idiosyncrasy).

56 Sentimental heroism, loyalty and martial vigor, the qualities of Fingal and company, are also the clearest associations of Bonny Prince Charlie and the '45. We might also remember that Napoleon was an avid reader of Ossian, and his career more than anything else expresses the explosive and dangerous qualities of the primitive virtues; see P. Van Tiegham, *Ossian en France* (Geneva, 1967), vol. II, pp. 1–13.

2 ROBERT BURNS

1 From *The Letters of Robert Burns*, ed. J. Delancey Ferguson and G. Ross Roy (Oxford, 1985), vol. I, p. 17. All further citations from the letters will give volume number and page number, as well as the letter number. I give the number because Roy has conveniently retained the numbering of Ferguson's edition, which is widely available.

2 Quoted from *The Poetical Works of William Shenstone*, ed. William Gilfillan (New York, 1854), stanza 7, p. 2.

3 Taken from Jeffrey's review of Cromek's *Reliques of Robert Burns* (1809), conveniently excerpted in *Robert Burns: The Critical Heritage*, ed. Donald Low (London, 1974), p. 187. The early reviews Low presents almost all include some such reference to the poem; see, for instance, nos. 4, 5 and 7. Some of the most interesting of all contemporary praise comes from Burns' highly intelligent if quirky correspondent, Mrs. Dunlop of

Dunlop. Worn out by the death of her husband and the faithless bankruptcy of her eldest son, Mrs. Dunlop recovered her health and spirits after reading "The Cottar's Saturday Night":

An event to which I have since owed inestimable pleasure, and for which I shall ever retain the sincerest gratitude to that power which endowed the author with capacity to write…

See *Robert Burns and Mrs. Dunlop*, ed. William Wallace (New York, 1898), vol. II, p. 155.

4 Stanzas 17 and 20 respectively; quoted from *The Poems and Songs of Robert Burns*, ed. James Kinsley (Oxford, 1968), vol. I, poem no. 72. In all future references, I will simply give Kinsley's poem number.

5 The nature of Burns' current readership would be an interesting subject for investigation. In some ways his readership is certain to be broader outside of academia than within, a remarkable feat for a poet of the eighteenth century, and a direct result of the convivial strategies I outline in this chapter. His close identification with Scotland (again a Burnsian strategy) insures, too, that the relationship of Scottish readers to Burns' poems will be closer than that of other readers (though perhaps also still contained, to some extent, by the posturing that I attribute to him).

6 Quoted in Low, *Critical Heritage*, item no. 15b, p. 91.

7 For information on the linguistic status of Scots, see the following: two essays in *The Languages of Scotland*, ed. A. J. Aitken and T. McArthur (Edinburgh, 1979): David Murison, "The Historical Background," pp. 2–13, and A. J. Aitken, "Scottish Speech: A Historical View With Special Reference to the Standard English of Scotland," pp. 85–118. See also another essay by Aitken, "The Good Old Scots Tongue: Does Scots Have an Identity?" in *Minority Languages Today*, ed. E. Haugen, et al. (Edinburgh, 1981), pp. 112–36.

8 In Low, *Critical Heritage*, p. 186.

9 See J. H. Millar, *Scottish Prose of the 17th and 18th Centuries* (Glasgow, 1912), pp. 180–1, and Janet Smith, "18th Century Ideas of Scotland," in *Scotland in the Age of Improvement*, ed. R. Mitchison and N. T. Phillipson (Edinburgh, 1970), pp. 110–11. Two more specific but extremely informative studies may be found in *Aberdeen and the Enlightenment*, ed. J. S. Carter and J. H. Pittock (Aberdeen, 1987): David Hewitt, "James Beattie and the Languages of Scotland," pp. 251–60; and J. Derrick McClure, "Language and Genre in Allan Ramsay's 1721 Poems," pp. 261–9.

10 From Kinsley, *Poems*, vol. III, p. 971.

11 Low, *Critical Heritage*, item no. 4, p. 71.

12 Wallace, *Burns and Mrs. Dunlop*, vol. I, pp. 17–18.

13 Clarinda's letters may be found in many collected editions of Burns' works, especially those printed in the last half of the nineteenth and the first half of the twentieth centuries.

14 For a sharp discussion of the function of personification in this period, see

Clifford Siskin, *The Historicity of Romantic Discourse* (Oxford, 1988), pp. 68–84 and passim. Siskin's notions of the role of personification in the creation of "communities" runs very close to my formulations; this is true of other features of his argument too.

15 Again, see Siskin, *Historicity*, on this subject.

16 Delancey Ferguson, *Pride and Passion* (New York, 1939), p. 161. Ironically, in spite of his contempt for the episode, the title of Ferguson's book comes from a letter from Sylvander; in fact, it is from one of Sylvander's parades of personifications: "My great constituent elements are Pride and Passion ... " (vol. I, pp. 189–90, no. 166). Is the artificial Burns an unreal Burns?

17 Commission in the Excise comes before appointment, as a license comes before practice. The appointment itself is the subject of the poem and letter discussed above.

18 One of the best illustrations of the elaborate fictions Burns was toying with at this point is the contrast between two descriptions of his reunion with Jean Armour. The description he gives to Clarinda is feeling and quite shocked at Jean's "vulgarity of soul" (vol. I, p. 244, no. 210); a letter to a coarse friend is full of repulsive bravado, singing out over how he "f—d her till she rejoiced with joy unspeakable and full of glory" (vol. I, p. 251, no. 215). There is no reason, as far as I can see, to credit either of these accounts with truth or falseness.

19 From the review of Cromek, *Reliques*, p. 182.

20 See *Letters*, vol. II, p. 242, no. 586 and vol. II, p. 316, no. 644 respectively.

21 I put the "it" in brackets because the original deletes this word and substitutes "many," which does not make (to me) very much sense.

22 See Kinsley, *Poems*, vol. III, p. 1171.

23 Blair's suggestions are reprinted in Low, *Critical Heritage*, pp. 81–2.

24 Wallace, *Burns and Mrs. Dunlop*, vol. I, p. 35.

25 The Earl of Buchan, quoted in David Craig, *Scottish Literature and the Scottish People* (London, 1961), p. 105.

26 Again, qualification of this statement might well be required when speaking of Scottish readers, or British readers generally, especially with reference to the longer "Scotch" poems. But I would stick to the claim that any real *critical* life Burns is to have now must rest on his best lyrics: his songs.

27 There were many editions of this work, with varying authority (if authority is to be had in such a venture). For a summary, see the prefaces to *The Merry Muses of Caledonia*, ed. James Barke and Sydney Smith (Edinburgh, 1959).

28 This song was enclosed in a letter (vol. I, p. 51, no. 45) and also included in *The Merry Muses of Caledonia*. For the confusing history of Burns' interest in this old song, see Kinsley's commentary (vol. III, pp. 1210–11).

29 From his review of Cromek's *Reliques*, in the brand-new *Quarterly Review*; quoted in Low, *Critical Heritage*, p. 206.

30 Interestingly, several authors, contemporary and Romantic, claim that songs also experienced an unusual social freedom in eighteenth-century

Scotland. They went everywhere, and were enjoyed by an unusually broad spectrum of classes. For a quick discussion of this subject, see Thomas Crawford's "Lowland Song and Popular Tradition in the Eighteenth Century," in *The History of Scottish Literature, 1660–1800*, ed. Andrew Hook (Aberdeen, 1987) vol. II, pp. 123–39. Crawford's article contains good references to more thorough discussions.

31 See F. B. Snyder, *The Life of Robert Burns* (New York, 1932), pp. 125–6.

32 See the commentary to the poem in Kinsley, *Poems*, vol. III, p. 1139.

33 See Kinsley's commentary, *Poems*, vol. III, p. 1139.

34 *Scottish Song in Two Volumes* (London, 1794), pp. lxxix and (i) respectively.

35 This often quoted letter may be found in its entirety in many older editions of Burns' works; I quote here from *The Works of Robert Burns* (London, 1891), vol. VI, p. 216.

36 Barke and Smith (eds.), *Merry Muses*, p. 114. The version in Johnson is signed.

37 From the edition cited above (London, 1891), vol. VI, p. 254.

38 The circle of anonymity around the poems in the *Scots Magazine*, discussed in the previous chapter, bears a fascinating resemblance to that around song. I think that in fact the dynamics are very similar: both circles are examples of highly conventional, modest poetry, happy if minor poetic ground. This happy minority is precisely what MacPherson had no use for.

39 The edition I have seen is London, 1820; this six-volume edition absorbs Cromek's *Reliques of Robert Burns*, 4th ed. (London, 1817) as vol. VI. This quotation is from p. i of the Preface to vol. II.

40 Quoted from Cromek's *Reliques*, 4th ed. (London, 1817), Preface, p. iv. That Cromek did not particularly admire this quality is made clear in a detailed study by Dennis Read, "Practicing 'The Necessity of Purification': Cromek, Roscoe and *Reliques of Burns*," *Studies in Bibliography* 35 (1982), 306–19.

3 JAMES HOGG

1 *The Shepherd's Guide* (Edinburgh, 1807), introduction, pp. 3–4.

2 Published in the *The Scots Magazine* for October 1794 (vol. 56), p. 624. The authority for this attribution of the unsigned poem is an auto-biographical letter published by Hogg in *The Scots Magazine* for July 1805 (vol. 67), p. 503. This letter is signed "Z"; Hogg did write it, though, and I will give the evidence for this second attribution later.

3 From the *Memoir of the Author's Life and Familiar Anecdotes of Sir Walter Scott*, ed. Douglas Mack (Edinburgh, 1972), p. 18. Further references to the *Memoir* will simply give the page number of this edition.

4 See, for instance, an account quoted by E. C. Batho in *The Ettrick Shepherd* (Cambridge, 1927), p. 60.

5 Batho, *Shepherd*, p. 74.

6 From his review in the *Edinburgh Review* for November 1814 (vol. 34), p. 161.

7 I quote from Thomas Thomson's collected edition, *The Works of the Ettrick Shepherd* (London, 1865), vol. II, p. 12; future citations will give the page number, with the understanding that they are always from vol. II. This edition, reprinted by AMS (New York, 1973), is reliable enough for the poetry, though it lacks the many interesting notes Hogg wrote for his songs. The reader should not depend upon it for the prose, though, since almost every story and novel has been expurgated or changed in some way.

8 *The Poetic Mirror* (London, 1817), pp. iii–iv.

9 It was originally supposed to go by the name of *The Poetical Repository*, and then briefly metamorphoses into the interestingly British *The Thistle and the Rose*.

10 From a letter to Byron dated June 3, 1814; quoted in *The Life and Letters of James Hogg* by Alan Lang Strout (Lubbock, 1946), p. 73.

11 Strout, *Life*, p. 77.

12 There is also, of course, the long history of collections of "friends" verse; MacPherson published things in such a collection, and many song books are, in the end, collections of this type.

13 In the *Noctes Ambrosianae* no. 17, *Blackwood's* 16 (November 1824), 585.

14 *Memoir*, p. 70.

15 From the 1830 introduction to *The Lord of the Isles*, here taken from *The Poetical Works of Walter Scott* (Boston, 1880), vol. III, p. 9.

16 From "Parody, Pastiche, and Allusion" in *Lyric Poetry: Beyond New Criticism*, ed. Chaviva Hosek and Patricia Parker (Ithaca, 1985), p. 331.

17 Bromwich, "Parody," p. 331.

18 *Memoir*, p. 37.

19 *Memoir*, p. 39.

20 Quoted by Strout, *Life*, p. 114n. For some comments by Hogg on the composition of some of the poems, see the note to "O, Weel Befa' the Maiden Gay" in *Songs of the Ettrick Shepherd* (Edinburgh and London, 1831), p. 117.

21 *The Spy* (Edinburgh, 1810–11), p. 1. The copy of this rare item that I looked at is in the Beinecke Library at Yale University, amongst the many things in the James Hogg collection housed there. I would like to thank my friend Steve Parks, curator of the Osborne collection, for his invaluable help in making my trip to see *The Spy* a productive one.

22 Scott's Muse is depicted on a stage, watched by his audience: "Though many of them are screwing up their noses as if in derision, yet it is easily seen, by the eagerness with which they are watching and scrutinizing her every motion, that they cannot help admiring her, whatever they may pretend ... Everyone is holding out his hand expecting some favor from her; which, you see, she is distributing liberally: yet these are not her own productions; but such is the effect of gawky admiration, that if it but come through her hands it is received with avidity" (p. 10).

23 Quoted in Louis Simpson's *James Hogg, A Critical Study* (New York, 1962), p. 17. "Sheep-smearing" is a way of marking sheep; it is not a typo for "sheep-shearing."

24 *Memoir*, p. 21.
25 56 (October 1794), p. 624.
26 vol. 66, pp. 572–3.
27 After covering his early life in the first official memoir (1807) – the same period covered by the letters in the *The Scots Magazine* – Hogg says: "The above is the substance of three letters, written in the same year, and alluding mostly to Poetical Trifles" (p. 16).
28 67 (January 1805), p. 16.
29 In books already referred to, see *Memoir*, p. 16n, Strout, *Life*, pp. 24–6, and Batho, *Shepherd*, p. 14. The basic conflict is already present in the *Memoir*, where he claims to both have planned the volume and to have tossed it off (p. 15).
30 The *Noctes* themselves begin in 1822; I include the earlier date because two issues in 1819 (August and September) contain the beginnings of the sketches. These beginnings are the episodes associated with the "Tent."
31 Reality and creation become quite confused when visitors attempt to describe their nights at Ambrose's. For an example, see the description of R. P. Gillies, quoted in Strout, *Life*, pp. 269–70.
32 For a good general description of the birth and popularity of the *Noctes*, see Mrs. Oliphant, *William Blackwood and His Sons: Their Magazine and Friends* (New York, 1897), vol. I, ca. p. 199.
33 From 13 (May 1823), p. 592. Alan Strout claims that Lockhart was primarily responsible for this *Noctes*: see *A Bibliography of Articles in Blackwood's Magazine* (Lubbock, 1959), p. 108.
34 William Howitt, quoted in the introduction to the *Memoir*, pp. viii–ix.
35 *Memoir*, pp. 77–8.
36 Contra Hogg, Scott does not seem to have entirely enjoyed the process of absorption by *Blackwood's*. He wrote some letters of complaint to Blackwood, discussing, interestingly, the abuse of his "person." See Mrs. Oliphant, *Blackwood and His Sons*, vol. I, p. 211.
37 From a note appended to the song in the collected edition of 1831 (*Songs by the Ettrick Shepherd*, Edinburgh and London).
38 In the *Noctes* version the music is printed along with the words, and the song is untitled.
39 "'I made the thing,' added the Poet; 'God knows how I have forgot it. Since I have come to the top of this cursed tower, the wind has blown it out of my head'" (p. 293). See *The Three Perils of Man: Wine, Women and Witchcraft*, ed. Douglas Gifford (Totowa, N.J., 1973).
40 These anecdotes are given as notes to the song in the edition of 1831 (pp. 3–5), alluded to above. For more of Hogg's thoughts concerning the performance of songs, see the Preface to *The Forest Minstrel* (Edinburgh, 1810).
41 "Donald M'Donald" was apparently published as a song-sheet, to be sold by itself, and without an indication of author.
42 For a list of the songs involved, see Batho, *Shepherd*, pp. 151–4.
43 From the *Songs* of 1831; p. 73. I quote Moore from an American edition,

The Poetical Works of Thomas Moore (Boston, 1881), vol. IV, p. 105. The note to the poem I refer to is also on this page.

44 *Songs*, p. 71.

45 Letter dated November 6, 1813, quoted from *The Letters of Sir Walter Scott 1811–1814*, ed. H. J. C. Grierson (London, 1932), p. 373.

46 "By a Bush," in *The Forest Minstrel*, p. 196. This song was first published in *The Edinburgh Magazine*, New Series, 21 (January 1803), 52–3.

47 He was certainly reading magazines, especially *The Scots Magazine*, oldest of Scottish periodicals. The poetry of this magazine is a veritable compendium of hackneyed poetic diction.

48 Hogg took this route too, in some ways: he did receive the gift of a lease on a farm (in 1814) from the Duke of Buccleugh, in response to Hogg's attentions to the recently deceased Duchess. See *Memoirs*, pp. 52–3.

4 WALTER SCOTT

1 This remarkable fact, especially remarkable given the commercial difficulty of several periods within this span, makes it all the more wondrous that Scott's financial house should have collapsed in 1825, bringing down that most solid of publishers, Archibald Constable, with it. Of the many accounts of Scott's ruin, I like that of Leslie Stephen the best: see "The Story of Scott's Ruin" in *Studies of a Biographer* (London, 1898), vol. II, pp. 1–38.

2 From a letter to Wordsworth in early October of 1810. It is conveniently extracted in *Scott: The Critical Heritage*, ed. John O. Haydon (New York, 1970), p. 57. It is important to note that Coleridge approved much more of the novels, and in fact was willing to give Scott a sort of greatness; but never for his poetry, which pained his fine ear and high sensibilities.

3 Lockhart, somewhat coyly, says: "I am sure it is right for me to facilitate the task of future historians of our literature by preserving these details as often as I can. Such particulars respecting many of the great works even of the last century, are already sought for with vain regret; and I anticipate no day when the student of English civilization will pass without curiosity the contemporary reception of the Tale of Flodden Field." *Life of Scott* (Philadelphia, 1837), vol. I, p. 304 (chapter 16).

4 As anyone who has read these fascinating prefaces knows, this is not entirely accurate. That is, there is a tension between a sort of easy amateurism and severe professional interest throughout Scott's self-descriptions. Thus, while relating his decision to abandon the law, he both thinks seriously about how to be an author, and also insists that the income from his writing would never become his primary source of income: a sadly ironic (and strangely blind) statement from a man ruined by publishing speculations and who was trying to erase that debt by writing. The central point is that his career as an author looks like a sort of consumer's choice (from the range of available employments).

5 In the American edition I am using – *The Poetical Works of Walter Scott*

(Boston, 1880) – this is on pp. 15–16 of vol. I. All subsequent citations of Scott's Introductions and his poetry will be from this edition, unless otherwise noted. Because there are so many editions of Scott's poetry, and because there is no authoritative edition, I will cite the poetry by canto and stanza.

6 Letter to Ellis, November 1804, quoted in Lockhart, *Life*, vol. I, p. 238.

7 For a much more thorough discussion of the ways in which the Minstrel figures Scott, see the appropriate chapter in *Scott the Rhymer* by Nancy Moore Goslee (Lexington, 1988).

8 Reviewers often complain of this, and also of Scott's habit of salvaging rhymes through reconstruction, or worse, through repetition. See Francis Jeffrey's review of the "Lay" in the *Edinburgh Review* 6 (April 1805), 19–20, and see also *Literary Journal*, in Haydon, *Critical Heritage*, pp. 29–31.

9 Jeffrey, "Lay," pp. 1–2; see also *Literary Journal*, pp. 25–6.

10 By claiming an "old" status for the Minstrel's poem, Scott also includes a kind of editorial atmosphere, less aggressively obtruded than the imitative part, but still contributing to the subtle evaporation of the responsibility of the author.

11 Scott, about a year later, echoes Jeffrey's description in the same magazine: "The story is generally rambling and desultory, utterly incapable consequently of exciting the pleasure arising from a well-conducted plan, all the parts of which tend, each in due degree, to bring on the catastrophe ... so far is this from being the case, that in a long romance, the adventures usually are all separated and insulated; only connected with each other, by their having happened to the same hero; just as a string of beads is combined by the thread on which they are strung." From a review of two editions of romances, "Romances by Ellis and Ritson," *Edinburgh Review* 7 (January 1806), 411. See also his review of *Amadis of Gaul* (translated by Robert Southey), *Edinburgh Review* 3 (October 1803), 109–36, and his essay on "Romance," available in various editions of Scott's Miscellaneous Prose, originally written for the *Encyclopaedia Britannica* in 1813–14; it is in vol. VI (pp. 127–216) of Chamber's Edinburgh edition of 1834–44.

12 H. J. C. Grierson (ed.), *The Letters of Walter Scott* (London, 1932–7), vol. I, p. 242 (March 21, 1805; to Anna Seward); Jeffrey, "Lay," p. 19.

13 Nancy Goslee also identifies the wanderlust of Scott's stories with the wanderings of romance plots, though with fairly different aims. Scott's working out of romance interests constitutes the theme of her whole book, *Scott the Rhymer*, but see especially the chapters on *Marmion* and *The Lady of the Lake*.

14 For a similar discussion of these issues and facts, in a slightly different key, see Susan Stewart, *Crimes of Writing* (Oxford, 1991), esp. the chapter "The Scandals of the Ballad."

15 From the essay "Remarks on Popular Poetry," written in 1830 and placed before the original introduction to the *Border Minstrelsy*. The most

generally available edition of the *Minstrelsy* is the reprint of the 1902 Scribner's edition, ed. T. F. Henderson, issued by the Singing Tree Press (Detroit, 1968), here p. 13. All further references to the "Remarks" refer to this text. I feel confident of the authenticity of this essay, in spite of its late date, because it is in fact very conservative; it hearkens back thirty years to the ideas that were circulating when the *Minstrelsy* was produced. For instance, Jeffrey's review of *The Lady of the Lake*, of 1810, rehearses, as accepted fact, the same notions.

16 For a compact description of many important features of these romances, see the first chapter of Lee C. Ramsay's *Chivalric Romances* (Bloomington, 1983); for specifics on the Auchinleck MS, a book it is thought that Chaucer knew, see the sources indicated in Ramsay's endnote, p. 236.

17 Wordsworth, *Prose Works*, ed. W. J. B. Owen and J. W. Smyser (Oxford, 1974) vol. I, p. 160.

18 Wordsworth, "Appendix," p. 160.

19 The best illustration of Percy's methods is to be found in Ritson's *Ancient Metrical Romances* (London, 1802), where Ritson puts the material from Percy's MS on one side, and what Percy actually published on the other.

20 From the Introduction to the *Minstrelsy*, p. 167. This is the original introduction, written in 1802. A complete description of Scott's methods can be found in two articles by Charles Zug III: "Sir Walter Scott and Ballad Forgery," *Studies in Scottish Literature* 8:1 (July 1970), 52–61; and "The Ballad Editor as Antiquary: Scott and the *Minstrelsy*," *Journal of the Folklore Institute* 13:1 (1976), 57–73.

21 The practical results of Scott's editorial methods are various. He tends to eliminate repetition, though this is not a rule. In his "Clerk Saunders" (first collected in the *Minstrelsy*; Child Ballad no. 69) for instance, which is constructed from at least three versions, he eliminates an elaborate example of ballad repetition (where the description of someone fulfilling directions repeats the directions themselves). For the Child Ballads, see the condensed version prepared by H. C. Sargent and George Lyman Kittredge, *English and Scottish Popular Ballads* (Boston, 1932). Scott tends to heighten dramatic cohesion, by filling in holes in the story; he tends to downplay heavily Scots passages in favor of represented Scots, familiar from Burns' poems. In general, Scott's genuine love for ballads wins out over his history, and he is softer in practice on the faults of ballads than he is in theory. For a more forward looking collector, see William Motherwell, *Minstrelsy, Ancient and Modern* (Glasgow, 1827).

22 On this point see Bertrand Bronson, "Mrs. Brown and the Ballad," in *The Ballad as Song* (Berkeley, 1969), pp. 74–5; see also David Fowler, *A Literary History of the Popular Ballad* (Durham, 1968). For additional material on the ballad revival in general, see *The Ballad Revival* by Albert Friedman (Chicago, 1961).

23 This is described in Hogg's *Memoirs of the Author's Life and Familiar Anecdotes of Walter Scott* (Edinburgh, 1972) pp. 136–7. This theme is discussed in an article by David Vincent, "The Decline of the Oral

Tradition in Popular Culture," in *Popular Culture and Custom in 19th Century England*, ed. Robert Storch (London, 1982), pp. 20–47 (he quotes this anecdote from Hogg).

24 Letter to Scott, June 30, 1802; printed in *The Ettrick Shepherd* by C. K. Batho (Cambridge, 1927), p. 26.

25 Witness, for example, Scott's comments about the worn-out appeal of the ballad stanza, quoted above. A stanza which had offered constant pleasures to its largely oral practitioners over a span of hundreds of years lasts only ten or so on the market.

26 *Edinburgh Review* 12 (April 1808), 1.

27 He spends some time reflecting on the imperfections of readerly memories, and draws lessons for publishing history from these reflections; see pp. 1–2.

28 His vow takes the form of an interesting will to repeat: "If I ever write another poem, I am determined to make every couplet of it as perfect as my uttermost care and attention can possibly effect. In order to ensure the accomplishment of these good resolutions I will consider the whole story in humble prose, and endeavour to make it as interesting as I can before I begin to write it out in verse... " From a letter to Lady Abercorn, June 9, 1808; Grierson, *Letters*, vol. II, p. 69. Scott would have read Jeffrey's review before writing this letter.

29 *Edinburgh Review* 16 (August 1810), 263.

30 Much of this review is strikingly Wordsworthian, though it is also an odd Wordsworthian mixture. Passages such as this remind one of the bitter "Essay, Supplementary" of 1815; other parts, such as the rehearsal of the anthropomorphic history, sound very much like the "Appendix on Diction" of 1800.

31 Quoted by Lockhart, from Ballantyne's *Memoranda*, in *Life*, vol. I, p. 562.

32 Grierson, *Letters*, vol. I, pp. 242–3.

33 As Nancy Goslee discusses throughout *Scott the Rhymer*.

34 "Preface" of 1830, pp. 16–17.

35 "Christabel," of course, had not yet been published; Scott heard it from a friend with an excellent memory, a Mr. John Stoddart. And so oral circumstances creep into *The Lay of the Last Minstrel* in this small way too.

36 This is from the poetry that is outside of the canto proper, and hence without stanza numbers.

37 Scott's accommodation of history and progress, from a broader ideological perspective, has been the center of many contemporary discussions of his novels; see Avrom Fleischman, *The English Historical Novel* (Baltimore, 1971), Harry Shaw, *The Forms of Historical Fiction* (Ithaca, 1983) and James Kerr, *Fiction Against History* (Cambridge, 1989).

38 I might be willing to exempt *Harold the Dauntless* from this sweeping generalization; but even there, Harold's transformation looks more like someone simply changing his mind. It is not clear that the stalwart Dane we see through most of the story is not simply a good British hero

behaving in a rather poor way: that is, we are never invited to detest Harold.

39 For more about the specifics of the relationship to romance plots, see Goslee, *Rhymer*, pp. 67–94.

40 This scene occurs again in *Rokeby*, but there the participants are both human beings.

41 Goslee, *Rhymer*, p. 81. Though I disagree entirely with this statement, I agree with all sorts of things Goslee has to say about the poem. See particularly her discussions of the relationships between medieval, renaissance and "modern" conceptions of romance.

42 *Guy* is in the Auchinleck MS; I assume Scott knew it well.

43 This, it seems to me, is truer, even, of the novels; think of Edward Waverly's wonderful passivity, or the conflict between the untroubled Morton and the constricted Burley in *Old Mortality*. I have discussed this feature of Scott's novels elsewhere, in "Scott's Disappointments: Reading the *Heart of Mid-Lothian*," *Modern Philology* (forthcoming).

5 WILLIAM WORDSWORTH

1 Most notably, Jon Klancher in *The Making of English Reading Audiences, 1790–1832* (Madison, 1987). Other writers have not Klancher's pure interest, but still insist on the interactive nature of Wordsworth's poetry, and especially the *Lyrical Ballads*. Don Bialostosky's Bahktinian *Making Tales* (Chicago, 1984) is rigorously aware of the reader throughout; this book is the product of the surge of interest in the *Lyrical Ballads* that began in the late 1950s with Stephen Parrish (for references see Bialostosky). Another product of this surge is Mary Jacobus' *Tradition and Experiment in the Lyrical Ballads* (Oxford, 1976), which is full of information and from which I have learned much.

2 Quoted from *The Prose Works of William Wordsworth*, ed. W. J. B. Owen and Jane Worthington Smyser (Oxford, 1974), vol. I, pp. 157–9. One complication: in all cases I cite the text from the 1802 edition of the Preface. This edition, which varies only in small (but occasionally important) ways from the 1850 edition, may be reconstructed from the textual apparatus that Owen and Smyser provide. The easier way, though, is to refer to Stephen Gill's selection of Wordsworth's poetry in the Oxford Authors Series (*William Wordsworth* [Oxford, 1984]), where the 1802 text is given directly. For purposes of standards, however, I refer to the standard edition, with this alteration understood. All other citations of Wordsworth's prose are from Owen and Smyser also.

3 Reading 100 times leads to well-thumbed copies of books, like the copy of *The Seasons* that Coleridge and Hazlitt saw lying on a window-sill in an inn; Coleridge exclaimed "*That* is true fame!" See "My First Acquaintance with Poets," in *Selected Writings*, ed. Ronald Blythe (Harmondsworth, 1970), p. 62. The quotation is from the Preface to the *Lyrical Ballads*, vol. I, p. 151.

4 This application has actually been attempted by Bialostosky, in *Making Tales*, pp. 51–5.

5 This passage is not in the 1850 edition, which removes almost all specific references to the poems. It was in the 1800 edition, and the 1802; I presume it was lost, along with other things, in the thoroughgoing revisions of 1836.

6 *Wordsworth's Poetry* (New Haven, 1971), p. 141.

7 *Zoonomia*. See the note to the poem in the reprint of the *Lyrical Ballads*, ed. R. L. Brett and A. R. Jones (New York, 1963), p. 276, which gives the specific sources in full.

8 Mayo makes this observation in his article "The Contemporaneity of the *Lyrical Ballads*," *PMLA* 69 (1954), 520. I take the information on "Peter Bell" from the useful introduction by John E. Jordan in the Cornell Wordsworth edition of "Peter Bell" (Ithaca, 1985), esp. pp. 17–18.

9 Quoted from Gill's selection in the Oxford Authors Series, referred to above; p. 58.

10 From Southey's review of the *Lyrical Ballads* in *The Critical Review*. Southey makes this complaint just after his famous complaint about the tiresome loquacity of "The Thorn." The italicized "*well-authenticated*" comes from a sentence in the "Advertisement" (Owen and Smyser, vol. I, p. 117), which says only this, and does no explaining. The review can be found in Donald Reiman, *Romantics Reviewed* (New York, 1973), part A, p. 308. Mary Jacobus (p. 235) thinks of this worry as extra or unimportant; my argument is that it is in fact central. *The Monthly Review* contains another interesting example; it has other interesting political features, and so I will give a fullish extract:

> Distress from poverty and want is admirably described, in the "*True Story of Goody Blake and Harry Gill*": but are we to imagine that Harry was bewitched by Goody Blake? The hardest heart must be softened into pity for the poor old woman; – and yet, if all the poor are to help themselves, and supply their wants from the possessions of their neighbors, what imaginary wants and real anarchy would it not create? Goody Blake should have been relieved from the *two millions* annually allowed by the state to the poor of this country, not by the plunder of the individual.

This review can be found in Reiman, *Romantics Reviewed*, Part A, vol. II, pp. 713–17.

11 Quoted from Jordan (ed.), *Peter Bell*, p. 41. All page numbers and line numbers referring to *Peter Bell* are from this text; I use the first edition as my reading version.

12 Add to this Hazlitt's description of Wordsworth reading "Peter Bell" (which I will discuss later) to him: "Whatever might be thought of the poem,'his face was a book where men might read strange matters,' and he announced the fate of his hero in prophetic tones. There is a *chaunt* in the recitation of Coleridge and Wordsworth, which acts as a spell upon the hearer, and disarms the judgement. Perhaps they have deceived

themselves by making habitual use of this accompaniment." From "My
First Acquaintance With Poets," in Blythe (ed.), *Selected Writings*, p. 59.

13 This quick trip through the plot of "Peter Bell" depends upon the more
detailed readings of others for its implied detail; see, for instance,
Jacobus, *Tradition and Experiment*, pp. 262–72.

14 Klancher, *English Audiences*, depicts this movement in his terms:
"Wordsworth's effort to remake the existing audience of 1800 ends, in
1815, by inventing an audience in imagination he was unable to find in
the world" (p. 143).

15 *Minstrelsy of the Scottish Border* (London, 1839), p. 304.

16 *Wordsworth: The Sense of History* (Stanford, 1989), pp. 119–30.

17 This text may be found in the Cornell Wordsworth series; it is also
conveniently available in Gill (ed.), *William Wordsworth*, p. 7.

18 Child Ballad no. 20; see H. C. Sargent and G. L. Kittredge (eds.),
English and Scottish Popular Ballads (Boston, 1932), p. 37.

19 See Jacobus, *Tradition and Experiment*, pp. 240–50.

20 See Bronson's many works on this subject, referred to in previous
chapters; especially a few of the essays in *The Ballad as Song* (Berkeley,
1969) and the Introduction to *The Traditional Tunes of the Child Ballads*
(Princeton, 1959).

21 This is Child Ballad no. 74; I quote from version A, Sargent and
Kittredge (eds.), *Ballads*, p. 157.

22 Because it is the simplest and most available source for an accurate early
text, I again quote from Gill (ed.), *William Wordsworth*, here p. 594. My
text for "The Thorn" is also taken from this volume.

23 See Jacobus, *Tradition and Experiment*; there is also an interesting
"rhetorical" discussion in Francis Ferguson's *Language as Counter-Spirit*
(New Haven, 1977), pp. 11–16.

24 Obviously, the note to "The Thorn" shares characteristics with the
addendums to "Goody Blake and Harry Gill." In particular, the note to
"The Thorn" fastidiously adds in context (narrator as seafarer, etc.) in
order to compensate for the dramatic isolation produced by the faithful
reproduction of the seafarer's voice, the isolation of monologue.
Interestingly, "The Thorn" was also criticized by Southey in his 1798
review, and the note appears in 1800 along with the additional material
for "Goody Blake."

25 "To Wordsworth," lines 11–14; quoted from *Shelley's Poetry and Prose*,
ed. Donald Reiman and Sharon Powers (New York, 1977), p. 88.

26 *Minstrelsy*, pp. 305–6.

27 In a letter to Scott, January 16, 1805; referred to in *The Poetical Works of
William Wordsworth*, ed. E. De Selincourt and H. Darbishire (Oxford,
1946), vol. III, p. 446. "Leader Haughs" itself can be found in Allan
Ramsay's *The Tea-Table Miscellany*; in the edition I have (Glasgow,
1876), it is on page 188 of vol. I, though in the original it is in vol. II. For
another discussion of this material, see Stephen Gill, "'The Braes of
Yarrow': Poetic Context and Personal Memory in Wordsworth's

'Extempore Effusion on the Death of James Hogg,'" *Wordsworth Circle* 16:3 (Summer 1985), 120–5.

28 From Percy's *Reliques*, Second series, book III. In the edition that I have (London, 1859), it is on p. 368. It can also be found in later editions of Ramsay's *Tea-Table Miscellany*.

29 Ernest De Selincourt (ed.), *The Letters of William and Dorothy Wordsworth: The Middle Years* (Oxford, 1937), vol. II, p. 611.

30 From Gill (ed.), *William Wordsworth*.

31 From Gill (ed.), *William Wordsworth*.

32 *Poetical Works*, vol. III, pp. 525–6; also quoted in Gill (ed.), *William Wordsworth*, p. 725.

33 This is a bald summary of Marjorie Levinson's reading, in *Wordsworth's Great Period Poems* (Cambridge, 1986), which I admire especially for its working of historical context with poetic necessity and accomplishment; as she says, she restores our enjoyment of the poem. Alan Liu offers a sharp summary of the recent interest in "Tintern Abbey," and the motives of that interest, in *Wordsworth: The Sense of History* (Stanford, 1989), pp. 215–17.

34 "Tintern Abbey" provides an opportunity to note that ways in which I have described the force that interrupts Wordsworth bear a close though figurative relationship to the forces of "history" that other recent readers have found in this poem. I am thinking especially of the nuanced and poetically active sense that Alan Liu gives to this word; see *Wordsworth*, esp. chapter 1.

CONCLUSION

1 Levinson, *Great Period Poems*, p. 10.

2 This essay is in *Beyond Formalism* (New Haven, 1970), pp. 283–97. This quotation is from p. 296.

3 This phrase appears in two crucial places, near the beginning of the essay and near the end; pp. 285 and 296. Different versions of it appear in the various essays about the progress of poetry and the "westering" of the imagination that appear in *The Fate of Reading*.

4 That is, Wordsworth's fear that the reflective mind is captive in the reflective person, unable to reach out and startle in the way the archaic poet (like Bürger) does so easily. I hope it is clear how thoroughly I am indebted to Hartman's picture of Wordsworth's interaction with "magic" and archaic powers.

5 The tug of mortality is presented in more complex ways in other of Hartman's writings, of course; most notably, for my purposes, in *Wordsworth's Poetry*. But even in his sadder essays, death and mortality are sublimed away into psychological or even philosophical conflict, spiritual instead of material forces. Like Wordsworth, Hartman purifies his world in order to accomplish his ends.

6 From Gill (ed.), *William Wordsworth*.

7 He also adds the typical Romantic touch, by seeing the death of the tradition in the death of his source; see the Fenwick note, quoted by Gill (ed.), *William Wordsworth*, p. 695.

8 As Clifford Siskin has so convincingly argued, one of the things we like about Wordsworth is his "lyric turn." My version of this turn is the turn towards transcendence, the escape from the limits of mortality. Recognizing that love is the same as demystifying it: transcendence does not "appear" in Wordsworth. It is imposed, it is itself part of a strategy. Though the final features of my argument are quite different from Siskin's, I think our motives are very similar: we both want to portray Wordsworth as in some way imposing himself upon literary history, instead of being a "natural" link in it. See *The Historicity of Romantic Discourse* (Oxford, 1988), passim.

Bibliography

Aitken, A. J., "Scottish Speech: A Historical View With Special Reference to the Standard English of Scotland," in Aitken and McArthur (eds.), *The Languages of Scotland*, pp. 85–118

"The Good Old Scots Tongue: Does Scots Have an Identity?" in Haugen, et al. (eds.), *Minority Languages Today*, pp. 112–36

Aitken, A. J. and T. McArthur (eds.), *The Languages of Scotland*, Edinburgh: Ward R. Chambers, 1979

Barke, James and Sydney Smith (eds.), *The Merry Muses of Caledonia*, Edinburgh: M. McDonald, 1959

Batho, E. K., *The Ettrick Shepherd*, Cambridge: Cambridge University Press, 1927

Bialostosky, Don, *Making Tales*, Chicago: University of Chicago Press, 1984

Black, George, "President Jefferson and MacPherson's Ossian," *Transactions of the Gaelic Society of Inverness* 33 (1925–7), 355–61

Blacklock, Thomas (ed.), *A Collection of Original Poems*, Edinburgh, 1760

Blair, Hugh, "A Critical Dissertation on the Poems of Ossian," in James MacPherson, *Poems of Ossian*, Boston, 1860, pp. 88–188

Lectures on Rhetoric and Belles-Lettres, 3 vols., London, 1781

Bromwich, David, "Parody, Pastiche and Allusion," in *Lyric Poetry: Beyond New Criticism*, ed. Chaviva Hosek and Patricia Parker, Ithaca: Cornell University Press, 1985, pp. 320–41

Bronson, Bertrand, *The Ballad as Song*, Berkeley: University of California Press, 1969

The Traditional Tunes of the Child Ballads, 4 vols., Princeton: Princeton University Press, 1959–72

Brooks, Cleanth, *The Well Wrought Urn*, New York: Harcourt Brace Jovanovich, 1975

Brown, Mary Ellen, *Burns and Tradition*, Chicago: University of Chicago Press, 1984

Burns, Robert, *Works*, 6 vols., London, 1891

Byron, George Gordon, Baron, *The Complete Poetical Works*, ed. Jerome McGann, 5 vols., Oxford: Oxford University Press, 1980–6

Bysveen, Josef, *Epic Tradition and Innovation in James MacPherson's Fingal*, Upsala: University of Upsala, 1982

Campbell, R. H., *Scotland Since 1707*, 2nd ed., Edinburgh: J. Donald Publishers, 1985

Campbell, R. H. and J. B. A. Dow (eds.), *Source Book of Scottish Economic and Social History*, Oxford: Oxford University Press, 1968

Carter, J. S. and J. H. Pittock (eds.), *Aberdeen and the Enlightenment*, Aberdeen: Aberdeen University Press, 1987

Christensen, Jerome, "From Rhetoric to Corporate Populism: A Romantic Critique of the Academy in an Age of High Gossip," *Critical Inquiry* 16 (1990), 438–65

Clerk, Archibald (ed.), *The Poems of Ossian, in the Original Gaelic*, 2 vols., Edinburgh, 1870

Cottom, Daniel, *The Civilized Imagination*, Cambridge: Cambridge University Press, 1984

Craig, David, *Scottish Literature and the Scottish People*, London: Chatto and Windus, 1961

Crawford, Thomas, "Lowland Song and Popular Tradition in the 18th Century," in Hook (ed.), *History of Scottish Literature*, pp. 123–39

Cromek, Robert, *Reliques of Robert Burns*, 4th ed., London, 1817

Curley, Thomas, "Johnson's Last Word on Ossian," in Carter and Pittock (eds.), *Aberdeen and the Enlightenment*, pp. 375–93

Currie, James (ed.), *The Works of Robert Burns*, 6 vols., London, 1820

Damrosch, Leopold, "Blake, Burns and the Recovery of Lyric," *Studies in Romanticism* 21 (1982), 637–60

De Selincourt, Ernest (ed.), *The Letters of William and Dorothy Wordsworth: The Middle Years*, 2 vols., Oxford: Oxford University Press, 1937

Dodgshon, R. A., "'Pretense of Blude' and 'Place of Their Dwelling': The Nature of Highland Clans, 1500–1745," in Houston and Whyte (eds.), *Scottish Society*, pp. 154–76

Dorian, Nancy C., *Language Death: The Life Cycle of a Scottish Gaelic Dialect*, Philadelphia: University of Pennsylvania Press, 1980

Ferguson, Francis, *Language as Counter-Spirit*, New Haven: Yale University Press, 1977

Ferguson, J. Delancey, *Pride and Passion*, New York: Oxford University Press, 1939

Ferguson, J. Delancey and G. Ross Roy (eds.), *The Letters of Robert Burns*, Oxford: Oxford University Press, 1985

Fitzgerald, Robert, "The Style of Ossian," *Studies in Romanticism* 6 (1966), 22–33

Fleischman, Avrom, *The English Historical Novel*, Baltimore: Johns Hopkins University Press, 1971

Folkenflik, Robert, "MacPherson, Chatterton, Blake and the Great Age of Ballad Forgery," *The Centennial Review* 18 (1974), 378–91

Fowler, David, *A Literary History of the Popular Ballad*, Durham: Duke University Press, 1968

Friedman, Albert, *The Ballad Revival*, Chicago: University of Chicago Press, 1961

Gaskill, Howard, "'Ossian' MacPherson: Towards a Rehabilitation," *Comparative Criticism* 8 (1986), 113–46

Gill, Stephen, "'The Braes of Yarrow': Poetic Context and Personal

Memory in Wordsworth's 'Extempore Effusion on the Death of James Hogg,'" *Wordsworth Circle* 16:3 (Summer 1985), 120–5

Gill, Stephen (ed.), *William Wordsworth*, The Oxford Authors Series, Oxford: Oxford University Press, 1984

Goslee, Nancy Moore, *Scott the Rhymer*, Lexington: University of Kentucky Press, 1988

Gray, Malcolm, *The Highland Economy, 1750–1850*, Edinburgh: Oliver and Boyd, 1957

Grierson, H. J. C. (ed.), *The Letters of Sir Walter Scott*, 12 vols., London: Constable, 1932–7

Grimble, Ian, "The Reverend Alexander Pope's Letter to James Hogg," *Scottish Gaelic Studies* 9, pt. 1 (1961), 98–104

Guillory, John, "Canon," in Lentricchia and McLaughlin (eds.), *Critical Terms*, pp. 233–49

Hartman, Geoffrey, *Beyond Formalism*, New Haven: Yale University Press, 1970

The Fate of Reading, Chicago: University of Chicago Press, 1985

Wordsworth's Poetry, New Haven: Yale University Press, 1971

Haugen, Einar, et al. (eds.), *Minority Languages Today*, Edinburgh: Edinburgh University Press, 1981

Hayden, John O., *Scott: The Critical Heritage*, New York: Barnes and Noble, 1970

Haywood, Ian, *The Making of History*, Rutherford: Fairleigh Dickinson University Press, 1986

Hewitt, David, "James Beattie and the Languages of Scotland," in Carter and Pittock (eds.), *Aberdeen and the Enlightenment*, pp. 251–60

Hobsbawm, Erik and Terrence Ranger (eds.), *The Invention of Tradition*, Cambridge: Cambridge University Press, 1983

Hogg, James (ed.), *The Forest Minstrel*, Edinburgh, 1810

Memoir of the Author's Life and Familiar Anecdotes of Sir Walter Scott, ed. Douglas Mack, Edinburgh: Scottish Academic Press, 1972

(ed.), *The Mountain Bard*, Edinburgh, 1807

The Poetic Mirror, London, 1817

The Shepherd's Guide, Edinburgh, 1807

Songs by the Ettrick Shepherd, Edinburgh and London, 1831

The Spy, Edinburgh, 1810–11

The Three Perils of Man: Wine, Women and Witchcraft, ed. Douglas Gifford, Totowa: Rowman and Littlefield, 1973

Hook, Andrew (ed.), *The History of Scottish Literature, 1660–1800*, vol. II, Aberdeen: Aberdeen University Press, 1987

Houston, R. A. and I. H. Whyte (eds.), *Scottish Society 1500–1800*, Cambridge: Cambridge University Press, 1989

Hull, Mr., *Select Letters by Mr. Hull*, London, 1778

Jacobus, Mary, *Tradition and Experiment in the Lyrical Ballads*, Oxford: Oxford University Press, 1976

Jeffrey, Francis, "*The Lady of the Lake*," *Edinburgh Review* 16:30 (August 1810), 263–93

"*The Lay of the Last Minstrel*," *Edinburgh Review* 6:11 (April 1805), 1–20

"*Marmion*," *Edinburgh Review* 12:23 (April 1808), 1–35

Johnson, James (ed.), *The Scots Musical Museum*, 6 vols., Edinburgh, 1787–1803

Johnson, Samuel, *A Journey to the Western Islands of Scotland*, Harmondsworth: Penguin, 1984

Kerr, James, *Fiction Against History*, Cambridge: Cambridge University Press, 1989

Kinsley, James (ed.), *The Poems and Songs of Robert Burns*, 3 vols., Oxford: Oxford University Press, 1968

Klancher, John, *The Making of English Reading Audiences*, Madison: University of Wisconsin Press, 1987

Lentricchia, Frank and Thomas McLaughlin (eds.), *Critical Terms for Literary Study*, Chicago: University of Chicago Press, 1990

Levinson, Marjorie, *Wordsworth's Great Period Poems*, Cambridge: Cambridge University Press, 1986

Lockhart, John G., *Life of Walter Scott*, 2 vols., Philadelphia, 1837

Low, Donald (ed.), *Robert Burns: The Critical Heritage*, London: Routledge & Kegan Paul, 1974

Mackenzie, Henry (ed.), *Report of the Committee of the Highland Society of Scotland, Appointed to Inquire into the Nature and Authenticity of the Poems of Ossian*, Edinburgh, 1805

MacPherson, James, *Fragments of Ancient Poetry*, Augustan Reprint Society Publication no. 122, Los Angeles: Clark Memorial Library, 1966

Poems of Ossian, Boston, 1860

Mayo, Robert, "The Contemporaneity of the *Lyrical Ballads*," *PMLA* 69 (1954), 486–522

McClure, J. Derrick, "Language and Genre in Allan Ramsay's 1721 Poems" in Carter and Pittock (eds.), *Aberdeen and the Enlightenment*, pp. 261–9

McElroy, George, "Ossianic Imagination and the History of India," in Carter and Pittock (eds.), *Aberdeen and the Enlightenment*, pp. 363–74

Millar, J. H., *Scottish Prose of the 17th and 18th Centuries*, Glasgow, 1912

Mitchison, Rosalind, "The Government in the Highlands, 1707–1745," in Mitchison and Phillipson (eds.), *Scotland in the Age of Improvement*, pp. 203–29

Mitchison, R. and N. T. Phillipson (eds.), *Scotland in the Age of Improvement*, Edinburgh: Edinburgh University Press, 1970

Moore, Thomas, *Poetical Works*, 6 vols., Boston, 1881

Motherwell, William (ed.), *Minstrelsy, Ancient and Modern*, Glasgow, 1827

Murison, David, "The Historical Background," in Aitken and McArthur (eds.), *The Languages of Scotland*, pp. 2–13

Nutt, Alfred, *Ossian and Ossianic Literature*, New York: AMS, 1972

Oliphant, Mrs. Margaret, *William Blackwood and His Sons: Their Magazine and Friends*, 2 vols., New York, 1897

Percy, Thomas, *Reliques of Ancient Poetry*, London, 1859

Potkay, Adam, "Virtue and Manners in MacPherson's *Poems of Ossian,*" *PMLA* 107 (1992), 120–30

Prebble, John, *The Highland Clearances*, Harmondsworth: Penguin, 1969

Ramsay, Allan (ed.), *The Tea-Table Miscellany*, 2 vols., Glasgow, 1876

Ramsay, Lee C., *Chivalric Romances*, Bloomington: Indiana University Press, 1983

Read, Dennis M., "Practicing 'The Necessity of Purification': Cromek, Roscoe and *Reliques of Burns,*" *Studies in Bibliography* 35 (1982), 306–19

Reiman, Donald (ed.), *The Romantics Reviewed*, 3 vols., New York: Garland Publications, 1972

Reiman, Donald and Sharon Powers (eds.), *Shelley's Poetry and Prose*, New York: Norton Critical Editions, 1977

Ritson, James (ed.), *Scottish Song in Two Volumes*, London, 1794

Ritson, Joseph, *Ancient Metrical Romances*, London, 1802

Ross, Neil, *Heroic Poetry from the Book of the Dean of Lismore*, Edinburgh: Scottish Gaelic Texts Society, 1939

Sargent, H. C. and G. L. Kittredge (eds.), *English and Scottish Popular Ballads*, Boston: Houghton Mifflin, 1932

Scott, Sir Walter (ed.), *Minstrelsy of the Scottish Border*, 4 vols., Detroit: Singing Tree Press, 1968

Scott, Walter, "Amadis of Gaul," *Edinburgh Review* 3 (October 1803), 109–36

Miscellaneous Prose Works of Walter Scott, 28 vols., Edinburgh, 1834–44

Old Mortality, Harmondsworth: Penguin, 1975

Poetical Works, 5 vols., Boston, 1880

"Romances by Ellis and Ritson," *Edinburgh Review* 7 (January 1806), 387–413

Tales of a Grandfather, 3rd series, London, 1923

Shaw, Harry, *The Forms of Historical Fiction*, Ithaca: Cornell University Press, 1983

Shaw, William, *An Enquiry into the Authenticity of the Poems Ascribed to Ossian*, London, 1781

Shenstone, William, *Poetical Works*, ed. William Gilfillan, New York, 1854

Simpson, Louis, *James Hogg, A Critical Study*, New York: St. Martin's, 1962

Siskin, Clifford, *The Historicity of Romantic Discourse*, Oxford: Oxford University Press, 1988

Smart, T. C., *A History of the Scottish People 1560–1830*, 2nd ed., London: Collins, 1970

Smith, Janet, "18th Century Ideas of Scotland," in Mitchison and Phillipson (eds.), *Scotland in the Age of Improvement*, pp. 100–20

Snyder, F. B., *The Life of Robert Burns*, New York, 1932

Stafford, Fiona, *The Sublime Savage: A Study of James MacPherson and the Poems of Ossian*, Edinburgh: Edinburgh University Press, 1988

Stephen, Leslie, *Studies of a Biographer*, 4 vols., London, 1898

Stern, Ludwig, "Ossianic Heroic Poetry," trans. J. L. Robertson, *Transactions of the Gaelic Society of Inverness* 22 (1897–98), 257–325

Stewart, Susan, *Crimes of Writing*, Oxford: Oxford University Press, 1991
Strout, Alan Lang, *A Bibliography of Articles in Blackwoods Magazine*, Library
    Bulletin no. 5, Lubbock: Texas Tech Press, 1959
    The Life and Letters of James Hogg, Lubbock: Texas Tech Press, 1946
Swedenberg, H. T., Jr., *The Theory of the Epic in England, 1650–1800*,
    Berkeley: University of California Press, 1944
Thomson, Derick, *The Gaelic Sources of MacPherson's Ossian*, Aberdeen
    University Studies no. 130, Edinburgh: Oliver and Boyd, 1952
    "The MacMhuirich Bardic Family," *Transactions of the Gaelic Society of
    Inverness* 43 (1966), 276–304
Thomson, George (ed.), *A Select Collection of Scottish Airs*, 5 vols., Edinburgh,
    1793–1814
Thomson, Thomas (ed.), *The Works of the Ettrick Shepherd*, 2 vols., New York:
    AMS Press, 1973
Trevor-Roper, Hugh, "The Invention of Tradition: The Highland Tra-
    dition of Scotland," in Hobsbawm and Ranger (eds.), *The Invention of
    Tradition*, pp. 15–41
Van Tiegham, P., *Ossian en France*, 2 vols., Geneva: Slatkine Reprints, 1967
Venis, Linda, "The Problem of Broadside Balladry's Influence on the
    Lyrical Ballads," in *Studies in English Literature* 24:4 (1984), 617–32
Vincent, David, "The Decline of the Oral Tradition in Popular Culture,"
    in *Popular Culture and Custom in 19th Century England*, ed. Robert Storch,
    London: Croom Helm, 1982, pp. 20–47.
Wallace, William (ed.), *Robert Burns and Mrs. Dunlop*, 2 vols., New York, 1898
Wordsworth, William, *Peter Bell*, ed. John Jordan, Ithaca: Cornell
    University Press, 1985
    The Poetical Works, ed. E. De Selincourt and H. Darbishire, 5 vols.,
    Oxford: Oxford University Press, 1940–59
    Prose Works, ed. W. J. R. Owen and J. W. Smyser, 3 vols., Oxford:
    Oxford University Press, 1974
Wordsworth, William and Samuel Coleridge, *Lyrical Ballads*, ed. R. L.
    Brett and A. R. Jones, New York, 1963
Young, Edward, *Conjectures on Original Composition*, reprinted in *Edward
    Young's "Conjectures on Original Composition" in England and Germany*, by
    M. W. Steinke, *Americana Germanica* no. 28, New York: Stechert, 1917
Zug, Charles III, "The Ballad Editor as Antiquary: Scott and the
    Minstrelsy," *Journal of the Folklore Institute* 13 (1976), 57–73
    "Sir Walter Scott and Ballad Forgery," *Studies in Scottish Literature* 8
    (1970), 52–61

Index

267